The Voice of the Hammer

NICOLA MASCIANDARO

The
VOICE *of the*
HAMMER

The Meaning of Work in Middle English Literature

University of Notre Dame Press
Notre Dame, Indiana

Library of Congress Cataloging-in-Publication Data

Masciandaro, Nicola, 1969–
The voice of the hammer : the meaning of work in Middle English literature /
Nicola Masciandaro.
p. cm.
Includes bibliographical references and index.
ISBN-13: 978-0-268-03498-6 (pbk. : alk. paper)
ISBN-10: 0-268-03498-2 (pbk. : alk. paper)
1. English literature—Middle English, 1100–1500—History and criticism.
2. Work in literature. 3. Working class in literature. 4. Social classes in
literature. 5. Labor—England—History—To 1500. 6. Chaucer, Geoffrey,
d. 1400. Canterbury tales. I. Title.
PR275.W67M37   2006
820.9'355—dc22

                    2006024201

To my parents

> . . . quand' ella ti parrà soave
>
> tanto, che sù andar ti fa leggero
>
> com' a seconda giù andar per nave,
>
> allor sarai al fin d'esto sentiero.
>
> (Dante, *Purgatorio* 4.91–94)

Contents

Acknowledgments

This book started as my dissertation in the Medieval Studies program at Yale. Many thanks to my advisor, Lee Patterson, and readers, Paul Freedman and Traugott Lawler, for their encouraging support, thoughtful glossing, and ongoing interest in this work. I would also like to acknowledge the other professors who made those years an enjoyable, fruitful experience and contributed to this project in more subtle ways, especially Robert G. Babcock and Giuseppe Mazzotta. I send my sincere thanks to the anonymous readers of my manuscript for their intelligent commentary and suggestions. This work was supported in part by a grant from the City University of New York PSC-CUNY Research Award Program.

I am especially grateful to my wife, Heather, whose wisdom and beauty help me prove true Augustine's words, *nullo enim modo sunt onerosi labores amantium.*

A Note on Citations

All citations from Chaucer's works are from Larry D. Benson, gen. ed., *The Riverside Chaucer,* 3rd ed. (Boston: Houghton Mifflin, 1987). Translations are mine unless otherwise noted. The following abbreviations are used:

CA	John Gower, *Confessio amantis,* in *The Complete Works of John Gower,* ed. G. C. Macaulay, 4 vols. (Oxford: Clarendon Press, 1899–1902).
CkT	*Cook's Tale*
ClT	*Clerk's Tale*
CYT	*Canon Yeoman's Tale*
EETS, e.s.	Early English Text Society, Extra Series
EETS, o.s.	Early English Text Society, Original Series
Form Age	*The Former Age*
Gent	*Gentilesse*
GP	*General Prologue*
HF	*House of Fame*
LCL	Loeb Classical Library
ME	Middle English
MED	*Middle English Dictionary*

Mel	*Tale of Melibee*
MerT	*Merchant's Tale*
MilT	*Miller's Tale*
MkT	*Monk's Tale*
ModE	Modern English
NPT	*Nun's Priest's Tale*
OED	*Oxford English Dictionary*
OF	Old French
PardT	*Pardoner's Tale*
ParsT	*Parson's Tale*
PL	J.-P. Migne, Patrologia Cursus Completus: Series Latina. 221 vols. (Paris: Migne, 1844–91).
PPl	William Langland, *The Vision of Piers Plowman*, 2nd ed., ed. A. V. C. Schmidt (London: J. M. Dent, 1978).
PrT	*Prioress's Tale*
ShipT	*Shipman's Tale*
SNT	*Second Nun's Tale*
Sted	*Lak of Stedfastnesse*
SumT	*Summoner's Tale*

Introduction

In the alliterative poem known as the *Complaint against Black-smiths,* the rhythmic noise of forging is transmuted into the music of po-etry: "Swarte smekyd smeþes smateryd wyth smoke / Dryue me to deth wyth den of here dyntes. / Swech noys on nyghtes ne herd men neuer: / What knauene cry, and clateryng of knockes!"[1] In another Middle English poem, a carpenter's tools actually speak, debating how to reform their un-thrifty master: "'With grete strokys I schall hym pelte [says the mallet]. / My mayster schall full well thene, / Both to cloþe [and] fede his men.'"[2] These similar representational moments drive home in complementary ways that late medieval English literature had something to say about work, that it gave voice to labor as a significant category of experience. This is not labor's voice as the self-expression of medieval laborers, which is so difficult to find in medieval texts.[3] In the *Complaint* it is precisely the inarticulate and wayward speech of workers that is judged and controlled by the superior voice of poetry: "'Huf, puf!' seith þat on; 'haf, paf!' þat oþer. / Þei spyttyn and spraulyn and spellyn many spelles; / Þei gnauen and gnacchen, þei gronys togydere" (7–9). In the *Debate of the Carpen-ter's Tools,* the carpenter himself is conspicuously absent.[4] Rather, these instances of poetic animation, in which work becomes more than work, speak to the meaningfulness of work itself, as an activity that has its own structure and significance as well as complex relationships to other values. As the *Complaint* is constituted and caused by the industry that keeps its author awake at night, so does it present a homology between manual and poetic labor that reenacts the legend of music's discovery at the forge and underscores the more general interdependence of material and intellectual production within human culture.[5] And the arguing tools of the *Debate*, faithful and unruly, dramatize tensions inherent to the process of work—above all, the conflict between the economic need for efficient production and the deep inertia all work must overcome.[6]

This book seeks to understand several ways Middle English literature made meaning out of work. The cultural landscape of late medieval England was fertile territory for the representation of work, shaped as it was by the new possibilities for economic self-determination among the laboring classes created by the plague, the ongoing attempts by government to control the labor market in the interest of landlords and employers, the political agitation of artisans and agriculturalists in 1381, the growing formalization of status consciousness, and increasing commercialization. The appreciation of this fact by literary scholars has been dominated, for obvious reasons, by the study of *Piers Plowman*. But that a poem so focused on the issue of work would be made at this time also attests to a more general consciousness of its significance. Part of my intention in this study has been to take the interpretive conversation about late medieval literary representations of work in new directions, and it is encouraging to find other recent studies doing the same.[7] The following chapters examine three areas of such representation: the Middle English lexicon, accounts of the history of work, and Fragment VIII of Chaucer's *Canterbury Tales*. Their common premise is that late medieval English society, through its language and literature, conceptualized work as a distinct, problematical feature of life and that the work-related crises of the period effected corresponding needs to articulate and question work's meaning and value.

The Middle English vocabulary of work offers rich and challenging evidence of how late medieval people conceived of work, how they gave meaning to it at the most fundamental level. Chapter 1 investigates both the semantic structure of the vocabulary and its cultural significance. The vocabulary is divisible into terms that emphasize the subjective, effortful dimension of work and those that emphasize work's objective, productive dimension. This dichotomous structure, I argue, originates chiefly in the intersection of status-based and class-based attitudes toward work. The influence of social attitudes on the vocabulary is demonstrated, for example, by the fact that Middle English adopts from Anglo-French only words for work that are associated with servitude and pain. I then show how this rich vocabulary reflects late medieval society's broad awareness of the nature and processes of work, an awareness that is corroborated, for example, by medieval discourse on the related concepts of *artes illiberales, artes mechanicae,* and *opera servilia.* Last, I address the question of how ME *werk,* in light of its subsequent semantic history, might be considered a cultural keyword. I propose that the substantial polysemy of *werk*—its signification of both labor and action in general—attests not to a lack of distinction between the economic and the noneconomic in medieval culture but to a cultural habit of perceiving relations between work and life, between occupational and personal agency.

It is natural that periods in which work is foregrounded as a force of history would be especially interested in imagining the history of work. Where the Victorian age projected its dreams of humane industry onto medieval workers, late medieval authors envisioned the origins of work in no less creative ways, using the past to define work's meaning and value. Chapter 2 examines several Middle English representations of work's history. It demonstrates that the history of work, though rooted in biblical, classical, and earlier medieval traditions, was malleable and contested, that it constituted a significant form of discourse on the meaning of work in contemporary society. After reading John Ball's use of the proverb "Whanne Adam dalfe and Eve span / Who was þanne a gentil man?" as a sign of the ideological nature of work's history, this chapter looks closely at three texts: the history of masonry contained in the Cooke MS (British Museum, Add. MS 23198), John Gower's account of the history of work in book 4 of the *Confessio amantis,* and Chaucer's *Former Age.* The uniqueness of the Cooke MS lies in its opposition to the general concealment of the world of work within medieval historiography. It defends the dignity of masonry by rewriting legendary and biblical material into a genealogical narrative of craft progress. It also defines masonry in ways that blur the boundary between the liberal and mechanical arts. These moves, I suggest, were fostered by three distinguishing characteristics of late medieval masonry: its close association with the ruling classes, its itinerancy, and the relatively permanent and hence historic nature of its products. By contrast, Gower's history of work constructs parallel but discrete histories for intellectual and physical labor. In doing so, Gower both upholds the social legitimacy of intellectual work as a form of production and preserves its superior value and dignity vis-à-vis material production, thus showing his characteristic devotion to the morality of social order, hierarchy, and place. Gower also prefaces his history of work with a discourse on true nobility that identifies *gentilesse* with *besinesse.* In this context, Gower's history of work also articulates a specifically bourgeois work mentality, a simultaneous valorization of industry and subordination of it to higher noneconomic values. Last, this chapter offers a revisionary reading of *The Former Age.* I argue that Chaucer's primitivist lyric is not so much a critique of contemporary civilization as a critique of contemporary primitivism, that its effective strategy both lures its reader into nostalgia for an atechnic past and exposes the irrationality of such nostalgia.

Complementing these historicizing impulses, late medieval authors also sought work's meaning in the self by representing work as a subjective necessity, a fulfillment that the individual requires over and above labor's fulfillment of material and moral responsibility. This search, my concluding chapter argues, was encouraged by the attention the labor problems of the fourteenth century generated around the issue of the motive for work. First, I demonstrate the general currency of interest in work's subjective dimension through a series of examples: the broadening of the concept of *acedia* or sloth to include occupational laziness, Gower's representation of work as a moral necessity, and Langland's vocational self-examination in the *apologia* (PPl C.5.1–104). I then show how Fragment VIII of *The Canterbury Tales,* comprising the *Second Nun's Tale* and *Canon's Yeoman's Tale,* is Chaucer's deepest reflection on work as a requirement, not only of the conditions of life, but of human nature itself.

"Labour of Tonge"

The Middle English Vocabulary of Work

[G]o forth again to gaze upon the old cathedral front, where you have smiled

so often at the fantastic ignorance of the old sculptors: examine once more

those ugly goblins, those formless monsters, and stern statues, anatomiless

and rigid; but do not mock at them, for they are signs of the life and liberty

of every workman who struck the stone.

John Ruskin, "The Nature of the Gothic,"
in *The Stones of Venice*

The seductiveness of Ruskin's invitation to nostalgia may have waned, but the polarized construction of medieval and modern work on which it is based is one of the more durable legacies of romantic medievalism. Since the eighteenth century, work in the Middle Ages has been repeatedly imagined in opposition to its modern counterpart, usually in terms of the relation of economic to social life: where modern work is separated from the life of the household, or even life itself, medieval work was fused with social and personal experience.[1] The idea that medieval people lived within a now lost unity of work and life is the necessary counterpart to the claim that the separation of work from "life" is specifically modern. Whatever its truth value, this idea contributes to the reduction of the

5

history of work to an antithesis between then and now, a narrative of loss
and inversion centered on the rupture of past and present.[2] And despite
the general lack of evidence as to how work was experienced in the Middle Ages, the designation of medieval work as traditional, communal, and
intrinsically satisfying is buttressed by a number of now classic theoretical formulations of fundamental differences between capitalist and precapitalist society: Polanyi's account of precapitalist economic activity as
embedded in other social and political institutions and capitalism's re-
verse embedding of social relationships in the economic system, Tönnies's
description of urban industrialism's replacement of *Gemeinschaft* ("community") with *Gesellschaft* ("society"), Durkheim's model of transition
from *mechanical* to *organic* social solidarity through the increasing division of labor, Weber's description of the rational organization of free labor
and the separation of capitalist enterprise from the household, and (behind them all) Marx's account of the alienation of the modern worker.[3]

The oppositional understanding of medieval and modern work has
had a decisive influence upon studies of the medieval vocabulary of work.
While there have been relatively few analyses of medieval words for work
as cultural, as opposed to simply linguistic, artifacts, what has been said
on the subject is characterized by an emphasis upon semantic alterity and
supports the view that medieval and modern concepts of work are radically different. According to Ruzena Ostrá, the history of the French work
vocabulary is defined by the genesis of a general, objective, occupationally
nonspecific term *(travail)* and the proportional loss of medieval semantic
distinctions between artisanal conceptions of work as a professional and
creative activity and agricultural conceptions of work as "un triste devoir
de l'homme condamné á gagner son pain á la sueur de son front."[4] Similarly, Jacques Le Goff draws attention to the absence of a general concept
of work and corresponding word in the Middle Ages and deduces that
work per se was not a medieval value: "Le travail n'était pas une 'valeur,' il
n'y avait même pas de mot pour le désigner."[5] For both Ostrá and Le Goff,
the *lack* of a general term and concept is the medieval work vocabulary's
defining and essential feature.

Intentionally or not, these accounts follow the logic of Marx's comments on the abstract conception of work in the *Grundrisse,* in which the
oppositional understanding of modern and premodern work is brought to
bear upon the issue of semantic change. Just as the imperfections and im-

precisions of the Gothic style were for Ruskin reflections of the medieval worker's nonalienation ("signs of the life and liberty of every workman who struck the stone"), so the lack of an abstract term for work was for Marx a sign of premodern man's inability to alienate the concept of work, a semantic reflection of a mentality that conceptualized work only in particular forms. Discussing the economic conception of labor in general first represented by Adam Smith,[6] Marx explains how "the simplest abstraction . . . which modern economics places at the head of its discussions, and which expresses an immeasurably ancient relation valid in all forms of society, nevertheless achieves practical truth as an abstraction only as a category of the most modern society."[7] Marx is concerned, then, with the abstract sense of *labor* not only as a discursive tool of political economy but as the semantic manifestation of significant social and conceptual change. How words reflect such change is no small question, but Marx constructs a correlation between changes in *labor* (the word) and changes in labor (the activity) by connecting the process of abstraction with the experience of indifference: "[T]his abstraction of labour as such is not merely the mental product of a concrete totality of labours. Indifference towards specific labours corresponds to a form of society in which individuals can with ease transfer from one labour to another, and where the specific kind is a matter of chance for them, hence of indifference. Not only the category, labour, but labour in reality has become the means of creating wealth in general, and has ceased to be organically linked with particular individuals in any specific form."[8] In other words, the abstract conception of labor, as a freeing of the concept of labor from specific forms of labor, is formally related to the development of free labor. Marx does not explain the two modern abstract senses of *labor*—"first the economic abstraction of the activity; secondly the social abstraction of that class of people who performed it"[9]—as reflecting a dehumanized, exploitative conception of labor by its capitalist organizers (though we may consider this point implicit). Instead, Marx locates the semantic change more broadly in the socioeconomic situation of workers and in doing so reveals his interest in the organicism of the past. The explanation illustrates the point, fundamental to Marx's thinking, that "the more deeply we go back into history, the more does the individual, and hence also the producing individual, appear as dependent, as belonging to a greater whole."[10] As one form of the absence of this belonging, "indifference towards specific labours"

characterizes the alienated perspective of the worker for whom the meaning of work is absorbed by the exchange of labor for livelihood. With this
indifference as the middle term in his equation, Marx identifies the individual worker's experience of the meaning of work as the meeting place of
semantic and social changes in work, as the conceptual agency that reveals the relation of word to thing.[11]

Marx's explanation of the socioeconomic context of *labor*'s modern
abstract sense remains compelling, but it should not serve as a starting
point for the interpretation of the medieval work vocabulary. Like other
oppositional accounts of medieval and modern culture, it succeeds in understanding a particular feature of the present by defining it against generalized and romantic assumptions about the past, in this case the idea
that work in earlier times was "organically linked" with individuals. In
this regard, it is as problematic as the Polanyi thesis, which, as Todd Lowry
explains, implies that "we cannot study ideas about the economy in ancient and medieval times, but only ideas that had economic content and
that may have cumulatively contributed to the eventual comprehension of
the economy as an independent functioning entity."[12] Not surprisingly,
Marx's account has been read as implying the impossibility of studying
medieval words for work in general.[13] If one accepts this, it is easy to produce an analysis of the medieval work vocabulary that validates the oppositional view of medieval work. One need only describe the occupational
and cultural associations of the various terms, the social relations they described and supported, and their positive and negative connotations and
then conclude that the propriety of every term to particular situations and
definitions of work reflects a state of affairs in which work and life were
fused and that the absence of a dominant, general, abstract term (such as
work, travail, Arbeit, lavoro) results from the concreteness of medieval
work, its subordination to use value, and its task orientation.

The problems with such an approach are manifold and irremediable.
First, the oppositional construction of medieval and modern work is in
general problematic. The comparison of medieval to modern work is a
valid, though incomplete, means of historical representation, but there is
no self-evident reason why such comparison should take the form of opposition. Instead, the oppositional construction of medieval work is rooted
in nostalgia, in the belief that the ills of today are a corruption of the health
of yesterday. Nostalgia obscures both historical similarity and real histori-

cal difference. Where historical similarity blurs the distinction between traditional and modern upon which nostalgia rests, historical difference—difference per se, or diversity, irreducible to simple opposition—depolarizes it, frustrating the dream of a return to tradition and draining the past of immediate polemical value. A historically legitimate estimation of the medieval experience of work, one that is optimally aware of both its familiarity and its alterity, can emerge only from the acceptance of the fluidity of the traditional-modern distinction.[14] Specifically, the a priori view of medieval people as less aware than we of work as a distinct realm of experience and consequently less aware of the relation of work to other aspects of life should be set aside. If we are to understand and not only imagine the medieval experience of work, the possibility that the relation of work to life was as problematic in the Middle Ages as today must remain open. Second, the application of the oppositional approach to the study of the medieval work vocabulary is methodologically crippled. To assume that the most culturally significant lexical features are those that appear to the present most alien is to disregard the whole for the part. Such analysis can at best produce an incomplete and distorted picture of the conceptual structure of medieval work. Specifically, the isolation of the medieval work vocabulary's lack of a dominant, general term as its essential, most "medieval" characteristic disregards the value of the general meanings it does possess. Moreover, there is no clear basis for the comparison of the cultural significance of terms across periods. With respect to Marx, the fact that the abstract sense of *labor* corresponds within modern society to indifference toward specific labors does not necessarily imply that the absence of such a term is possible only in a society where there is no such indifference.

The medieval vocabulary of work comprises fundamental evidence of medieval attitudes toward work, evidence that has its own story to tell and that should not simply be assigned a place within a preexisting historical framework. It is the linguistic equivalent of the other types of cultural products—textual, visual, and material—through which the medieval experience of work may be understood, and its analysis is not ancillary but complementary to the study of these other kinds of representations. The uniqueness of vocabulary as cultural evidence lies in its very generality. A vocabulary is to a superior degree a collective product, not a statement but the medium and the result of myriad statements, not an idea but the

vehicle and breeder of ideas. To historical study the generality of vocabulary is both a strength and a weakness. On the one hand it constitutes a
severe limit on the nature of the cultural evidence that vocabulary contains. On the other hand it ensures that the evidence vocabulary contains
is cultural, a reflection not of a particular life but of a way of life, not of a
particular mind but of mentalities.

As the medieval artifact points to the history of the nature of work, so
the medieval work vocabulary points to the history of the concept of work.
The meaning of work and the meaning of *work* are historically relative.
What is their interrelation? What can words tell us about the attitudes
and conceptions of the people who use them? How does mentality shape
the meaning of words? My purpose in this chapter is to address these
questions as they relate to the conceptual structure of work in late medieval England.[15] Some attention will be given to Latin and French terms,
but Middle English words are my focus. This choice is not arbitrary, as several things suggest that among the languages current in the period Middle English is the most fitting for the study of work mentalities. English
was the language most closely aligned to the experience of those who
themselves engaged in that multitude of productive activities that we col-
lectively term *work*. As William of Nassyngton wrote around 1325, "Bothe
lered and lewed, olde and ʒonge, / Alle understonden English tonge."[16] Extant statements by peasants and artisans may be lacking, but we may look
at the language they spoke and shaped. Middle English also displays to a
higher degree than Anglo-Latin or Anglo-French the double movement of
linguistic change—growth and stabilization—that links it in form more
closely to its historical situation. As a language of increasing textual production and formal use, English was least anchored to norms of expression
controlled by bureaucratic and academic tradition. To the extent that developments in attitudes toward work are reflected at the lexical level, we
may reasonably expect to find them in the language that was developing
the most.

The analysis that follows consists of two parts. The first part briefly
describes the Middle English work vocabulary term by term. My objective
here is not interpretation but a synthetic representation of the vocabulary
that will enable its interpretation *as a whole*. The Middle English lexicon
embodies a multiplicity of perspectives on the nature of work, and as an
undifferentiated mass of meanings this multiplicity is unintelligible. Some

conceptual framework or measuring rod is necessary to disclose the relationship between its elements. For this I have chosen a definition of work as a four-part concept built around the subjective and objective dimensions of action and end.

The second part assesses the cultural significance of the vocabulary. My primary concern here is with the work vocabulary as a reflection of ideology and mentality, as a complex of socially contingent meanings. The preponderance of Middle English words for work that emphasize the difficulty and painfulness of work, for instance, relates not only to Christian belief in the fallen nature of work and to the palpable experience of work's difficulty, but to status-conscious and especially upper-class conceptions of work as degrading and ignoble. The formative influence of social structure upon lexicon is clearly demonstrated in this regard by the fact that English takes from Anglo-French only words for work that are associated with servitude and pain (*travail* and *labour*)—a particular instance of the well-known fact that upper-class words (e.g., military and bureaucratic terms) predominate in the French portion of the English vocabulary. My conclusions in this section are several, but I hope to demonstrate above all that late medieval conceptions of work were significantly more complex and sophisticated than the polarized construction of medieval and modern work allows and that the Middle English work vocabulary is the product of a culture that was highly conscious of work as a distinct and problematic realm of experience, a culture attuned to the question of its meaning.

THE SEMANTICS OF WORK

Concepts of work per se are reflected primarily in those words that signify work in general. Among the multitude of work-related words in Middle English, these are *travail, labour, swink, werk*, and *craft*, with their verbal forms *travailen, labouren, swinken, werken*, and *craften*.[17] The most direct method of understanding the semantic structure of these words in relation to each other is to measure them against the immeasurably old and current conception of work as a particular kind of action directed to a particular kind of end, namely the definition of work as "action involving effort or exertion directed to a definite end, esp. as a means of gaining one's livelihood."[18] A division of this idea into its essential parts will furnish the types of features according to which the Middle English work vocabulary may be most clearly studied.

Work, then, consists of an action and an end. The action and the end of work are each of a certain character, and each may be considered with regard either to the agent or to the act of work itself. That is, we may think of work either in terms of the worker's experience of and motive for work or in terms of the nature of the process and the product of work. I will refer to these two aspects of work as work's subjective and objective dimensions. Subjectively, the action of work is characterized by effort, exertion, and the overcoming of inertia (as opposed to leisure, which is characterized by ease). Objectively, the action of work is characterized by productivity and utility, especially material productivity and utility, making and doing things necessary to life (as opposed to leisure, which involves doing things whose utility is less apparent). Subjectively, the end of work is first and foremost livelihood, the meeting of basic needs through compensation or the products of work (as opposed to play, which is not motivated by basic needs). Objectively, the end of work consists of a product or service, especially a materially necessary product or service (as opposed to play, which is its own end).

The boundaries between these dimensions may not always be apparent, but distinguishing between them helps to reveal the complex character of work and its concepts. This complexity is not only conceptual and semantic but very real, a material characteristic of the work process that is of necessity apparent to the worker. As an agent, the worker is aware of the materialization of his effort as something that satisfies a need. As a witness to the work process, he is aware of the transformation of the material worked upon into a product.[19] The complexity of the concept of work derives from the nature of work itself, as an activity that encompasses a double doubleness: the double end of livelihood and the work task itself plus the double nature of the work act as both effortful and useful. Like most human action, work is always doing one thing to achieve another. But work seems especially susceptible to tension and contradiction between its aspects. This owes, at the simplest level, to work's participation in the fundamental contraries of the life process: living and dying, growth and decay. As Hannah Arendt points out, "Labor assures not only individual survival, but the life of the species. Work and its product, the human artifact, bestow a measure of permanence and durability upon the futility of mortal life and the fleeting character of human time."[20] At the same time, work paradoxically enacts human mortality and frailty, both by being a necessary, imposed means of sustaining life, and thus an expression of weakness, and more palpably by involving the loss of energy, time, and life, by producing weakness. As work is the means of life, life is the means of death—a transactional complex that is succinctly expressed in the Adamic curse, "In the sweat of your face you shall eat bread till you return to the ground" (Gen. 3:19).

Similar tensions within the nature of work are visible in the way the major work-related problems of society can be defined in terms of an improper or unbalanced relation among work's dimensions. Alienation, for example, involves the outweighing of work's subjective by its objective dimension, whereby the worker is reduced to an object in the work process and all sense of continuity between the subjective and objective ends of work is lost. Professionalization concerns the displacement of work's objective by its subjective end, so that the inherent value of the work done suffers or ceases altogether to matter. Social justice issues concerning work revolve around the proper proportion between the subjective action and ends of work, between effort and compensation, as well as between work's objective and subjective ends, between what the worker accomplishes and earns. Last, ideas about the dignity and indignity of work are often expressible in terms of an emphasis upon one of work's dimensions, as in the indignity of needing to earn a living (an emphasis on work's subjective end) or the dignity of being a producer (an emphasis on work's objective action).

These kinds of interrelational complexities bring to light how naming work, more than signifying something that is simply there, involves taking a perspective on its nature, a perspective that may express a range of attitudes and realities. Work has multiple identities and requires several names. In the Middle Ages as now, an array of terms has served the purpose of signifying work's different dimensions as well as communicating its more abstract qualities like differences in status and class situation. Indeed, the question of what constitutes work within a particular period is sufficiently complicated that in a sense it is more proper to speak of work as constituted by its names. However naturally determined the forms of work are, its social and cultural nature ensures arbitrariness within the category as it is defined across class and gender boundaries. Distinctions between what is work and what is not are to a significant degree conventional and perceptual. Even at the individual level, it can make a real experiential difference whether one thinks of a particular action as "work" or not.

Conceived of universally, labor is, as Marx says, a process "in which man of his own accord starts, regulates, and controls the material reactions between himself and Nature."[21] But however immanent such a general idea may be in human concepts of work, a work vocabulary gives evidence of how work concepts are much more partial and historically contingent. As human beings create both their world and themselves through work, they also create their concepts of work and the words that express them. Old words for work are important, not only for what they can reveal, historically, about the culture that used them, but for how they represent the ongoing process whereby humans give meaning to, and find meaning in, work.

Travail

Travail is first attested in English near the end of the thirteenth century, and most of its derivatives appear during the last quarter of the fourteenth century.[22] The most striking semantic feature of *travail* is the degree to which it remains true to its prehistory. The established etymology is that *travail* derives from Late Latin *trepalium,* a three-staked device of torture.[23] Accordingly, *travail* primarily expresses work as an action in the subjective sense, as effort, especially painful effort. ModE *travail* strongly retains this sense, whereas the development of the word in French has taken an opposite course.[24] But ME *travail*'s range of meaning is much broader than its Modern English version, and the combined range of the Modern English and French versions of the word is a good indication of that earlier broadness. Particularly, ME *travail* signified work per se to a greater degree than now. It first enters English as a term for work rather than as a term for any type of trying or painful experience.[25] Likewise, *travail* is found signifying work in most of its four aspects.[26]

It is the association of *travail* with pain, suffering, and distress, then, that most calls for explication. To say that *travail* concerns work as effort is correct but imprecise. Effort may be considered as something expended, with stress on the agency of effort, or as something experienced, with stress on the patiency (the state of being acted upon, as opposed to agency) of effort, and it is the latter sense that *travail* primarily communicates. *Travail* is centered on work as something that is suffered through, endured. It is the personal price of work, the toll it takes on the worker. As something paid, *travail* has currency and may be stolen, squandered, or weighed.[27]

As *travail* is focused on the painful experience of work, so may it signify any type of arduous or distressing activity. Hence the *Catholicon Anglicum,* composed in the latter half of the fifteenth century, defines *travail* as "labor vel—bos, sudor, vexamen, operia, angor, laboramen, opera."[28] As these definitions make clear, *travail* may be used to signify both mentally and physically trying activities. "Þere is double maner trauaile, of spirit and of wittis and bodely trauaile," writes John of Trevisa, supplying "studiynge, wakyng, wreþþe, sorewe, and busines" as examples of the former.[29] Applications of *travail* to activities in which the physical component is secondary, however, are rarer and should be considered as metaphoric extensions of the physical sense. As a rule, such usage necessitates the addition of some qualifying phrase.[30] Likewise, the only specific activity commonly signified by *travail* without qualification is travel, whose physical difficulty was the grounds for such usage: "traveillynge men are ofte wery and their horses to."[31]

In sum, *travail* expresses above all the unavoidable difficulty of human work, not the technical difficulty of its processes or the social difficulties of the worker, but its most palpable pains. Viewed through the lens of *travail,* the nature of work appears narrowly focused on the suffering subject, a subject who, like one who is tortured, experiences pain as something forced upon him from without. Thus centered on the patiency of effort, *travail* encompasses the most undesirable aspects of work, those that are most often rationalized in terms of individual spiritual, particularly penitential, benefit, those whose material utility is least apparent. *Travail* is what is left behind in Augustine's imagination of work before the Fall,[32] just as it is the *mot juste* in the Wycliffite translation of Genesis 3.17: "cursid is the erthe in thi werk; in traueyls thow shalt ete of it alle the daies of thi lijf."[33]

Labour

Though the *MED* records one use of *labour* as early as 1300 (s.v. "labour n.," 3a), it generally appears in English during the last quarter of the fourteenth century, at the end of the period of the greatest assimilation of French words.[34] The lateness of its adoption may be partially explained by both the previous existence of *swink* and *werk* and the earlier assimilation of *travail.* Evidently another term for work was not what English usage most required, particularly one whose Latin equivalent was already commonly translated by *travail,* as the above citations from the *Catholicon Anglicum* and Wyclif's Bible show.[35] Like *travail, labour* is strongly tied to effort and pain. Etymologically, *labor* has been compared to the verb *labor,* meaning to slip or fall[36]—a homographic coincidence that ties into one elegant knot the *primorum parentum lapsus* and the double labor imposed upon them. In the *Aeneid,* Labos, labor personified, is in infernal company with Luctus, Curae, Morbi, Senectus, et al. (6.273ff), though positive valuations of *labor* are equally easy to find. The equivalent of Greek *ponos, labor* is the suffering that exalts Hercules and makes a hero of Virgil's farmer: "Herculem duri celebrant labores"; "labor omnia vicit / improbus et duris urgens in rebus egestas."[37]

How did *labour* enrich the Middle English work vocabulary? A preliminary answer can be found by looking at the semantic relationship between OF *laborer* and *travailler.* According to Ostrá, the general features of this relationship are as follows: *laborer* and *travailler* both represent work as effort, as fatigue, and as torment; *laborer* stresses the result and the utility of work, whereas *travailler* does not; *laborer* is more closely tied to agriculture and does not stress the negativity of work as much as *travailler.*[38]

These conclusions generally hold for Middle English as well. *Labour* was used to signify work generally, as effort or exertion, and as product.[39] The relationship of *labouren* to work as production is revealed most clearly in its transitive senses. Though *labouren,* like *travailen,* may denote harassment,[40] it is primarily used in connection with the object of work (what labor is expended upon) and, more rarely, with the subjective end of work (what is earned or achieved by labor).[41] *Labour* is not used to signify livelihood or professional occupation (as *craft, mister, lif-lode,* and *werk* are), but it comes closer than *travail* to doing so through its close connection to agriculture, which is especially clear in *labour*'s cognates.[42]

As a term for work as effort, *labour* is distinguished from *travail* through the emphasis it places on the agency, rather than the patiency, of effort. This defines its uniqueness. *Labour* emphasizes more the effort expended *on something*, the directed exertion of the worker, and less the pain per se of that exertion. While both *travailen* and *labouren* may be used to signify the endurance of pain generally, the multifarious transitive senses of *labouren* that *travailen* does not admit indicate the preoccupation of *labouren* with pain not simply as an effect but as an intrinsic element of the process of work.[43] Like *travail*, *labour* is unequivocally postlapsarian,[44] but it places less emphasis on the negativity of work because it is more holistic. *Labour* signifies work as both experience and as act, and reflects above all the fundamental productive work that constitutes man's nourishing and painful relationship to the earth:

> Ffor the erthe was made of erthe
> At the first begynnynge,
> That erthe schuld labour the erthe
> In trowthe and sore swynkynge.[45]

Swink

Before the late medieval adoption of *travail* and *labour*, *swink* was the term of choice for translating Latin *labor*—a fair indication of its focus on work as effort.[46] Like *travail* and *labour*, *swink* signifies the postlapsarian nature of work, its specifically human character.[47] God does not *swink*, as Ælfric makes clear in his commentary on the seasons: "His nama is *omnipotens*, ðæt ys, ælmigtig, for ðan ðe he mæg eall þæt he wille, and his miht nahwar ne swincþ."[48] Often found in alliteration with *swete* (in both alliterative and nonalliterative texts), *swink* signifies work primarily as physical exertion. Etymologically, *swink* is "a collateral form of *swingan*, 'to beat, strike, whip.'"[49] *Swink* is thus strongly tied to the notion of work as a type of bodily act. But it is also flexible enough to signify work both generally and more specifically as effort, production, or product.[50] *Swink*'s semantic uniqueness lies in the emphasis it places on the physical activeness of work, its motion and athleticism. Where *travail* and *labour* emphasize the patiency and the agency of effort, respectively, *swink* completes this trio of effort-centered terms by emphasizing the act of effort itself.

Another prominent feature of s*wink* is its relative rarity in texts, as compared with *travail* and *labour.* The word does not occur once in such large prose texts as Wyclif's Bible, the works of Malory, or *An Alphabet of Tales,* a rarity that the propensity of translators to employ cognates cannot alone explain, particularly in the case of the Bible, which contains numerous references to work. Chaucer, Gower, and Langland all used *swink* much less frequently than *travail* and *labour,* despite their significant intersection in meaning.[51] Since there is no indication that *swink* was simply losing its currency, except to the degree that some of its earlier functions were being shared by *travail* and *labour,* this suggests that *swink* is both the most colloquial and the most narrow in meaning of the Middle English terms for work as effort.

Evidence for *swink*'s colloquialness is not hard to find. For example, *swink* is almost entirely unrepresented in fifteenth-century lexicographical books, indicating that the word had little place in the textual life of the schools such works served.[52] And in the *Canterbury Tales, swink* occurs more often both in reported speech and in syntactical connection with a first-person subject or pronoun than either *travail* or *labour.*[53]

Swink's narrower semantic range must also be counted as influencing the relative infrequency of its attestations. All of the meanings that the *OED* and *MED* provide for *swink* are also provided for *travail* and *labour* but not vice versa, except those related to sexual intercourse, which *labouren* alone may also signify. This semantic "deficiency" is to some degree a function of *swink*'s minimal transitivity. OE *swincan* is wholly intransitive, and the transitive senses of *swinken* do not appear until the early thirteenth century, and generally later.[54] But there are also more telling differences. Most striking is *swink*'s relative lack of associations with textual, intellectual, and legal practice, a difference with *travail* and *labour* that reflects the latter's origin in the language of administration and privilege.[55] *Swink*'s use in military contexts is also relatively limited. *Swink, travail,* and *labour* were all used to signify the toil of battle, but *travail* and *labour* could also signify military and heroic action objectively as military service, knightly competition, siege, or feat of strength, revealing their affiliation with the language of the court and its literature.[56]

Altogether, these distinctions reveal how *swink* expresses the very real continuity between the corporeality of work and the colloquial. In the late medieval period, *swink* was and had the aura of being the common worker's word for the most common kind of work. Words that stress the agency and the patiency of effort may carry ineradicable associations with manual labor, but exertion and pain are common to all types of work, both manual and mental, and are thus easily assimilated to a wide range of contexts and values. This is not so true of the physical act of work itself, especially those iterative acts of agricultural labor (*diching, delving, threshing,* etc.) that in their singularity make up the process of production. It is this kind of physicality that is the basis for the striking continuity in the restricted use of *swink* in two vocational portraits written almost four hundred years apart. In both Ælfric's *Colloquy on the Occupations* and Chaucer's *General Prologue* it is the plowman who swinks: "La leof, þearle ic swince!" (8) and "A trewe swynkere and a good was he" (I.531).[57]

Werk

Werk is preeminent among the Middle English terms for work in its generality. Though not as general as *don* or *maken, werken* may also signify action or production per se, *werk* an act or a product. Where *travail, labour,* and *swink* are all anchored in the concept of work as effort, *werk* frees work, as it were, from its difficulty by stressing the creativity of its process and the tangibility of its product. This "positive" emphasis is succinctly evident in *werk*'s application to divine creation and its equivalence to *opus*.[58] The objectivity of *werk* is not so absolute as to preclude association with suffering—*werken* may simply mean "to tax and exert oneself physically"[59]—but it is the basis for its marked association with craft, particularly the architectural and ornamental crafts.[60] *Werk*'s objectivity is the basis for this association more specifically in the sense that *werken*'s transitivity and *werk*'s substantive sense express the nature of artisanal work as a creative working upon some material that produces a conceptually and functionally distinct object: for example, the making of leather into shoes or stone into a building. ModE *werk* has lost much of this craft association, which survives conspicuously in the past-participle-turned-adjective *wrought*. More than its Modern English descendant, *werk* distinguishes itself from nonproductive types of work and those in which the worker, as agent, does not appear as the prime cause of production, such as agricultural cultivation. Craft, as ordered toward and valued by the object it creates, is preeminently a transitive activity. As the crafted product objectifies the labor and skill of the craftsman, so the semantic representation that craft elicits is objective.[61]

Werk's generality is also greater than that of ModE *work*, whose most general senses are now obsolete or archaic.[62] A significant *rapprochement* between *werk*'s general and specific senses may be found within specific contexts, such as the cycle plays' representation of Noah as a good worker in both senses.[63] But *werk* was frequently used, more than *travail* or *labour*, without any reference to work and could indicate just about any action whatsoever. From the perspective of this generality, *werk*'s signification of work may appear as simply one application among many of a term more broadly rooted in the concept of effective action. Yet the centrality of *werk*'s connection to work is indicated by the fact that nearly all of its derivatives, such as *werkman, werkday, werkhouse,* and *werkless,* concern productive, occupational labor.

The special value of *werk* within the Middle English work vocabulary lies in its being a holistic and versatile term that places relatively balanced emphasis on the subjective and objective dimensions of work. *Werk* involves effort, but that is not its defining attribute. In this respect *werk* is unlike *craft,* which, being more purely objective, carries little connotation of the difficulty of work. Yet like *craft, werk* is rooted in the productivity and utility of work. *Werken* is not only to labor but to accomplish. Hence *werk,* unlike the effort-centered terms, gets at the purposes of work, both subjective and objective. *Werk*'s signification of the objective end of work, built around its substantive sense, is particularly evident in such phrases as *worke of thy handes* and *clerk of the werkes* and in a variety of compounds such as *handwerk, castyn-werk,* and *iren-werk. Werk*'s signification of the subjective end of work, livelihood, which is now often taken for granted in ModE *work,* is less obvious. For the noun, the meanings "labor" and "occupation, employment" are often only contextually distinguishable. But from the fourteenth century onwards, *werken* is found meaning "To do one's ordinary business; to pursue a regular occupation"[64]—a striking indication that the development of a content-neutral, strongly economic concept of work was well underway during this period.

Craft

The most original meaning of *craft* is "strength, power, might, force."[65] This sense dies out in the sixteenth century, while the derivative meaning, "skill, skillfulness, art," which is also attested from the Old English period, does not.[66] *Craft*, like *werk*, was thus a flexible term whose basic meaning extended well beyond the sphere of work. Yet its association with productive, economically oriented labor is strong and pervasive.[67] Moreover, as its general meanings testify, *craft* embodies a concept of work not only free of any association with suffering but rooted in the appreciation of its power.

Beyond its basic work-related meanings, *craft*'s strongest association with work is its signification of economic institutions of work, especially those of manufacture. Like *mister*, *craft* signifies trade or occupation, especially those of the artisan, and by the end of the fourteenth century an organization of craftsmen or tradesmen, or a guild.[68] In opposition to *labourer* and *swinker*, which generally signify an agricultural worker, and in contrast to the more versatile *travailour* and *werker*, *craftesman* is almost always used to denote an artisan or, after the adoption of *craft* to denote a guild, a member of a guild. But this, like other derivatives, is built upon only the primary connotation of its root, and many nonartisanal or marginally artisanal occupations are indicated by compounds that employ *craft*: *gleo-craft*, *leche-craft*, *wode-craft*, *baking-craft*, *scrivener-craft*, *tilling-craft*, and so on. From this perspective, we may say that *craft* designates the skill necessary to work in general. Langland, extending St. Paul's enumeration of the spiritual gifts of the Holy Spirit (1 Cor. 12.4–10) to include all occupations, uses *craft* to signify both occupation and occupational skill in general.[69]

Craft's semantic flexibility also reflects its more general designation of art. *Craft* translates Latin *ars* and likewise crosses the boundary between *artes liberales* and *artes mechanicae*, whence the terms *seven craftes* and *craftes mechanic*.[70] But Middle English also had *art*, which could likewise designate industrial pursuits. Gower, for example, refers to "hem that ben Artificiers, / Whiche usen craftes and mestiers, / Whos Art is cleped Mechanique" (*CA* 7.1691–93). While *craft* and *art* are thus comparable within specific contexts, above all within schematic organizations of theoretical and practical types of knowledge, their difference lies in the deeper affiliation of the former to the practical side of things. *Art* and *craft* both imply knowledge, but *craft* to a superior degree implies its use. As Reginald Pecock puts it, *craft* is essentially know-how: "Craft . . . is a kunnyng wherbi we knowen how þis or þat is to be maad of þe newe in sum outward abidyng mater: as is kunnyng to make an hous, a schipp, a knyf, a cloke, and so forþ of oþire lijk."[71]

Craft's most important contribution to the Middle English work vocabulary lies in its expression of the rationality of work and the worker. Of all the Middle English terms, *craft* places the least emphasis on the effort of work and stresses instead both its intellective, technical component and the tangibility of its product. *Craft* is not only production but *making*, the purposive creation of a new and exceptionally human product. Accordingly, *craft* does not share in the negativity of the other terms, the negativity that attaches to the painfulness of work. The negative sense that *craft* does carry, that of trickery and deception, derives from its rationality and has no relation to work, except in specific contexts.[72] Perhaps the strongest indication of *craft*'s rationality and positivity is that it is attributable to divinity, both as God's creativity—"after þis haþ crafte of God so medlid mannis partis togidere þat noon contrarieþ to anoþer"—and as the partial revelation of that creativity to man: "God . . . ȝeueþ wit in alle craftes."[73]

BETWEEN VOCABULARY AND CULTURE

What does the Middle English work vocabulary reveal about attitudes toward work in late medieval England? To try to answer this question presupposes that the relationship of language to culture is intelligible and meaningful, that lexical structure is more than linguistic but is in some significant way *about* culture. But this is far from obvious. Like artifacts, words both embody and conceal the conditions of their formation. Verbal meaning is not static but is subject to continual modification through usage, which both applies and creates the current meanings of words. As Gadamer puts it, "[T]he general concept meant by the word is enriched by any given perception of a thing, so that what emerges is a new, more specific word formation which does more justice to the particularity of that act of perception. However certainly speaking implies using pre-established words with general meanings, at the same time, a constant process of concept formation is going on, by means of which the life of a language develops."[74] But however much words are thus shaped by and tuned to their historical situation, they also obscure it. The word reflects life but also has a life of its own. Verbal meaning preserves particular perceptions not in their particularity but in the objectified form of modifications in general, available meaning. As the work that goes into making an artifact is concealed by the artifact's distinctive form and utility, the concept formation that fashions verbal meaning is concealed by the generality and versatility that enable meaning's usefulness. But a word conceals the circumstances of its formation even to a greater degree than the artifact. Where the artifact is the product of particular situations and intentions and is shaped by design, the shape of a word is not designed but is the product, or more accurately the by-product, of innumerable and diverse events. Like other social institutions, a vocabulary is generated and sustained by a complexity of forces and thus resists simple, causal explanation.

The existence of language-specific names for things (e.g., material objects, customs, institutions) and untranslatable words offers the simplest evidence for the cultural embeddedness of language. But such examples are only the most obvious manifestations of a more pervasive and close relation between vocabulary and culture. As Edward Sapir, Raymond Williams, and many others have recognized, vocabulary both shapes and is shaped by culture, both organizes and reflects material and conceptual experience.[75] Numerous studies in historical semantics, anthropological linguistics, and sociolinguistics have confirmed in diverse ways the validity of Sapir's general observation that "vocabulary is a very sensitive index of the culture of a people and changes in meaning, loss of old words, the creation and borrowing of new ones are all dependent on the history of culture itself."[76] But interpreting vocabulary as cultural evidence, as evidence of mentality, of ideology, of the modes of thought whereby a society articulates itself, poses many problems. As Malcolm Crick has warned, "[L]anguage and culture do not mirror one another. . . . Language is *in itself* a highly complex organizational structure."[77] Because the first function of meaning is simply signification, there is always a gap between the meaning of words and the conceptions of those who use them. A lexicon is not in itself an adequate means of expression but contains deficiencies and surpluses of meaning that syntax, rhetoric, and context must continually remedy. For instance, it may be true, as Le Goff argues, that "Le mot *travail* est . . . né dans des conditions pas particulièrement optimistes, celles du travail considéré comme une torture,"[78] but the fact that *travail* carries the sense of torture (as it still does in some Modern French locutions, e.g., *se travailler*) does not imply that the society that uses it generally experiences or conceives of work as torture. A relationship between different meanings of the same word may or may not be evidence of a real cultural relationship between their referents. Even if the relation between such meanings is of cultural significance, it may not match up with their historical development. The double reference of ME *craft* and *gin* to technology and trickery, for example, may be plausibly situated within late medieval attitudes toward technology,[79] though neither of these senses develops out of the other. Changes in the meaning of a word do not smoothly document changes in attitudes toward its referent. Semantic change, the process by which words attain the meanings they may be said to "have" within a given period, as any brief consideration will show, is an extraordinarily irregular and messy phenomenon.[80] The passage of semantic features from *parole* to *langue* is always the work of multiple causes, and the "*origin* and *dissemination* of new meanings are often due to widely different factors."[81]

In the study of the cultural content of vocabulary, two related concepts have enabled analysis to negotiate the complexities of semantic structure and change: the semantic field and the keyword. *Semantic field* was first used by Gunther Ipsen to denote the complex of meanings proper to a particular conceptual sphere, but it was Jost Trier's study of German intellectual terminology that put the field theory on firm footing and established its usefulness as a method of historical study.[82] As Stephen Ullmann explains,

> Trier elaborated his conception of fields as closely-knit sectors of the vocabulary, in which a particular sphere is divided up, classified and organized in such a way that each element helps to delimit its neighbors and is delimited by them. In Ipsen's picturesque formula,

their contours fit into each other like pieces of different shapes in a mosaic. In each field, the raw material of experience is analyzed and elaborated in a unique way, differing from one language to another and often from one period to another in the history of the same idiom. In this way, the structure of semantic fields embodies a specific philosophy and a scale of values.[83]

By recognizing semantic features as both expressions of their historical situation and functional elements in a system of expression, this model guards against the dangers of reading too much into the single word. Each word presents but one perspective on the subject of the field, and its relation to other terms deserves consideration as much as its positive content. The demise of *travail* and *swink* in English, for example, does not appear so strongly as evidence of a general shift from negativity to positivity in the work vocabulary when set against the advent of *toil* and *drudgery*.[84] Additionally, the field model recognizes the need to understand not only the meanings of the field but all of its general features as evidence of the way a culture or period understands a particular area of itself. The number and type of conceptual distinctions marked by the structure of the field, the shape of the structure itself, and the relationships between the connotations and social contexts of its terms are all important. In short, the field theory of vocabulary correctly emphasizes the cultural importance of not only what society has words for but how it has them.

The term *keyword (mot-clé)* was first used by Georges Matoré to signify a word that both dominates a particular semantic field and is a "unité lexicologique exprimant une société . . . un être, un sentiment, une idée, vivants dans la mesure même où la société reconnaît en eux son idéal."[85] Although this definition privileges abstractions and the study of keywords has a strong association with the history of ideas, the concept of the keyword has been broadened, notably by Anna Wierzbicka and Raymond Williams. While recognizing that there is no objective procedure for identifying keywords, Wierzbicka suggests that a keyword is generally "a common word" that is "very frequently used in one particular semantic domain" and that is "at the center of a whole phraseological cluster."[86] Williams offers similar but more acute criteria, characterizing keywords as words "we share with others, often imperfectly, when we wish to discuss many of the central processes of our common life," "significant, binding words in certain activities and their interpretation," and words for which "the problems of [their] meanings" become "inextricably bound up with the problems [they are] used to discuss."[87] The keyword is, in these terms, a real phenomenon of linguistic experience. But its main interest to scholarship has been as an interpretive category that exposes relationships between language and culture, thus enabling an understanding of deeper, unobvious connections between elements of culture and mentality.

The semantic field and keyword concepts concretize and validate the sense, so well explored by C. S. Lewis's *Studies in Words,* that in examining old words "all the while one seems to be learning not only about words."[88] The crucial issue, of course, is the truth and content of this seeming. For word study to achieve its interpretive promise, its claims and methods must be clarified, especially with regard to two issues: the relationship between language and culture in general and the significance of polysemy. Toward the first, Peggy A. Knapp's recent study of words across the late medieval/early modern boundary rightly emphasizes the interplay of language and social history: "[S]emantic and social changes must be seen in a dynamic and fluid relationship, in which new social formations modify the range or inflection of verbal signs and those signs in turn impel or retard social change."[89] Words offer evidence, then, not of things outside language but of cultural developments that happen in and through language, of how, in Knapp's words, "social change is being naturalized into the life-worlds of men and women" (8). Toward the second issue, Williams's definition of keywords as words whose problems in meaning become complicated with the issues they are used to address offers a way of distinguishing between culturally significant and merely linguistically significant polysemy. This criterion may be generalized to include words whose differing meanings have an important and more than logical relationship or anywhere there seems to be a crisis in the relationship between *res* and *verba,* as is clearly the case, for instance, with the word *gentilesse.*

The analysis that follows seeks to apply these methods and principles to three features of the Middle English work vocabulary that seem especially significant: (1) the divided structure of its semantic field, (2) the multiplicity of the vocabulary, and (3) the polysemy of *werk.* As a semantic field, the Middle English work vocabulary is divisible into two areas, the relative domains of *swink-travail-labour* and *werk-craft,* as may be illustrated by a simple table:[90]

Dominant Meanings		*Swink*	*Travail*	*Labour*	*Werk*	*Craft*
Subjective	Effort	■ (black)	■ (black)	■ (black)	▨ (grey)	□ (empty)
	Livelihood	□ (empty)	▨ (grey)	▨ (grey)	▨ (grey)	■ (black)
Objective	Production	□ (empty)	□ (empty)	▨ (grey)	■ (black)	■ (black)
	Product	□ (empty)	□ (empty)	▨ (grey)	■ (black)	■ (black)

The first area emphasizes the subjective, effortful dimension of work, and the latter emphasizes work's objective, productive dimension. Boxes filled with black indicate relatively full emphasis, grey represents relatively partial emphasis, and empty boxes indicate scant or no emphasis. The semantic field is "divided" in the sense that it lacks a fully extensive term, a feature shared with its Old French counterpart.[91] This structural division encompasses both the meanings and the social associations of the terms. *Swink, travail,* and *labour* are strongly associated with manual labor, servitude, and agricultural work, *werk* and *craft* with artisanal manufacture and the liberal arts. The vocabulary thus constitutes a homology between the division of the concept of labor and the division of labor. It represents a fragmentation, as it were, of the work process and a projection of those fragments onto particular types of work. This structural division extends as well to the vocabulary's linguistic origins. During the period under question, English adopts from Anglo-French only terms that describe work as effort and pain and whose strongest associations are with servitude and agriculture, maintaining words of English origin to signify work more objectively as production. The multiplicity of the vocabulary is not formally separable from this structural division, but it merits separate consideration as the *degree* of division in the vocabulary. We may ask, in other words, why Middle English developed as many terms for work in general as it did and what this implies about the work vocabulary's function within society as a system of expression. Finally, the polysemy of *werk* is a significant feature of the vocabulary in that *werk* is both its most extensive term and the one most used to signify acts other than work. In contrast to ModE *work,* which both is fully extensive and primarily denotes occupational activity, *werk* appears as simultaneously the most and the least work-related word in Middle English. The word thus raises important questions about the boundaries of the concept of work in the late medieval period.

Taking these features in turn, I shall argue, first, that the divided structure of the Middle English work vocabulary, while generally representative of the complex nature of work itself, is rooted above all in a combination of class-based and status-based conceptions of work; second, that the multiplicity of the vocabulary, as a system of expression, reflects a cultural recognition of the value and nature of the work process itself, a *phenomenal* awareness of work that is characteristically medieval; and third, that *werk*, as a cultural keyword, figures not an incapacity for making distinctions between the economic and the noneconomic but a cultural habit of perceiving relations between work and life, between occupational and personal agency.

The Dichotomous Structure

Ruzena Ostrá has argued that the dichotomous structure of the Old French work vocabulary is its defining, specifically medieval characteristic. Lacking a fully extensive term that dominated usage in the manner of ModFr *travail*, the semantic field may be conceived of as having two centers, *laborer* and *ovrer*, its two most extensive terms, the one emphasizing the effort of work, the other its utility.[92] The fundamental cause of this dualism, says Ostrá, is the currency of two opposed conceptions of work in medieval society, one agricultural and negative, the other urban and positive. The *laborer* group represents the conception of work as "une punition que Dieu infligea à l'homme en le chassant du Paradis et en le condamnant à une vie remplie de labeur, donc d'un travail fatigant, pénible et sans joie" (37). The *ovrer* group, on the other hand, represents the "conception qui correspondait aux opinions et sentiments des artisans et des milieux urbains en général et qui considérait le travail en tant qu'activité ayant pour but de produire quelque chose d'utile (ou de beau), donc un ouvrage" (38). These alternate conceptions of work are, according to Ostrá, more or less independent. The first is born out of the difficult conditions, "primitives and dures" (37), of medieval, especially agricultural, labor. The *ovrer* conception departs from this negativity and reflects, on the part of artisans, "la conscience de leur individualité et de leur valeur professionnelle, le sentiment nouveau de la dignité du travail."[93]

The merits of this account, as a possible explanation for the structure of the Middle English work vocabulary, are outweighed by the problems it poses. First, while it is obvious that the Middle English work vocabulary embodies contrary conceptions of work and that this contrariety extends to occupational associations of terms, there is little to suggest that such contrariety is uniquely medieval. Such distinctions, at once occupational and social, reflect divergent conceptions of work as either honorific or demeaning, personally or merely economically satisfying, professional or servile, intelligently creative or merely physically productive. They obtain, in one form or another, in ancient, medieval, and modern societies. As Birgit van den Hoven has demonstrated, classical conceptions of work were as ambivalent, as simultaneously positive and negative, as medieval.[94] Similarly, P. D. Anthony's exploration of the ideology of work, of "the various exhortations that have been made for its efficient or enthusiastic performance," demonstrates the interrelatedness of modern conceptions of work as alienating and satisfying.[95]

Divergent conceptions of work are perennial, not least because of the complex nature of work, which is, as Anthony says, "a dialectic in itself."[96] As the socialist Hendrik De Man explains, "Every worker is simultaneously creator and slave. He is the latter, even if he be the happiest of creators, for he is a slave of his own creation. Freedom of creation and compulsion of performance, ruling and being ruled, command and obedience, functioning as subjects and functioning as objects—these are the poles of a tension which is immanent in the very nature of work."[97] In the deepest sense, this dualism results from the fact that work is both an objective and a subjective necessity, both something that must be done and something that *one* must do. Work is at once an affliction, an act forced upon humans by material conditions, and an expression, a self-directed exercise of specifically human powers.

This idea may be most familiar to us through Marx, for whom man is *animal laborans,* a creature that creates, realizes, and distinguishes itself through work.[98] But medieval religious and philosophic tradition also articulated in comparable ways work's vitalness to human nature. In addition to more commonplace notions about the physical, moral, and spiritual benefits of work that define it in a weaker sense as necessary to individual life—for example, "Usage of labour is a greet thyng, for it maketh, as seith Seint Bernard, the laborer to have stronge armes and harde synwes; and slouthe maketh hem feble and tendre" (Chaucer, *ParsT* X.689)—there is the Augustinian idea that work was not a consequence of the Fall but a divinely ordained feature of Edenic life (see n. 32). According to Augustine's authoritative exegesis, man not only must work but was created by God *to* work.[99] The divine origin of work was also represented visually in scenes showing Adam being taught how to plow by an angel or in some cases God himself.[100] Related currents of thought defined work by analogy to higher forms of production, natural and divine. The church fathers generally conceived of work as a participation in divine creativity, as Charles Munier explains: "Faithful to Jewish and NT tradition, the Fathers rehabilitated labour in all its forms, and laid down its obligations. For them, labour is a divine institution written into the work of creation. 'Man,' writes Irenaeus, 'has received hands from God to grasp and work. Who participates in God's art and wisdom, participates also in his power' [*Adv. haer.* V, 3, 2]. Through his labour, man in some way continues God's work; like God, he must use wisdom, force and beauty."[101] In the twelfth century, the centrality of work to human nature received influential elaboration by Hugh of St. Victor, who emphasized that all forms of work both express man's rationality, "so that we look with wonder not at nature alone but at the artificer as well," and are ordered toward the perfection of his fallen nature: "This, then, is what the arts are concerned with, this is what they intend, namely to restore within us the divine likeness, a likeness which to us is a form but to God is his nature."[102]

Ostrá's conception of the independence of the alternate conceptions of work represented by the *ovrer-laborer* dichotomy is also problematic. Work as pain and work as production are neither true opposites nor mutually exclusive. Nor are the attitudes most associated with these aspects of work, disdain for work as degrading and servile on the one hand and appreciation of work as creative and useful on the other, incompatible. As Paul Freedman has demonstrated regarding medieval attitudes to agricultural work, "One might praise the diligence of the laborer without thereby crediting him with spiritual dignity. It was quite possible to maintain an image of the plowman as a worthy and patient worker while considering physical toil itself the punishment of Adam's sin. . . . The modern tendency to equate productivity with moral character makes it difficult to see how medieval observers might acknowledge the utility, the necessity, and even the *virtue* of agricultural labor while expressing a frank contempt for those who engaged in it."[103] Indeed, to think of work as simultaneously useful and demeaning is at the heart of the aristocratic attitudes toward it. As the means of generating what is to be consumed and displayed work is useful, but as a mark of servility, of powerlessness, it is base. The social meaning of the conspicuous consumption and leisure proper to aristocratic life lies in their being signs of someone else's work. Leisure is honorific because it testifies to another's toil, just as the aristocratic appreciation of fine workmanship, however aesthetic, involves the predatory pleasure of possessing another's labor.[104]

A coincidence of conceptions of work as painful and valuable is also broadly proper to all workers, agricultural and artisanal alike. Pride and pleasure in work have long been obsessively and nostalgically attributed to the medieval craftsman as someone who, owning, overseeing, and being the means of production, conceived of his product as an externalization of himself and was highly conscious of the importance of his work.[105] This attribution is as much an admixture of truth and romantic exaggeration as the equally perdurable depersonalized image of the medieval peasant as simply an exploited toiler. Direct documentary evidence of how agricultural and artisanal laborers conceptualized their work may be slim, but their social and economic situations in late medieval England point to greater similarity than difference in this regard. The common unit of both agricultural and artisanal production was the family (nuclear or three-generational), augmented in some cases with wage workers and either an apprentice or journeyman, respectively.[106] While commodity production and monetization were naturally more dominant in towns and cities than in the countryside, and were more typical of artisanal than agricultural work, "in the countryside as well as in the towns petty commodity production was established very early," and "there existed since at least the twelfth century a vigorous, monetized, and even credit-based peasant land market."[107] Urban and rural communities were mutually permeable and similarly stratified.[108] The occupational distinction between peasant and craftsman was not a firm one, since most peasants "were able to repair, and even to make, many necessary tools" and a rural craftsman "usually had some agricultural land as well as his workshop."[109] Last, both peasant and craftsman were subjects of feudal exploitation.[110] According to the dominant social model of the time and in reality, both were *labora-tores* to whom "it falleþ to trauayle bodily and wiþ here sore swet geten out of þe erþe bodily lifelode for hem and for oþer parties," and both participated in the Rising of 1381.[111] In short, there are many reasons to imagine the peasant and artisan—by virtue of their common small production of both use values and exchange values, the tangibility and apparency of those values, and the appropriation of them by the ruling class—as mutually conscious of the pain and usefulness of their work and as comparably capable of experiencing it as either demeaning or dignified.

The dichotomous structure of the Middle English work vocabulary is derivable neither from generalizations about the strenuous nature of medieval agricultural work nor from the professional pride of craftsmen. These generalizations are important, but the diverse features of the vocabulary cannot be realistically localized to particular occupational groups as if their experience of work were responsible piecemeal for their lexical presence. To attempt to do so would be to ignore both the dialectical structure of work itself and the fact that the way individuals understand this structure, in their own work and in the work of others, is significantly conditioned by social factors. It is evident, for instance, that "the aversion to labor is in great part a conventional aversion" and that the "distastefulness and even physical irksomeness of an activity are decisively modified by the context in which this activity is placed by society."[112] The polarity of aristocratic attitudes toward manual work and warfare offers the most conspicuous example of this modification. Work and warfare are both physically taxing, and both satisfy economic need, yet engaging in one is as much a requirement of the nobility as abstaining from the other.

To understand the dichotomous structure of the Middle English work vocabulary and, more specifically, why its terms both privileged particular aspects of work over others and were associated with particular types of occupations, it will be necessary to examine more closely the social contingency of concepts of work, specifically their relation to status and class. Work is not only a relation between man and nature but a relation between men, a social relation. The forms of social differentiation that most express this fact are status and class. Status and class constitute the most fundamental connection between work and social structure. The place of individuals within society, both the honor and prestige that are accorded them (their status) and their economic situation (their class), are inextricably bound to the nature of the work they perform and the rewards it brings them. As articulated by Max Weber, status and class in essence concern the division of labor and the distribution of the products of labor in society: "[C]lasses are stratified according to their relation to the production and acquisition of goods; whereas status groups are stratified according to the principles of their *consumption* of goods as represented by special styles of life."[13] Accordingly, perceptions and expressions of the nature and value of work are related to status and class interests. That is, just as work itself is not a private and autonomous act but is formally bound to the worker's status and class situation, so concepts of work carry social and ideological force and are tied to status- and class-based attitudes.

Because "stratification by status goes hand in hand with a monopolization of ideal and material goods," status consciousness, concerned with the "specific, positive or negative, social estimation of *honor*," always involves perceptions of the worth and nature of the production and the producers of goods as well as invidious comparisons between them.[14] As status-defining acts, possession and consumption are not separable from the question of the social origin of the goods that are possessed and consumed. Rather, the dependence of material privilege upon production is the basis for the conventional designation of abstention from work as a sign of privilege and status, a designation that in turn diminishes the honorableness of work. As Veblen explains,

> *Nota notae est nota rei ipsius.* According to well-established laws of human nature, prescription presently seizes upon this conventional evidence of wealth [abstention from work] and fixes it in men's habits of thought as something that is in itself substantially meritorious and ennobling; while productive labour at the same time and by a like process becomes in a double sense intrinsically unworthy. Prescription ends by making labour not only disreputable in the eyes of the community, but morally impossible to the noble, freeborn man, and incompatible with a worthy life.[15]

But the disdain for work that thus emerges—most strongly and inclusively from the most privileged groups and less inclusively but not necessarily less strongly from all status groups toward inferiors—also constitutes a

definition of what work is. Status consciousness is capable of disqualify-
ing work only by *defining* it as evidence of a lack of wealth, as the sign of
inferior force. It appreciates the reality of work and the worker only insofar as they may be understood as such signs and conceptually prefers, as
most suited to its desire to articulate to itself and others its superiority,
those aspects of work that most naturally and with the least misrepresen-
tation signal inferior force.

The aspect of work that most signifies inferior force is the subjective
dimension of the action of work, namely effort. All aspects of work may be
understood as signs of need, and semblances of material utility and productivity are rigorously avoided in the conventional display of material
privilege. But effort signifies inferior force and lack of wealth to a superior
degree by virtue of its being an expenditure, a loss of force. As an expression of the gap between the will and its object, effort is a sign of imperfect
power.

As an expression of the struggle of human agency for something it
needs, effort is a sign of imperfect possession. The Latin word that best
captures effort in this full sense is *difficultas,* a combination of distress
and want. In Augustine's oft-cited expression for the dual punishment imposed on Adam and his descendants, *ignorantia et difficultas,* it is the corporal dimension of man's fallen nature and the specific feature of postlapsarian work.[116] Understood in this characteristically medieval fashion,
effort is thus rooted in sinfulness. As the "supplicium mortalitatis," the
punishment, the painfulness of mortality, imposed "ad animi expenden-
dam miseriam," for the expiation of the spirit's wretchedness, effort is a
kind of sweating out of vicious nature.

Cultural articulation of the effort of work as a sign of powerless and
sinful inferiority, as postlapsarian *difficultas,* emerges most clearly, and
in a form eminently suited to the conceptual reduction of work to effort
by status consciousness, from the medieval understanding of Cain. The
fourth book of Genesis narrates, among other things, a transformation of
the nature of work in the person of Cain. From the description of Cain as
a husbandman *(agricola)* who offered "de fructibus terrae munera Domino"
(Gen. 4.3) to God's curse that Cain's work upon the earth will no longer be
fruitful, work deteriorates from utility to futility, from productivity to
mere effort.[117] Exegetical opinion has differed as to how the defectiveness

of Cain's offering and God's rejection of it should be precisely interpreted, but commentators consistently held that the fault lay not in the offering but the offerer.[118] Cain's fault, as emblematized in the derivation of his name from Hebrew *qanah* (to possess), was possessiveness.[119] According to the Septuagint reading of Genesis 4.7, in which God questions Cain's division of his offering, Cain's possessiveness was most commonly and simply understood as his desire to reserve for himself the best fruits of his labor. Augustine, interpreting Cain as the founder of the earthly city, describes his possessiveness compatibly but more deeply as a spiritual condition—"while he gave to God some possession that was his, he kept himself for himself"—a desire for self-possession and refusal of subjection that defines the earthly city: "[T]his city worships, not because it has any love of service, but because its passion is for domination."[120] The Cain story is thus governed by a kind of *contrapasso:* he who desired to possess himself becomes dispossessed; the worker who wishes to keep his product has it taken from him. Attached to effort as an expenditure that demands the full compensation of effort's product, Cain is reduced to effort. The deterioration of Cain's work appears as a kind of second Fall: the effort of work enters the world through the first man, the futility of effort enters through the second.

By ascribing to Cain the historical role of first peasant and progenitor of the peasantry, medieval authors transformed the moral and spiritual figure of Cain into an image of significant social and ideological force. Serfdom was generally held to originate with Noah's son Ham (himself of the race of Cain), but Cain was the forefather of the peasantry in general, of the class of agricultural laborers. As Freedman explains, both performed multiple and related historical roles: "Cain functioned as the originator of the monstrous races and also of peasants, whether free or unfree. Ham had two medieval roles: as the father of a number of peoples, including black Africans, and as the ancestor of European serfs. If Cain was an archetype of the peasant regardless of status, Ham was the progenitor of the unfree of whatever race."[121] Several studies have analyzed the complex of medieval representations of Cain and Ham and demonstrated their common support of "what Rodney Hilton calls 'the caste interpretation of peasant status'—the idea that serfdom is a permanent condition of moral inferiority inherent in the peasant's very being."[122] Of principal concern

here is the medieval representation of Cain as a worker and the evidence
it provides of the mentality that determined in the first place the preponderance of effort-centered terms for work in Middle English and secondly
the dominant association of these terms with agricultural work. Though
the book of Genesis does not actually represent the fruitless toil to which
Cain is condemned, a body of medieval visual representations do, such
that the figure of Cain constituted "an emblem of fruitless agricultural
labor."[123] This in itself attests to the consistency with which Cain was associated with contemporary peasants.

One of the fullest representations of Cain the worker occurs in the
drama *Mactatio Abel* from the Towneley cycle. In this play, Cain is introduced by his servant boy as a familiar and socially dominant yeoman:

> A good yoman my master hat.
> Full well ye all hym ken.
> Begyn he with you for to stryfe,
> Certis, then mon ye never thryfe;
> Bot I trow, bi God on life,
> Som of you ar his men.
> (lines 15–20)[124]

The play throughout gives special emphasis to the arduous nature of
Cain's work but locates that arduousness as much in Cain's ill-tempered
resentment of the effort of work as in the nature of work itself. He enters
the stage struggling with and cursing his plow team (25ff) and exits as
foully, swearing to his boy that if he gives him any trouble "I shall hang the
apon this plo" (459). His character is defined by selfishness ("Bi all men set
I not a fart" 369), indiscriminate violence ("Take the that, boy, tak the that!
[*Strikes him*] . . . Peas, man, I did it bot to use my hand" [387–93], not to
mention Abel's murder), and above all an awareness of the difficulty of
labor and a desire to possess its meager fruits:

> We! Wherof shuld I tend, leif brothere?
> For I am ich yere wars then othere;
> Here my trouth, it is none othere.
> My wynnyngys ar bot meyn,
> No wonder if that I be leyn;
> (108–12)[125]

Its moral and religious truths notwithstanding, the ideological force of the *Mactatio Abel,* and the medieval Cain in general, resides in its simultaneous evocation and foreclosure of peasant grievance. As much as the play gives voice to legitimate grievance over economic inequality, to the worker's consciousness of loss and futility entailed in the appropriation of his product by the social order, it brands such grievance as the illegitimate product of a selfish and sinful nature.[126] Cain's complaint about his work would belong to the tradition of lament over peasant sufferings, if it were not Cain's.[127]

The first and most general cause of the predominance of words signifying work as effort in the Middle English work vocabulary is not the "primitive" nature of medieval work but the conceptual reduction of work to effort as a sign of inferior possession and inferior power by the status mentality of a society in which possession and power define status. In this sense, *travail, labour,* and to a lesser degree *swink* represent an essentially noneconomic conception of work or, more precisely, an *un*economic conception of work that actively denies its economic reality in the interest of escaping economic forces in general and serves to articulate and justify economic inequality in noneconomic terms.[128] Accordingly, a fundamental characteristic of Cain the laborer, as one of the most extreme expressions of the status conception of work, is his economic unreality.[129] The medieval Cain is an impossible reduction of the *laboratores,* the heart of the medieval economy, to a sinful, suffering, singular mechanism.[130] He represents the most common type of medieval person, but he is hopelessly marginal, "vagus et profugus in terra" (Gen. 4.14). He represents the class of individuals who materially possessed the least, but he is *possessio.* His work represents the most productive form of labor in the world, but it is fruitless. Reversing the terms of inequality, status mentality defines its honor, "which always rests upon distance and exclusiveness," by faulting the commonality, however widely or narrowly perceived, with its own possessiveness and uselessness.[131]

To understand *travail, labour,* and *swink* as the semantic products of status mentality does not impugn the fact that late medieval workers experienced their work as difficult, nor does it imply that the aristocracy was solely responsible for their currency. Most forms of medieval work were physically taxing, but the strong association of these words with agricultural as opposed to other types of work itself testifies to the social and economic contingency of perceptions of the difficulty of work.[132] On the one hand, agricultural work was hit the hardest, as it were, by status mentality by virtue of its being the most common, necessary, and productive form of work. On the other hand, appropriation of the worker's surplus value in general, but particularly in the more palpable forms proper to agricultural labor (labor services, exactions in kind), intensified workers' perceptions of the difficulty of work. The anticlerical plowman of *The Plowman's Tale,* for example, confident in his capability for material and religious self-sufficiency and conscious of what his effort is worth, describes how the unrecompensed appropriation of his goods by the clergy brings the laboring laity to "payn."[133] Nevertheless, the Anglo-French origin of *travail* and *labour,* the fact that they emphasize work's difficulty more than the other terms, and the fact that they both occur in texts much more often than *swink* all predictably testify to the superior propriety of the status conception of work to the ruling and administrative classes.

Werk and *craft* embody a different perspective on the nature of work. Whereas *travail, labour,* and to a lesser degree *swink* represent the de-economizing reduction of work to difficulty by status mentality, *werk* and *craft* are the semantic products of a mentality that, through an appreciation of the economic and material value of work, conceptualizes it primarily as production. In this sense *werk* and *craft* embody a conception of work proper not to status but to class, understanding classes as groups that "are stratified according to their relations to the production and acquisition of goods."[134]

Status and class are by no means independent forms of social differentiation. Status and class distinctions frequently intersect, but they represent social relations according to different criteria. Where status mentality operates by conceiving of the social order in noneconomic terms, class mentality conceives of it economically and tends to perceive the economic bases of the status order. Where status mentality conceives of social identity as an essential, inborn, and enduring attribute of the individual rather than something that can be constructed or dismantled, class mentality views social identity in terms of an individual's (potentially alterable) social *situation.*[135] Accordingly, status and class differentiation are favored by different economic conditions. As Weber explains,

When the bases of the acquisition and distribution of goods are relatively stable, stratification by status is favored. Every technological repercussion and economic transformation threatens stratification by status and pushes the class situation into the foreground. Epochs and countries in which the naked class situation is of predominant significance are regularly the periods of technical and economic transformations. And every slowing down of the change in economic stratification leads, in due course, to the growth of status structures and makes for a resuscitation of the important role of social honor.[136]

It is well known that the fourteenth and fifteenth centuries generally follow just this pattern, namely that the economic changes precipitated by the Black Death led to a foregrounding of the class situation (above all in 1381) and that the relative demographic and economic stability of the fifteenth century was accompanied by a growth in status stratification. We may thus see in the polarity of the Middle English work vocabulary a reflection of these contrary but nonetheless concurrent historical movements, namely that "on the one hand English society in this period created new social barriers and new degrees of snobbery which remained into the modern period, particularly amongst wealthier income groups. On the other hand the withering away of serfdom, accompanied as it was by improvements in the economic welfare of the poorer classes in society, was social progress by both liberal and Marxist criteria."[137]

Like the status conception of work, the economic conception of work as use- and exchange-value-producing activity is not the peculiar property of any social group. But as the stronghold of the status conception of work is the class of individuals who consume more than they produce, so the stronghold of the economic conception of work is the class of individuals who produce more than they consume. This is attested to by the origin of *werk* and *craft* in the language of common speech, the multitude of compound forms of these words that denote everyday objects and activities, and the fact that the Anglo-French word for work as production, *ovrer,* did not pass into English. An economic conception of work, one that, in contradistinction to the one-dimensional reduction of work to *difficultas* by status mentality, recognizes work as both action and end (as

indicated by the superior extensiveness of *werk*), as an exchange of effort
for value, and thus also recognizes the worker's economic agency and
perhaps his agency in general, belongs not to any particular occupation
but to economic occupation itself. But if *werk* and *craft* broadly represent
such an economic conception of work, a conception most proper to the
producer, what accounts for their minimal association with agricultural
work, the most common form of production? All evidence is against Ostrá's proposition for Old French that such words owe their place in medieval language to the mentality of a minority occupational group, the
urban artisans.[138] Rather, remembering the commonness of words and
more specifically that words for work, in their association with a particular type of work, reflect not only the perceptions of those who engage in it
but also the perceptions of by everyone else (in this case a large majority)
regarding that form of work, one must take into account the phenomenal
and social natures of craft production and consider how these may have
brought about the strong association of the idea of production with artisanal work.[139]

Describing the place of craftsmen in village society, Rodney Hilton
has pointed out that the "ironsmith's forge was the focus of village life,
and, over and above this, the mysteries of his craft gave him an almost
magical prestige."[140] It is worth considering what makes the truth of this
seem obvious. First of all, craft production was related to lordship in a different manner than agricultural production. By the late medieval period,
the lord had long relinquished his claim on handmade articles.[141] To a superior degree the artisanal producer produced for the market. The more
completely he made his living by producing for the market (as in cities and
towns), the more his work appeared as specifically economic activity and
the more he became socially identifiable by his specific occupation.[142] Accordingly, the assessment terminology of the poll tax returns for 1380–81
attests to the superior occupational identity of craftsmen. While some tax
lists emphasize "tenures and legal status, and divide rural society into free
and servile tenants" and others make distinctions "based on the amount
of land held and the extent of wage earning," in both types "craftsmen
and traders in town and country alike were identified by their occupations . . . with an occasional payment at a higher rate to distinguish the
wealthy merchant or entrepreneur from the normal run of artisans and
small traders."[143]

Second, there are significant differences between the organization and nature of agricultural and artisanal production. The first reason that "the ironsmith's forge was the focus of village life" is that all the villagers needed its products. The visible singularity of their source would have promoted a recognition of a sickle not just as a sickle but as the *product* of so-and-so's forge. Such singularity does not belong to all forms of artisanal production, but in general craft production was a visible and defining characteristic of village and urban environments, as an Italian visitor to London in 1497 wrote: "[T]hroughout the town are to be seen many workshops of craftsmen in all sorts of mechanical arts, to such an extent that there is hardly a street which is not graced by some shop or the like."[144] Indeed, to practice a craft visibly was a significant form of advertisement, and the right to do so was legislated.[145] Formal differences between artisanal and agricultural production must also be counted as contributing to the superior association of the former with the production-centered terms *werk* and *craft*. The artisanal product is to a superior degree a form wrought by design. Its form and utility distinguish it as a specifically human product, and its durability and concentrated worth distinguish it as a labor-created value, as opposed to the agricultural product, which is prone to being confused with a natural resource. As Basil of Caesarea explained in his *Hexameron*, "In creative arts . . . the work lasts after the operation. Such is architecture—such are the arts which work in wood and brass and weaving, all those indeed which, even when the artisan has disappeared, serve to show an industrious intelligence and to cause the architect, the worker in brass or the weaver, to be admired on account of his work."[146] Also, the forms of artisanal products are less historically stable than agricultural ones, and this capability for newness promotes their perception as work products, as things made, things that were not there before. Craft production creates the antithesis between art and nature that marks it as the production of a person, an intelligence, a worker.[147]

Finally, force must be granted to several features of medieval religious and philosophical culture as both expressions of and/or influences upon the social experience of artisanal work and its apprehension as prepotent production. Briefly, these are pagan "traditions of artisanal techniques associated with particular socioprofessional groups and surrounded with an aura of religious belief,"[148] representations of God as a craftsman,[149] the relatively high status of artisanal as opposed to agricultural work within medieval classifications of the sciences,[150] and philosophical and theological tendencies to think in terms of craft production and to employ craft analogies and metaphors. Of the last Augustine provides one of the most developed and delightful examples, in which the figure of the world as God's workshop is used to underscore human ignorance and arrogance: "[M]en are very stupid. They do not dare criticize things in a human craftsman's workshop which they do not understand, but when they have seen them they believe they are necessary and made for certain uses. However, in this world, of which God is proclaimed the founder and administrator, they dare to criticize many things whose causes they do not see, and they wish to appear to know what they do not know concerning the works and tools of the omnipotent craftsman."[151] Similarly, medieval culture was readily capable of associating craft production with superior knowledge and power. This association is perceivable in both rarefied and quotidian forms, from Roger Bacon's prophetic dream of "machines [that] will make it possible to go to the bottom of seas and rivers" to habits of referring to "[t]he hye God, that al this world hath wrought."[152] Also, a correlative propensity of craftsmen to take special pride in their skill is indicated, for instance, by the special warning against craftsmen's pride in St. Benedict's *Rule* and in the fourteenth-century tale *The Smyth and His Dame,* in which a proud smith—"He called hymselfe the kynge, / Wythout any leasynge, / Of all maner of cunnynge"—is humbled by Christ, the *omnipotens artifex,* after attempting and failing to rejuvenate his wife in his forge.[153]

The "almost magical prestige" of artisanal production was less a supernatural aura than the merit accorded to conspicuous production by a society dominated by small producers. It was less a projection of the artisan than the social recognition of the value of work in the heightened form of conspicuous industry. As the status conception of work as effort emerges in the semantic association of effort with the most common form of work, the class-economic conception of work as production emerges in the semantic association of production with the least common form of work. The difference expresses both the difference and the relatedness of the two conceptions. On the one hand, status mentality, concerned with making invidious comparisons between persons with respect to wealth and force, with raising itself up and putting others down, and concerned thus with social proportions, with increasing the proportion of its self to the body of other selves, devalues the work of others and reduces useful production to a sign of inferiority. Class-economic mentality, on the other hand, concerned not with invidious comparisons and questions of honor but above all with the value of its own productive force, not with increasing the proportion of its self to others but with finding its way among them toward an optimal realization of the value of its own production, concerned, in short, not with a simple distribution of value toward itself but with the possibility of an exchange of values, openly values the work of others as a reflection of its own productive force through the exchange relation or its possibility and thus merits in particular those forms of production that appear both most productive in nature and most productive of value. At the same time, however, these alternate conceptions of work are only conceptually and not in reality separable, not simply because they are always mixed up in individuals but because each in some measure implies the other. As previously mentioned, the status-based conception of work as dishonorable effort not only is compatible with the appreciation of the value and utility of work but is based upon it. Work is dishonorable *because* it is productive and useful. It is incompatible with the display of superior wealth because it is the means of generating wealth. To status mentality, these are not contradictions. Work is anathema to the noble *person:* "[T]he laws say that a knight must not till the soil, or tend vines, or keep beasts, that is to say, be a shepherd, or be a matchmaker, or lawyer; otherwise he must lose knighthood and the privileges of a knight."[154] Yet his dependence on the work of others may be freely acknowledged, as in the well-known illuminations of the *Très riches heures du Duc de Berry,* in which "the juxtaposition of castles and scenes of aristocratic leisure with toiling peasants shows that the work of one class makes the ostentation of the other possible."[155] The class-economic conception of work as production is similarly bound to status concerns. As much as the exchange of values depends upon the mutual recognition of productive forces, it also requires their comparison and generally the attempt through hard bargaining to devalue the productive force of another, to claim, in effect, that another's labor is not worth as much as one's own. Comparison of persons with respect to their productive force, which involves comparison between both types of work and aptitudes of workers, can be just as invidious and serve status interests as much as comparison of persons with respect to wealth possessed. Moreover, the inextricability of these forms of comparison is particularly germane to agricultural contexts, where the distinction between productive force and wealth possessed tends to fall apart through the quantification of land.

The dichotomous structure of the Middle English work vocabulary exposes in a unique way the connections between concepts of work and social attitudes. This dichotomy per se is neither uniquely medieval nor uniquely English. Yet its diverse cultural associations, built around the distinction between work as effort and work as production, and above all its linguistic component, the consistent difference between terms of French and English origin, demonstrate how deeply related late medieval words for work were to status and class concerns. Quantification may not be possible, but the socioeconomic developments of the period and the parallel growth of the work vocabulary during it suggest that this relation was strengthening and that work in this sense was becoming more, not less, meaningful.

The Multiplicity of the Vocabulary

The Middle English vocabulary of work is not only an expression of concepts but a system of expression whose most basic function is to signify work in various aspects rather than reveal attitudes about it. The peculiar historical situation of Middle English in its rivalry with Anglo-Norman allows us to see with unusual clarity the formative impact of social divisions upon the lexicon. But the ubiquity and social diffusion of the vocabulary are witnessed by its most practical value: its capacity for making relatively fine distinctions between types and aspects of work.[156] As a system of expression, the vocabulary operates through a dialectic of the general and the specific, as each term both signifies work in general and emphasizes some aspect(s) of work over others. On the one hand, the complementarity of the terms constitutes a conceptual tool capable of manipulating work with significant dexterity, one that keeps open and available various dimensions of work. On the other hand, the diversity of the Middle English work vocabulary is not the absence of a general term but the presence of several and to some degree competing general terms for work, a kind of fossilized argument over what work is. Though medieval social theory tended to conceive of *werk* and *labour* as the proper activity of the *laboratores* and the dominance of this association is indicated by their agent forms *werkman* and *labourer,* all of the Middle English words for work, albeit to different degrees, were used without analogy to signify all sorts of activities. In this sense, the Middle English work vocabulary was significantly richer than its modern counterpart, in which the content-free conception of work as the category of remunerated activity dominates, for the former could more readily express both differences between types of work and formal connections between occupational and non-occupational activities.

The Middle English work vocabulary thus shows an affinity with the trifunctional model itself, which was a means of defining and reinforcing social boundaries as well as assimilating the duties of all estates to a broad notion of work as mutually necessary activity. As Freedman has shown, the "three orders" model of society was not only a model of domination but "a hierarchical model of society incorporating the importance of agricultural labor into an overall notion of mutual service."[157] Most importantly, the inescapable presence of *swinkeres, travailours, labourers, werkemen,* and *craftesmen* necessitated in the late medieval period, for the survival of the model itself, the articulation of this service as universal *travail.* Owst has shown, for instance, that a "favourite *figure* used by the preachers to set forth their political or social ideal is that of the Vineyard with its three Orders of Husbandmen."[158] Such a figure could be used to argue for work as the social and spiritual duty of all, as in Thomas Wimbledon's sermon of 1388: "So eueri man trauayle in his degre; for whanne þe euen is come þat is þe end of this worlde, 'þanne euery man shal take reward good oþer euyl, aftir þat he haþ trauayled here' [1 Cor. 3.8]."[159] While burying the reality of economic inequality in "in his degre" and reducing value-producing activity to a service whose rewards are beyond this world, such exhortation nevertheless recognized the dignity of the worker and refracted the critical optimism of the newly prosperous who a few years before had rallied around the old image of Adam and Eve at work. In this preacher's formulation, it is precisely the flexibility of the term *travail,* the interplay of its general and specific senses, that is performing the double rhetorical task of broadening the notion of work to include the functions of all three estates and lending the first and second estates' work the dignity and unquestionable legitimacy of manual labor, central to society and the biblical figure alike.

Just as the "three orders" model of society was a *functional* model, so the Middle English vocabulary of work was a *phenomenal* model, one that gave priority to the content and nature of work acts. This feature of the vocabulary is especially visible when we notice that the principal overall difference between the Middle English and Modern English work-related vocabularies is a difference in the proportion of content-based to content-free terms. Where Middle English has five general words for work that primarily denote the activity of work itself *(travail, labour, swink, werk, craft)*, Modern English has only two *(work, labor)*. By contrast, Modern English has many more general content-free terms for work than Middle English *(occupation, job, vocation, profession, employment, career)*. The multiplicity of the Middle English work vocabulary thus bears consideration as a reflection of late medieval society's phenomenal awareness of work, its interest in the nature of the work process and its objective function.

A society's phenomenal awareness of work—that is, its general consciousness of the nature of the work it performs—is in many ways opposed to a content-free conception of work—that is, to the conception of work not as a form of activity but as the category of remunerated activity or *whatever* one does for a living. Where the first views work according to the nature of the work process itself, the second disregards this nature and views work only according to its subjective end. Where the first, as an awareness of the objective structure of work, contributes to the awareness of work's use value, the second reduces work to an exchange value. A phenomenal awareness of work and a content-free conception of work are not mutually exclusive and are to some degree complementary, but it is clear that the predominance of one or the other will be favored by different conditions. The strength of one is the weakness of the other, insofar as a phenomenal awareness of work frustrates its content-free conception and vice versa. Numerous general factors may be counted as constituting the phenomenal presence of work in society and thus as contributing to the kind and degree of a society's phenomenal awareness of it. Among these the most obvious are the visibility of the work of others, the familiarity of individuals with different forms of work, the visibility of the sources of goods, the proportion of non-ready-made to ready-made articles in common circulation, the amount of labor involved in everyday activities, the intelligibility of the methods and purposes of work (one's own and others'), and the intelligibility of the use value of work (one's own and others'). The more these factors form a constituent part of general experience, the greater the propensity for society to conceive of work phenomenally.

It is obvious that the preindustrial conditions and organization of medieval work broadly favored such an awareness. The Middle English work vocabulary attests to this primarily through its overriding sense, in keeping with the predominance of manual labor during the period, of the physicality of work. *Travail, labour,* and *swink* all primarily signify work as physical difficulty and as an exercise of bodily power. *Werk* and *craft,* through their signification of the making and fashioning of objects, are also strongly tied to the physicality of work. At the same time, however, the vocabulary is structured around the important distinction between manual and nonmanual work. This distinction is not a strict one either in reality, where all types of work have both physical and mental dimensions, so that we can only say that one type is more physical or more mental than another, or in the Middle English vocabulary, where all terms could be used to signify all types of work. Still, both the dominant associations and the dominant meanings of the terms express this fundamental distinction. *Travail, labour,* and *swink* all primarily denote work as physical exertion and are most strongly associated with overtly physical forms of work. *Werk* and *craft* more readily signify the intellective dimensions of work and are most strongly associated both with forms of work in which the worker's ingenuity and skill are indispensable and with overtly intellectual activities. The manual versus nonmanual distinction within the vocabulary is thus defined by the same grouping of terms as the work-as-effort versus work-as-production distinction. More specifically, the distinguishing phenomenal meaning of each of the terms may be described as follows: patiency of effort *(travail),* agency of effort *(labour),* act of effort *(swink),* productive intention in action or the product of such intention *(werk),* productive process or the knowledge of such process *(craft).*

While medieval culture produced relatively little in the way of direct analysis of the nature of work, correlative evidence of a phenomenal interest in work is retrievable in several forms. First of all, the manual versus nonmanual distinction that the Middle English work vocabulary articulates has a long and variegated tradition. The related concepts of *artes illiberales, artes mechanicae,* and *opera servilia* all participate in this

distinction, and the classical and medieval discourse about these categories is grounded in concerns about the phenomenal character of work,
especially its bodily and mental effects. Emphasizing the prohibitive
character of labor, the sense in which it keeps one from other things, Aristotle had defined banausic or illiberal activities as follows: "[A]ny occupation, art, or science, which makes the body or soul or mind of the freeman
less fit for the practice or exercise of virtue, is vulgar; wherefore we call
those arts vulgar which tend to deform the body, and likewise all paid employments, for they absorb and degrade the mind."[160] Classical authors
unanimously ranked manual labor in this category. The ideological under-
pinnings of this categorization aside, its rationale lay not in the physicality
of manual labor per se but in its minimal exercise of intellectual powers.
As Elspeth Whitney explains, "The inferiority of the banausic arts is derived neither from their technological character nor their physicality alone
but from the idea that these particular arts do not involve the soul in either
its intellectual or its moral capacities but are practiced *merely* to satisfy
physical needs or pleasures."[161] Concern about the soul's freedom to pursue
higher things, then, was one possible starting point for phenomenological
descriptions of work. Exercised within the context of the liberal-illiberal
distinction, such concern could only produce negative characterizations
of work's effect on the individual (just as the term *artes illiberales* is itself
a negative definition), but outside this context other outcomes were possible. In the *De opere monachorum* Augustine argues, for the purpose of
refuting the Messalian rejection of work as a hindrance to the life of the
spirit, that in manual labor the mind is kept free to contemplate what it
will.[162] A conspicuous late medieval example of evaluating work in comparable terms is provided by Thomas Hoccleve, who compares the strenu-
ousness of writing, in which "Mynde, ee, and hand, non may fro othir
flitte," to the relative mental freedom of craft work:

> This artificers, se I day be day,
> In þe hotteste of al hir bysynesse
> Talken and syng, and make game and play,
> And forth hir labour passith with gladnesse;
> But we labour in trauaillous stilnesse;
> We stowpe and stare vp-on þe shepes skyn,
> And keepe muste our song and wordes in.[163]

Here may be seen an interesting reversal and permutation of what Stephen Knight has called the "clericalization" of labor in contemporary literary representations of work.[164] By showing the clerical labor of writing to be physically demanding and overall more taxing than the more purely manual labor of artisans, Hoccleve declericalizes it. Evoking the Aristotelian concept of the illiberal, he shows it to be deforming and degrading, physically and mentally. At the same time, the passage operates as an implicit claim about the superiority of the intellectual work of poetry, in which one's "song and wordes" are central and not peripheral to the work process. What makes this account most exemplary of a phenomenal awareness of work is that it accesses issues of the status and meaning of intellectual versus manual labor, not abstractly through notions of value, but through close attention to the experience of work itself.

Medieval developments in the classification of the arts and sciences, above all the growth of the concept of *artes mechanicae,* provided new impetus for phenomenal descriptions of work. The term *artes mechanicae* was first used by John the Scot in his commentary on Martianus Capella's *Marriage of Philology and Mercury,* and the central effect of this positive definition was a theoretical liberation of manual labor. As Whitney explains, "[U]nlike the classical idea of the banausic arts, which *opposed* unworthy physical and worthy mental arts, John's mechanical arts are *parallel* in form and function to the liberal arts. . . . Although John contrasts the two sets of arts, suggesting that the liberal arts are in some sense like the soul, 'divine,' while the mechanical arts are 'human,' they remain linked to each other and there is no trace of the pejorative tone associated with the banausic, or illiberal, arts."[165] It is within the project of fleshing out the nature of this link between liberal and mechanical arts, between intellectual and physical work, that twelfth- and thirteenth-century classifiers of knowledge came to bring unprecedented theoretical attention to the nature of work. This attention is evident most generally in the categorization and description of the mechanical arts themselves. Hugh of St. Victor divides the mechanical arts into seven types (fabric making, armament, commerce, agriculture, hunting, medicine, theatrics). "In this division," Hugh explains, "we find a likeness to the trivium and the quadrivium, for the trivium is concerned with words, which are external things, and the quadrivium with concepts, which are internally conceived."[166] Though Hugh does not develop this theme in any greater

detail—apart from describing commerce as a kind of rhetoric[167]—it forms
the starting point for his description of the seven mechanical arts, in which
the multiple forms of work that belong to them are not simply listed but
classified, however arbitrarily, according to their nature.[168] Hugh's classification was modified and refined by later authors, as the surveys of Elspeth Whitney, Birgit van den Hoven, and George Ovitt demonstrate.[169]
With respect to the phenomenology of work, the most significant of these
developments belongs to Robert Kilwardby, whose concern with the arbitrariness and imperfections of the Victorine classification stems from a
closer consideration of the nature of the mechanical arts than his predecessors'. Recognizing the complex diversity of the mechanical arts, Kilwardby found no "compelling reason why about so countless an array of
arts we should number them precisely as seven, save for certain superficial correspondence with the seven liberal arts."[170] Kilwardby also compli-
cates the distinction between intellectual and physical work by arguing
that "the speculative sciences are practical and the practical speculative."[171]
Though Kilwardby is not so much concerned with the mechanical arts
themselves as with their relation to the liberal ones, his exposition of this
relation succeeds in bringing out something of the multifaceted nature of
the various forms of work.[172]

The discussion of what forms of work ought to be counted among the
opera servilia prohibited by church law on Sundays and holy days provided another arena for the phenomenal examination of the nature of
work. "Fine distinctions drawn between that which was permissible and
that which was forbidden on holy days depended, in large measure, upon
an understanding of what constituted servile and non-servile employment."[173] And "the exact meaning of *servile work* remained a permanently
debatable point."[174] Spiritual interpretations of the prohibition on servile
work in light of John 8.34 ("omnis qui facit peccatum servus est peccati")
may have tempered the seriousness of the issue—whence Aquinas's (and
Augustine's) argument that "to sin on a feast day is more against this pre-
cept than to do some other but lawful bodily work" (*Summa theologica*
pt. 1–2, Q. 122, art. 4) and the *Rule of Benedict*'s allowance for the Sunday
labor of monks not disposed to reading—but the proliferation of holy days
made exacting definitions of servile work a practical necessity.[175] *Opus
servile* was commonly defined as work that was physical, that pertained to

material well-being, and that kept the worker from applying himself to spiritual matters.[176] In the words of Reginald Pecock, it was "al worldly wynful werk."[177] The complete cessation from all such occupation that a strict interpretation of these principles would have required, however, was not practicable, and an endless variety of allowances for work on Sundays and holy days was rationalized and legislated.[178] There was obvious theoretical justification for some such allowances—Aquinas, for example, allows for "corporal work pertaining to the preservation of one's own bodily well-being," "bodily work that is directed to the well-being of another," and "bodily work that is done to avoid an imminent damage to some external thing" (*Summa theologica* pt. 1–2, Q. 122, art. 4)—but the actual application of such principles posed its own problems, and many of the allowances approved by ecclesiastics show no clear affiliation with them. In London, for example, the "cordwainers . . . were not permitted to display their goods in the market on Sundays, but they might serve people within their dwellings."[179] Such manifestly utilitarian compromises, which restricted not so much work as its social visibility, may have involved consideration of the content of work, but with regard to the phenomenal awareness of work the most interesting allowances for holy day labor are those based in the evaluation of specific aspects of the work process. The amount of effort required by particular tasks, for instance, could be the grounds for their exemption. As Rodgers points out, several "activities commonly termed servile were sanctioned as necessitating an amount of labor too slight to hamper the freedom of the spirit in its devotion to God"—in effect, on the grounds that they were not *too* servile.[180] The subjective end of work or the worker's intention could also enter into this sort of consideration. Servile work undertaken for charity rather than personal gain was generally encouraged, as made clear in *Dives and Pauper*: "Netheles ȝif heryyng & sowynge, repynge, mowynge, cartynge & swyche oþer nedful warkys ben don purly for elmesse & only for heuenely mede & for nede of hem þat it arn don to in lythly haly dayys, it arn þan no seruyle warkys ne þe halyday is nout brokyn þerby" (278). Exemptions could also be made, somewhat paradoxically, at either end of the spectrum of utility, either for public works or for useful pursuits done recreationally.[181] The prohibition on servile work could also produce careful delineations of the boundary between servile and intellectual occupation.

Intellectual work was generally untouched by the prohibition insofar as it was considered a spiritual and liberal activity,[182] but the servile dimensions of professional intellectual work and textual production did not go unnoticed. In the calendars of most universities "Sundays and festivals enjoined upon the church as a whole were listed as 'non-legible' days"—that is, days on which the regular remunerated lecturing of doctors and masters was prohibited.[183] Though literary composition by students on holy days was considered unproblematic, the mechanical copying of a text (especially for profit) was prohibited, though "in the opinion of some authorities, this objection might be waived if the material was of a spiritual nature," as if the text's meaning would outweigh the servility of its transcription.[184]

Last, a phenomenal interest in work is evident in more general treatments of the relationship of work to sin, such as occur within the *sermones ad status* and other types of estates literature.[185] As a rule, these genres are most concerned with this relationship with regard to the opportunities for sin within particular occupations, but the moral nature of occupations themselves could also come into consideration. The fourteenth-century Franciscan Alvarus Pelagius, for example, attributes the wickedness of peasants to the earthiness of their labor.[186] Other authors could prove more insightful about the actual character of specific forms of work. Antoninus of Florence describes how agricultural work cannot, in itself, be performed fraudulently.[187] Similarly, John Bromyard contrasts the necessary orientation of material production toward the tangible good of the product with the arbitrariness of purpose that characterizes the work of lawyers.[188]

The multiplicity of the Middle English work vocabulary is a multiplicity of phenomenal meanings, a complex of content-based terms that reflects late medieval society's general awareness of the nature of the work it performed and its related tendency to conceive of itself functionally. This awareness should not be seen as isolated from the status- and class-based conceptions of work described in the previous section. Rather, the socially determined character and the phenomenal character of the vocabulary are mutually contingent. The phenomenal meanings of the vocabulary are both the medium and the expression of status- and class-based attitudes toward work, just as other representations of the nature of work cannot be divorced from ideological structures. Ideas about the status and class situation of work are inseparable from ideas about the nature of work. This inseparability is nowhere more obvious than in articulations of the distinction between intellectual and physical work. Kilwardby may see further into the fluidity of the intellectual-physical distinction than most medieval authors, but he is explicit about its social meaning: "Physical activity is more suited to insignificant and common people, the peace of meditation and study to the noble elite; in this way, everyone has an occupation fitting his station in life."[189] Furthermore, the affirmation of this distinction is especially appropriate to a society dominated by small producers, to a situation in which physical work was a highly visible feature of life. Throughout the Middle Ages, manual labor, the principal function of the *laboratores,* was the norm against which the socially superior functions of the *oratores* and *bellatores* had to be defined and justified, just as manual labor itself constituted the base notion of work. In a scholastic context, the priority of this concept could be worked out with reference to Aristotle's description of the human hand as a meta-instrument: "under manual labor are comprised all those human occupations whereby man can lawfully gain a livelihood, whether by using his hands, his feet, or his tongue . . . because, since the hand is the *organ of organs,* handiwork denotes all kinds of work, whereby a man may lawfully gain a livelihood."[190] But as this passage shows by alluding to and performing the "work of the tongue," the priority of physical labor was more deeply established within the medieval awareness of work. To live, in Langland's words, "by labour of tonge" (*PPl* B.19.233) is something both real and metaphorical, a distinct and legitimate act in itself as well as a suspect imitation of something more tangible, immediate, and necessary. In a similar way, the Middle English vocabulary of work, in its multiplicity, encompasses an array of forms of work, some of which are more "work" than others, yet links them all within a phenomenology of labor in its most essential form.

The Polysemy of *Werk*

If there is one feature of the Middle English work vocabulary that announces above the others its historical alterity, it is the polysemy of *werk,* specifically its signification of both work and action in general. On the one hand, *werk* is the most familiar and recognizable of the Middle English terms. Its extensiveness with respect to the work process is similar to that of ModE *work*. Like its descendant, *werk* was applied to all types of work, from God's to the peasant's. Also, *werk* was used, from the fourteenth century onwards, to express a content-free conception of work not too dissimilar from the modern conception of work as paid employment or whatever one does for a living. On the other hand, *werk* is the least familiar of terms, by virtue of its being so much more than its continuities with ModE *work*. As a glance at any Middle English concordance will show, *werk* was employed with much greater frequency to signify nonworking activities of many kinds. If one wanted concentrated and deeply emblematic evidence of the inextricability of work and life in the Middle Ages, of medieval society's difficulty in distinguishing between economic and noneconomic phenomena, between public and personal relations, and between what one did for a living and who one was, there seems no better candidate than ME *werk,* an amalgamation of occupational action and action in general.

Yet it is possible to look at *werk*'s polysemy in another way, not as evidence of a lack of distinction between its referents but as the sign of an awareness of their relation. The habit of making connections between disparate things, of perceiving similarity in dissimilarity, is, as Aristotle points out, not a sign of the unconsciousness of difference but of intelligence.[191] Awareness of difference is also a necessary precondition for the understanding of similarity. Accepting that the polysemy of *werk* attests to such a cultural habit, a habit of perceiving intersections between work and life, economic and noneconomic phenomena, and occupational and personal agency, we may then see it as the product not of *Gemeinschaft* or *Gesellschaft* but of something more realistic and intermediate, of a social situation in which the play between personal character and occupational role is often apparent and of consequence. The demise of *werk*'s polysemy would then represent the advent of the conceptual division of life into work and "life," a division often expressed in ways that deny the first personal significance and the second a more than personal meaning. By such an account, the restriction of *work* to work, however incomplete, represents, not the loss of an earlier unity of work and life, but simply a diminishment in the recognition and understanding of a unity that is perforce always there. Disenchantment with work as a personally and historically satisfying activity is, after all, also an acknowledgment of its personal and historical nature, its unity with the worker and the world he lives in. Such an interpretation of *werk*'s polysemy and its loss, like all schemes of cultural periodization, runs the risk of replacing one romanticism with another. Its significance can be realized only in specific contexts, and its validity cannot be demonstrated from semantic evidence alone. The postmedieval understanding of work, however, does indicate in some very general ways the viability of such an interpretation of the transformation from *werk* to *work*.

The possibility of there being a culturally and not only linguistically important relation between *werk*'s signification of work and its signification of action in general (hereafter referred to as *werk*'s specific and general senses) is suggested in a very general way by the fact that the modern division of life into work and "life" defines a disintegration of the concept of action represented by the general sense of *werk*. The conceptual division of life into earning a living and living, into work and "life"—a central feature of modern culture—does not represent a true division of the general and specific senses of *werk*. *Werk*, similar to ME and ModE *deed*, is essentially effective and consequential action. It represents action, not simply as doing something, but as the bringing into being of something done and the objectification of purpose. *Werk* thus involves a sense of the finality and durability of action as well as its disclosure of the agent's character. As evidenced by its frequent signification of moral, heroic, and spiritual deeds and their opposites, the word expresses action as both a publication of the self in the historical world and a recording of the self in the spiritual. In short, *werk* understands the human deed as a kind of making. Such a concept of action, which bears comparison to Hannah Arendt's analysis of action as the mode of political and historical life, is not readily admitted by the modern work/life dichotomy.[192] This dichotomy represents, by contrast, both the occupationalization of *work*, the restriction of effective and productive action to employment and profession, and the privatization of *life*, the restriction of life, as significant existence, to individual experience. That *werk*'s transformation into *work* entailed both the loss of this broader sense of effective action and in some measure the contradiction of it in *life* as the complement of *work* suggests that the polysemy of *werk* is not arbitrary but a cultural feature, an expression of a historicizable understanding of the relation of work to life.

Max Weber's *Protestant Ethic* provides a closer point of departure for the cultural interpretation of *werk*'s polysemy. Central to his analysis of the rapprochement between Protestantism and capitalism is the interdependence of attitudes toward good works and work, an interdependence that appears most strongly in Calvinism. According to Weber, Luther's "concept of the calling remained traditionalistic," and the importance of vocation as "something which man has to accept as a divine ordinance, to which he must adapt himself . . . outweighed the other idea which was also present, that work in the calling was a, or rather *the,* task set by God."[193] But within Calvinism, Luther's *sola fides* had a more revolutionary impact on attitudes toward work and resulted in a shifting of the balance between these two meanings of the calling. Calvin's insistence on not only justification by faith but *fides efficax,* a result of his spiritual suspicion of "all pure feelings and emotions, no matter how exalted they might seem to be," meant that "faith had to be proved by its objective results in order to provide a firm foundation for the *certitudo salutis*" (114). The resulting alteration in the significance of good works then becomes the means of an alteration in the meaning of work. The disqualification of the salvific efficacy of good works by *sola fides* and the unknowable *certitudo salutis,* and the correlative spiritual devaluing of "the concrete *intentio* of the single act" (116), transformed good works into the "technical means, not of purchasing salvation, but of getting rid of the fear of damnation" (115) and required "not single good works, but a life of good works combined into a unified system" (117). It is the contamination of work with this conception of good works that constitutes the Protestant work ethic or the worldly-ascetic approach to work. As Tawney makes clear in his discussion of the Puritan Richard Baxter, work comes to mean the precise opposite of the jettisoned medieval concept of good works: "It is not merely an economic means, to be laid aside when physical needs have been satisfied. It is a spiritual end, for in it alone can the soul find health, and it must be continued as an ethical duty long after it has ceased to be a material necessity. Work thus conceived stands at the very opposite pole from 'good works,' as they were understood, or misunderstood by the Protestants."[194]

Each of these postmedieval developments suggests a relationship between the transformation of *werk* into *work* and cultural changes in the conceptual relation of work to life. Moreover, these developments appear to be dialectically related. First, Protestant theology effected, through a reduction of the meaning of good works, a reduction of life to work. This, in turn, necessitated the "re-creation" of life as something that exists outside work. What kind of understanding of the work-life relation, then, lay behind this *rerum eloquentia contrariorum*?

The polysemy of *werk,* as a sign of awareness and concern about relationships between work and other aspects of life, offers at least the beginning of an answer to this question. That this is the correct way to interpret *werk*'s polysemy is corroborated by the word's fulfillment of Raymond Williams's definition of a keyword as a word for which the problem of its meaning gets bound up with the problem it is used to address. This is most clearly the case within late medieval discourse on idleness, one of the more important areas for the articulation of work ethics.[195] In this context, working and doing good works were bound to intersect, as in Chaucer's *Tale of Melibee,* which contains an elaborate and unmistakably middle-class *excursus* on the ethics of becoming and being rich.[196] Riches are praised as the means to noble status (1560), idleness is eschewed as a simultaneously ethical and economic vice (1586), and *bisinesse* is enjoined as the means to guilt-free wealth (1631–32). Within this mutual accommodation of economic and moral values, *goode werkes* become both the category through which work is moralized and a kind of temporary term for it: "And therfore seith Seint Jerome, 'Dooth somme goode dedes that the devel, which is oure enemy, ne fynde yow nat unoccupied.' / For the devel ne taketh nat lightly unto his werkynge swiche as he fyndeth occupied in goode werkes. Thanne thus in getynge richesses ye mosten flee ydelnesse" (1594–96).[197]

The opening vision of *Piers Plowman,* in which "alle manere of men" are seen "Werchynge and wandrynge as the world asketh" (B.Pro.18, 19), provides a more powerful, because more totalizing, instance of *werk*'s significant polysemy. Here the word serves to bring within one frame moral and occupational action, both to distinguish and to establish relationships between the two in society. With the general sense of *werk* as action considered from a moral perspective established by the poet's introduction of himself as an "heremite unholy of werkes" (3) a few lines earlier, "Werchynge and wandrynge as the world asketh" carries a double sense. Befitting such distinctions as that between those who "putten hem to the plough" (20) and those who "putten hem to pride" (23), the line represents both the hustle and bustle of necessary work and the multiplicity of entanglements with worldly attractions. This wordplay is especially appropriate because Langland's description of the "feeld ful of folk" emphasizes the *intersection* between occupational and moral distinctions within society. The peasants who "swonken ful harde, / And wonnen that thise wastours with glotonye destruyeth" (21–22), the "japeres and jangeleres" who "han wit at wille to werken if they wolde" (35, 37), the "Grete lobies and longe that lothe were to swynke" who "shopen hem heremytes hire ese to have" (55, 57) all speak to a pervasive absence of the ideal union of *werk* and *goode werkes* exemplified by Piers. Rather than indicating a lack of distinction between economic and noneconomic behavior, Langland's rhetorical use of *werk*'s polysemy highlights their relationship and functions overall as a reminder that work is always also *werk,* in the broader sense of ethically and historically consequential action.

Such moments of resonance within *werk*'s polysemy take the meaning of work in two complementary directions, one historical and the other individual. On the one hand, the significance of work is tied to its complex historicity, the way it is at once a major feature, an essential means, and a defining product of historical life. Work is a condition of history, as material and worldly life. It is thus also the means of history, as the continuity of society and culture. And work is history's product, not only because its forms and social organization are governed by the past, but because, in a deeper way, the way humanity works is part of its history making, its *werk* in the greater sense. On the other hand, the significance of work is related to its place within individual life. Here also work bears multiple meanings, since it both reveals and creates individuality. Work discloses individual nature, sometimes as a direct means of self-expression and always more generically as a display of a person's attitude toward working, of what kind and how good of a worker one is. And work also creates individual identity, both socially, as a distinguishing act of social and economic position, and subjectively, as the means of various kinds of fulfillment and self-objectification. The following chapters will explore the meaning of work in Middle English literature in each of these directions, first by looking at representations of the history of work and second by examining texts that articulate work's subjective significance.

"Cause & Fundacion of Alle Craftys"

Imagining Work's Origins

When John Ball took as the theme for his sermon at Blackheath the proverbial couplet "Whanne Adam dalfe and Eve span, / Who was þanne a gentil man?" he demonstrated both the complexity of late medieval views of the history of work and the ideological value of that history. As the radical meaning Ball made out of this couplet diverged from its dominant contemporary meanings, so the couplet itself was one of several diverse ways in which the history of work was imagined in late medieval England. Ball's sermon, as paraphrased by the chronicler Thomas Walsingham, is the only extant example of the proverb being used to argue for the injustice of serfdom. The proverb was generally used, not to question the hierarchical organization of society, but to point out the humble origin of all humanity and thereby argue against pride, especially pride in gentility and social status, and for the spiritual equality of men.[1] Its conventional function was not so much to evoke a purer time before oppressive and unnatural social institutions as to offer the consolation of an equality that transcends the social. Within this area of meaning, the proverb represents the work of Adam and Eve not positively as a divinely ordained and dignified activity worthy of imitation but negatively as a condition of fallen humanity. Extant examples of the proverb that elaborate upon the nature of work it represents, such as the following lines from a lyric of the school of Richard Rolle, fix this postlapsarian connotation:

> When adam delf & eue span, spir, if þou wil spede,
> Whare was þan þe pride of man þat now merres his mede?
> Of erth & slame als was Adam maked to noyes & nede,
> Ar we als he maked to be, whil we þis lyf sal lede.
> With I & E, born ar we als salomon vs hyght,
> To trauel here, whils we ar fere, als fouls to þe flight.[2]

As these lines make clear, the "when" of the proverb is a time between earthly paradise and civilization, a time when mankind, face to face with the fundamental material conditions of life, appeared most humble and its motives for work most elemental.[3] Work, as "noyes & nede," is here primarily a curse and a sign of exile in the historical world, less an expression of life than a condition of "*þys* lyf." Also, there is little reason to suspect that the other proverbial expression that this verse employs and mistakenly attributes to Solomon—"Homo nascitur ad laborem, et avis ad volatum" (Job 5.7)—here gives much positive meaning to work itself or expresses much beyond the idea that painful work ("trauel") is an unavoidable aspect of human life, or, as the *Cursor mundi* puts it, "To traiuail ordeint is þis liue" (line 23745).[4]

Ball's reading of the "when Adam delved" topos, and the work it represents, took a different direction. Contrary to its postlapsarian connotation, Ball interpreted his sermon text as an image of original, natural, and divinely instituted human society: "And continuing his sermon, he tried to prove, by the words of the proverb that he had taken for his text, that *from the beginning* all men were created equal *by nature,* and that servitude had been introduced by the unjust and evil oppression of men, against the will of God, who, if it had pleased him to create serfs, surely *in the beginning of the world* would have appointed who should be a serf and who a lord."[5] As Steven Justice explains, "Ball theorizes equality by equating the phrases 'by nature' and 'from the beginning': natural, rightly ordered human relations are those God established before social stratification."[6] Did Ball think of his sermon text as representing a time before the Fall? This is hardly possible. Only a very imaginative misinterpretation of Genesis 2–3 would identify the Augustinian concept of Edenic life as involving work with "whanne Adam dalfe and Eve span." Rather, Ball's interest in the proverb as an image of original man and his work is intelligible within the larger context of antediluvian history. Though the period of Adam and Eve's life within the world beyond Eden is part of the general movement of moral and physical decline defined by Genesis and its representation by medieval historiography, this period generally and Adam and Eve as workers specifically could have appealed to Ball for a number of reasons.[7] Indeed, it was by virtue of the idea that antediluvian history was unequivocally a period of decline and increasing corruption that newly fallen humanity and its work could be granted a positive status.

The logic of historical decline admits two contrary ways of viewing the period of Adam and Eve's labor: teleologically, as the seed and origin of later hardship, as archetypal hardship, or primitivistically, as a better, purer time than that which followed. As part of the curse for their disobedience, Adam and Eve's labor marks humanity's exclusion from Edenic life. In these terms, their labor has a negative meaning, being the end of a form of life that was, as Augustine says, "sine ulla egestate" and an expression of the disjunction between man and nature.[8] But the first parents' work also has the character of a new beginning and can be understood as a mode of life whose proximity to Eden and priority to later developments mark it as simpler, purer, and more natural. Each of these perspectives on Adam and Eve's labor is in its own way appropriate to Ball's argument. That work was established for humanity through Adam and Eve as a burdensome necessity lends itself to the principle that there is no a priori right to live off the labor of others. Work may originate in Eden, but work as the world knows it results from the Fall in which all share. At the same time, the originality of Adam and Eve's work facilitates its idealization, both generally as the defining act of man's essential material condition and specifically as labor without servility, as dignified labor. To trace peasant labor back to Adam and Eve is to trace it beyond the conventional origination of the peasantry in Cain and the origination of serfdom in Ham. To do so underscores the priority of labor, specifically material production, and locates work in human nature and its natural condition rather than in a particular branch of humanity.

While Genesis does not actually represent Adam and Eve working (other than sewing fig leaves together for aprons) and defines their work only in the context of God's curse upon them (Gen. 3.14–24), both of these dimensions of Adam and Eve's work, its difficulty and its dignity, were powerfully joined in the pseudepigraphical *Vita Adae et Evae* and its vernacular descendants.[9] According to these texts postlapsarian work is at once a curse upon the first parents, a divine institution established for humanity through them, and, from the perspective of fallen man's condition, a blessing and a power. They achieve this by relating how, after the banishment of Adam and Eve from Eden and their search for food, God sends the angel Michael to teach Adam agriculture and, in some versions, provide him with seeds to sow, as in the *Canticum de Creatione,* composed in 1375:

> Þo sente god Miȝhel
> To techen Adam to labouren wel,
> Boþe to diche and delue
> and sowe sedes on erthe to growe,
> ffor to fynden hem mete ynowe,
> his children and him selue;
>
> he tauȝte hem trauayle for here mete
> how þeȝ myȝte hem frutes gete
> with swet and swynkynge sore—
> þus bad þe angel to Adam,
> and al þe frut þat after him cam
> so sholde þeȝ euermore.[10]

Within this tradition, work is much more than an onerous necessity. It is also a providential institution, a responsibility of all mankind, and a form of knowledge. And as the word play here on *frutes* (the product of Adam's labor) and *frut* (future generations) emphasizes, work enables the continuity of human life and is the means of history itself. In the *Vita Adae et Evae* and its variants, the providential and specifically human character of work is underscored by the scene of Adam and Eve's search for food. Realizing that they are in a world that naturally provides for animals but not humans, Adam and Eve undertake penance for their transgression and pray to God that he provide them with a means of sustaining themselves.[11] Adam's reception of agricultural knowledge and the establishment of work as a defining aspect of human life thus also express the recovery of a right relation to God. In these ways, the story of Adam and Eve's life upheld the dignity of work. Moreover, by narrating a technological transformation from helplessness to self-sufficiency, these texts give expression to what Whitney terms the "man unarmed" topos, the classical and medieval tradition of "contrasting man's inferior physical condition 'naked and unarmed' with his unique possession of both hands and reason which together render him capable of the arts."[12] Man's natural inferiority and want are in these terms the providential complement of his rationality, the paradoxical source of his material progress and superiority over the natural world.[13] As the Fall necessitates labor, so labor remedies man's fallen condition. It is man's God-provided means of providing for himself and of living in the world as man, as a rational and purposive being.

On the basis of Walsingham's summary of Ball's sermon, it is possible to reconstruct the basic terms in which the image of Adam and Eve at work was significant to Ball and, to some unknown degree, his audience. Ball was interested in the proverb primarily as an image of social equality, and the proverb represents equality primarily as a time without gentility and its social counterpart, serfdom. Central to Ball's argument was the idea that this equality both once existed and could exist again, that it was not only original, natural, and divinely instituted but also recoverable in the present. "Let them consider, therefore," said Ball according to Walsingham, "that He had now appointed a time wherein, laying aside the yoke of long servitude, they might, if they wished, enjoy their liberty so long desired."[14] It is here that the historical position of Adam and Eve's work, what it follows and what it precedes, becomes crucial. The fitness of "whanne Adam dalfe and Eve span" as an image of recoverable equality consists in its representation of a time after the Fall and before the division of humanity into servile and free. To be recoverable, equality must have survived the Fall. To be remediable, inequality must be a specifically human institution. Ball's comparison between newly fallen humanity and contemporary society was thus a means of distinguishing between the natural and the socially determined condition of man.[15]

But "whanne Adam dalfe and Eve span" figures original and natural equality not only as the absence of gentility but as shared labor. That these two features of the proverb are functionally equivalent does not preclude the likelihood that at Blackheath the second carried its own significance. First, Adam and Eve's work is vital to the logic of Ball's sermon as an expression of the naturalness of original equality. The proverb identifies the division of labor as the medium of equality and portrays this division as natural, both in the sense of being ordered toward the production of primary necessities (food and clothing) and in the sense of being an application of gendered, innate capacities for work. Second, it is plausible that to Ball and his audience the proverb's representation of Adam and Eve at work, like that of the *Vita Adae et Evae,* carried the implication, consonant with "si quis non vult operari, nec manducet" (2 Thess. 3.10) and the critique of exploitative gentility, that work is a universal obligation. Freedman has suggested that "the proverb could be linked to the idea that all should labor, that work was the common obligation of humanity on the model of Adam and Eve."[16] While there are no extant examples of the proverb being used specifically in this manner, the labor of Adam and Eve more generally was frequently linked to the doctrine of work for all during the late Middle Ages, as in the following passage from a fifteenth-century sermon: "hit ys the wylle of Gode that every man and woman schuld labour besyly. For yf Adam and Eve had ben occupyed wyth labour, the serpent had not overcum them: for ydulnesse ys the devylles dyssyr. Wherfor ye may know well yt ys the wylle of Gode that we schuld labour and put our body to penaunce for to fle synne. Thus dyd Adam and Eve, to example of all tho that schuld come after them."[17] As these lines demonstrate, Adam and Eve at work could represent work not only as a necessary burden that justice requires all to share but also as a moral and spiritual duty in its own right.

Ball's sermon similarly upheld not only the rights but the righteousness of the worker. In a powerful analogy that echoes the agricultural parables of Matthew 13, Ball defined the violence of rebellion in terms of work: "[T]hey [the rebels] must be prudent, hastening to act after the manner of a good husbandman, tilling his field, and uprooting the tares that are accustomed to destroy the grain; first killing the great lords of the realm, then slaying the lawyers, justices, and jurors, and finally rooting out everyone whom they knew to be harmful to the community in the future."[18] From one perspective, this analogy is simply a means of arguing for and depicting the utility of revolt as well as justifying its violence as a practical process whose legitimacy is self-evident. By equating the killing of the great lords and others to the removal of so many weeds, the analogy affirms both the political efficacy and the moral validity of the violence it calls for. As husbandmen rather than insurgents, the rebels have only to uproot the weeds that choke their community and all will be well. From this perspective, the husbandman's goodness is his occupational responsibility, his knowledge and practice of efficient husbandry. But as much as Ball's analogy relies upon this primary meaning of the husbandman's goodness, it also elicits its potentially moral significance. Like the parable of the tares (Matt. 13.36–43), in which the wheat represents the "filii regni" and the tares the "filii . . . nequam" who, sown by the Devil, are to be separated from the former at the end of the world and burnt, Ball's analogy establishes a firm moral opposition between the community of rebels and the "weeds" that are harmful to it, an opposition to which the issue of work is central. Set against the materially nonproductive great lords and legal professions, the figure of the husbandman highlights the occupational and class identity of the rebels, specifically their collective productivity. In these terms, Ball's good husbandman operates as a figure of material and moral responsibility, an icon of both the dignity of productive labor and righteous antagonism toward the nonproductive.

We cannot be certain of the extent to which these ideas about work were associated with "whanne Adam dalfe and Eve span" at Blackheath. Ball's use of the proverb does not so much articulate specific ideas about work as invite consideration of the complexity of issues that attached to the history of work in late medieval England. Above all, it attests to the malleability of that history, the fact that the history of work subsisted within medieval culture less as narrative than as a multitude of relatively discrete episodes and topoi that achieved significance within particular and diverse contexts. It is impossible to speak of the history of work in the Middle Ages as a genre in its own right. Just as medieval labor had little in the way of a technical literature, so it almost entirely lacked a historical literature.[19] But however fitfully medieval culture represented the history of work, it also did so persistently, so that it is possible to speak of the history of work as a category of medieval thought. As work was essential to conventional representations of cyclical, seasonal time in the form of the labors of the months, so did it hold an established position within the articulation of linear, historical time.[20] Medieval attitudes toward history were dominated by the impulse "to connect, year by year, an originary

moment—the world's, a nation's or the writer's institution's foundation—
with the writer's present day, or at least point toward that connection with
the present."[21] Likewise, the medieval history of work is largely the story
of the origins of work. Genesis furnished a sequence of familiar, widely
represented episodes in the history of work—the labor of Adam and Eve,
the founding of various crafts by Cain's progeny, Noah's building of the
ark, the construction of the tower of Babel—and provided a fertile context
within which patristic and medieval authors worked out a variety of interpretations of the origins of work and the value of its technologies. As
transmitted through Virgil, Ovid, and Boethius, the classical model of the
Golden Age, during which the earth was spontaneously fruitful, and its
succession by the Silver Age, during which the diverse arts arose under
Jove's rule and "labor omnia vicit" (*Georg* 1.145), also played a prominent
role in the formation of medieval views of the origins of work.[22]

The prominence of these two traditions, one biblical and the other
classical, ensured the ubiquity of medieval representations of the origins
of work, but it by no means enforced their homogeneity. The work of
Adam and Eve might be depicted as punishment, as in a mosaic at the Pala-
tine Chapel at Palermo in which Eve looks sorrowfully on as Adam labors
under the words "in sudore vultus tui vesceris pane" (Gen. 3.19), or as a
gift from God, as in an illumination in the Carrow Psalter in which Adam
and Eve receive spade and distaff from a descending angel.[23] The Golden
Age might be conceived as a peaceful, primitive time without labor, as in
the *Roman de la Rose,* in which Amis, following Ovid, explains that "the
earth was not plowed at all then, but, just as God had prepared it, bore by
itself the things by which each person was made comfortable."[24] Or it
could be understood as a time of honest industry and commerce, innocent
of both idleness and superfluity, as in Lydgate's translation of Laurent de
Premierfait's version of Boccaccio's *De casibus virorum illustrium:*

> The trewe marchaunt be mesour bouhte & solde,
> Deceit was non in the artificieer,
> Makyng no balkis, the plouh was treuli holde,
> Abak stod idelnesse ferr from laboreer,
> Discrecioun marchall at dyneer & sopeer,
> Content with mesour, because attemperance
> Hadde in that world hooli the gouernaunce.[25]

In short, medieval representations of work's history share in the contrariety that characterizes medieval conceptions of work in general, which Ovitt has efficiently summarized: "God ennobled work by doing it himself; God punished postlapsarian man by making him earn his bread in the sweat of his brow. Nature was intended for man's use; nature is to be cared for and emulated by man. Monks must labor with their hands; monks must be preoccupied with the *opus Dei.* Technical knowledge is a gift of God; the mechanical arts are debased."[26]

This contrariety reveals, moreover, an ambiguity inherent in the concept of historical origin itself. The significance of historical origin lies in its archetypal character, in its being a foundational event that establishes and explains the repetition of what is original to it. But the originary event, by virtue of being the remotest moment in the historical development of what is original to it, is also open to an opposite meaning, to being an image, not of what is and must be, but of what is no longer and perhaps should or will be again. On these two dimensions of the historical origin, never wholly separable, are based the two dominant polemical uses of historical origins in the Middle Ages: first, to justify and legitimize something that is, as in the justification of serfdom on the basis of Noah's curse on Ham or the justification of political authority on the basis of its Trojan origins; second, to argue for a return to something that was, as in Ball's argument for a return to original equality or the many arguments for monastic reform. What is generally lacking in medieval historical representation is the historical origin as simply origin, as just a beginning or first stage in the development of something. Instead, the dominant medieval conception of the relation of historical origins to their derivatives is exemplary. As Mircea Eliade has explained, the originary concepts of traditional cultures are characterized by an identification of temporal and ontological priority, by the principle that "an object or an act becomes real only insofar as it imitates or repeats an archetype. . . . [and] everything which lacks an exemplary model is 'meaningless,' i.e., it lacks reality."[27] Similarly, medieval culture consistently sought for and defined the authenticity of things in terms of archetypal origin—that is, origin as the container and revealer of essential and ideal nature. Accordingly, "change was experienced as loss, development understood as reformation."[28] The rigidity with which models of historical decline assigned to successive ages increasing dissimilarity to their beginnings was counterbalanced by the hope, not of breaking with the past, but of renewal and its presupposition of "a relationship between the old and the new in the irreversible process of time."[29]

The archetypal value accorded to historical origins in the Middle Ages rendered the possibility of their disinterested representation remote. The vast array of claims substantiated on the basis of historical origin and its derivative categories (genealogy, custom, tradition, *auctoritas*) demonstrates the rhetorical and ideological, not to mention legal, force that attached to the representation of origins.[30] As a means of legitimization, the efficacy of the representation of origins resides in its deferral of questions of legitimacy. Having the logical structure of "as it was then so shall it be now," the tracing of something back to an archetypal origin both defines its present nature and presents that nature as inevitable, as the result of an inexorable historical process.

This chapter will thus examine late medieval English representations of the history and origins of work not simply as the detritus of diverse textual traditions but as a significant form of discourse on the place and meaning of work in contemporary society. Just as the structure of the Middle English vocabulary of work derives not only from the logical necessity for an array of terms capable of denoting various aspects of work but from socially contingent attitudes toward work, so the contrariety of histories of work in late medieval England derives not only from the inherent ambiguity of the concept of historical origin but from the diverse social and ideological affiliations of their authors. These histories may not constitute a public debate on the origins of work, but retrospectively at least they have the nature of a dialogue. Basically, this dialogue is built around two opposed types of narratives: first, those that look back to a better time before work and associate the beginnings of work with human viciousness; second, those that identify the origins of contemporary forms of work with their inventors as culture heroes. The first is essentially primitivist and defines work as a process of decline or falling away from origin. The second is progressive and defines work in terms of its own origin. The chief ideological value of the first is its valorization of a laborless or leisurely life and hence its legitimization of ruling-class pretensions to exemption from labor. The chief ideological value of the second is its representation of work and the worker as a civilizing force and hence its opposition to the superior status of the leisure class. Furthermore, these two types of narrative are differently affiliated with the dominant types of nonhistorical or marginally historical accounts of work's origins. While the first is easily assimilated to the derivation of labor from human sinfulness, the second is identifiable with the representation of labor and its technologies as products of necessity, as the realization of human potentialities, and as divinely ordained and inspired praxis.

Although these alternative structures of work's history, primitivist and progressive, are logically distinct, their literary origins are by no means separable. As George Boas has shown, Christian readers could find in the Old Testament "equally authoritative support for cultural primitivism and anti-intellectualism and for the opposite view—a natural consequence of the conjunction in these histories of different legends."[31] Similarly, Virgil's *Georgics* both looks back to a time when the fields, undivided and unplowed, "omnia liberius nullo poscente ferebat" (1.128) and, celebrating the gradual development of the arts through use (1.133–34), heroizes labor. That an appreciation of the value and creativity of labor and material progress is not incompatible with the recognition of its wayward and corrupt nature is perhaps best expressed by the famous passage in the *City of God* in which Augustine explains that in the "innumerable arts and skills which minister not only to the necessities of life but also to human enjoyment . . . even in those arts where the purposes may seem superfluous, perilous and pernicious, there is exercised an acuteness of intelligence of so high an order that it reveals how richly endowed our human nature is."[32] Late medieval accounts of the history of work do not so much diverge from such canonical narratives as abridge and elaborate upon them according to their own ends. As instanced by John Ball's use of the "when Adam delved" topos, this procedure of both repeating and refashioning authoritative texts was a subtle and potent means of simultaneously invoking their authority and transforming canonical into local meaning.

The analysis that follows is devoted to three Middle English accounts of the history of work that cover the spectrum from progressive to primitivist: the history of masonry contained in the Cooke MS, Gower's *Confessio amantis* 4.2363–700, and Chaucer's *Former Age*. The Cooke MS's progressive genealogy of the mason's craft, constructed out of disparate sources, traces the knowledge of masonry through famous personages and aligns it with the speculative and liberal arts. It thus represents an attempt to construct for masonry and craft in general a legitimacy and dignity comparable to those of aristocratic and clerical culture. Gower's history of work in the *Confessio amantis,* though also of the progressive type, is of a different order. Rather than closely associating physical and intellectual labor, it both opposes them and constructs for them parallel but discrete histories. This strategy articulates not only a conservative belief in traditional social boundaries and hierarchies but a specifically bourgeois work mentality. Where Gower's history of work barely imagines a time before productive labor when "Ther was no corn, though men it soughte" (4.2376), Chaucer's account of work's history in the *Former Age,* which remembers a better age when "corn up-sprong, unsowe of mannes hond" (10), is clearly of the primitivist type. Though the *Former Age* is thus aligned with nostalgia for a simple, atechnic life, it also, as we shall see, exposes the irrationality and contradictions of such nostalgia.

BUILDING HISTORY IN THE COOKE MS

Within medieval historiography, work occupied at best a marginal position. This marginality is more than the general rarity of representations of work and workers within sacred and secular historical narratives. For not only do these genres largely exclude the world of work from the movements of history, but where they do portray work they hide and subordinate its realities beneath their own primary values. This process is analogous to what Guy H. Allard has described as the "occultation des arts mécaniques" within medieval intellectual discourse, the way it both insists on the superiority of the liberal arts and "traite les arts mécaniques comme une résevoir et un répertoire où il va puiser des métaphores à l'appui de sa quête du savoir."[33] Similarly, as Paul Freedman points out, clerical work itself was simultaneously "endowed with more uniformly positive connotations" than peasant labor and "presented as a form of spiritual labor that borrowed metaphors from the agricultural world."[34]

A prominent example of this metaphorization of labor is the likening of preaching to plowing, as in Wit's statement in *Piers Plowman* that "Prelates and prestes and princes of holy churche" should "tulie þe erthe with tonge and teche men to louye" (C.10.196, 199).[35] Such metaphors are certainly not incompatible with a real and nonderisive appreciation of labor's value and the laborer's dignity. In the case of *Piers Plowman* they are firmly rooted in the poem's idealization of "Alle libbynge laborers that lyven with hir hondes / That treweliche taken and treweliche wynnen" (*PPl* B.7.60–61). But neither are they necessarily indicative of such appreciation, and on the whole it is Allard's interpretation of the tendency of medieval authors to employ them that rings true: "[Q]uand le discours savant-lettré utilise les arts mécaniques à ses fins littéraires, il n'atteste pas de leur ennoblissement mais plutôt de leur état d'infériorité et de dépendence envers les arts libéraux" (23).

It is all the more significant, then, that a late medieval text diverged from these norms and did so with confidence. The Cooke MS (British Museum Add. MS 23198) both counteracts the occultation of work by medieval historiography and corrects the conventional subordination of material to intellectual labor. As Lisa H. Cooper has observed, in this text "real artisans . . . appropriate an intellectual tradition to explain the venerably erudite nature of their labor."[36] But before examining the Cooke MS, it will be useful to observe two examples, sacred and secular, of the ideological forces against which its makers asserted the historical agency of the craftsman.

Augustine's authoritative formulation of the ages of the world in the *De Genesi contra Manichaeos* provides a clear example of the occultation of work within sacred historiography. For as much as this historical paradigm relies upon work as a structural principle, so does it elide the history of work itself. For Augustine, "the ages of history can be understood only in conjunction with the days of creation, the sixth or Christian age, especially, only in its parallelism with the sixth day on which man was created, and the end of history only by analogy with God's rest on the seventh day and with Christ's Resurrection on Easter Sunday."[37] The course of history is further defined as six "ages of work" that are to be followed by the seventh and eternal age of rest.[38] To this correspondence between the creation and the duration of the world Augustine also attaches six stages of individual life (*infantia, pueritia, adolescentia, iuventus, senioris aetas, senectus*) that mark man's corporeal and spiritual development. Actual, material human labor is not excluded from or entirely metaphorized within this parallel scheme of universal and individual history. As labor is established for all history through the Fall, the six historical ages are clearly *aetates operosae* in a literal sense. And universally and individually, the seventh age is an age of rest "ab omnibus operibus" (*De Genesi contra Manichaeos* 1.23, PL 34.193). Augustine also refers to occupational work in a general way by describing the fifth age of man as the time when the individual "should begin to work in the activities of this most turbulent world for the utility of brotherly society just as if he were in the waters of the sea."[39] Finally, the whole structure echoes the conventional weekly cycle of occupational work.[40] Yet despite the implicit and explicit presence of material work within this organization of history, the meaning and value of material work remain wholly absorbed into the more general and transcendent significance that work here carries. Above all, the work of the six ages is the work of refashioning man in the image of God, a work that is not simply part of history but the purpose of history itself. Elsewhere, Augustine compares this work to that of the sculptor: "We, therefore, . . . must after a fashion resculpt [the image] and reform it. But, who would be able to do this, except if he were the artist who shaped it? We could deform the image of God in us, but we cannot reform it."[41] The work of the six ages is ultimately divine, and human work, both material labor and action in general, is valued only through its participation in God's work. Accordingly, Augustine closes his discussion of the six ages by likening this assimilation of human to divine work to the building of a house by hired labor, where "a paterfamilias is rightly said to build a residence, though he makes it not through his own work, but through the work of those serving him whom he commands."[42]

A striking example of the occultation of work within secular historiography, Priam's rebuilding of Troy in John Lydgate's *Troy Book*, based on Guido delle Colonne's *Historia destructionis Troiae*, follows an analogous pattern. As Augustine's concept of the six *aetates operosae* transcendentalizes the meaning and agency of work, these accounts of Troy's reconstruction, as much as they laud the power of laborers and craftsmen, trace that power to the authority of the ruler who organizes them and who is glorified as the "builder" of the city. Lydgate's representation of the rebuilding of Troy lacks any emphasis on manual labor as debased and extols human industry in numerous ways. Emphasis throughout is placed on the skill and intelligence of workers, who are described, for example, as "Of wyt intentyf" (2.492), "sotyle in her fantasye" (2.494), and "excellyng in practik / Of any art callyd mekanyk" (2.528).[43] Likewise their work is of the highest quality, the ultimate combination of beauty and utility. The city walls, "Maskowed [machicolated] with-oute for sautis and assay" (2.580), shine with marble and alabaster so that Troy "alone was incomperable / Of alle cites þat any mortal man / Sawe euer ȝit, sithe þe world began" (2.586–88). Xanthus, the river that runs through Troy, is redirected by the laborers so that "it made a ful purgacioun / Of ordure & fylþes in þe toun" (2.749–50). In keeping with the scene's emphasis on the knowledge that guides labor rather than its difficulty, Lydgate identifies the mason's craft with the liberal art of geometry, naming Euclid as "þe maister and þe founder . . . / Of alle þat werkyn by squyre or compas, / Or kepe her mesour by leuel or by lyne" (2.555–57). Moreover, the city not only is raised by labor but is a laborer's paradise: "euery craft, þat any maner man / In any lond deuise or rekene can" (2.703–4) is practiced there, and all possess their own street "þat þei myȝt, for more comodite, / Eche be hym silfe werke at liberte" (2.709–10).

The ultimate source and recipient of all this urban splendor, however, is not the workers and citizens but Priam himself, who is consistently referred to as the builder, deviser, and maker of the city (2.484–85, 532, 539–40, 936, 974, 1058). These locutions may be natural and necessary to the representation of the organization of labor, but they encapsulate and solidify a transference of industrial agency that is expressed in more overt ways. More than praising the genius of workers, the scene glorifies Priam's power to impress the most ingenious workers from every region (2.489–530). Indeed, Troy is reconstituted through a series of three impressments, each more outrageous in its economic unreality than the last. After the initial impressment brings about Troy's reconstruction, "Kyng Priamus, of hiȝe discrecioun, / Ordeyned hath to dwellyn in þe toun" (2.705–6) every type of artisan known to man, evidently for no other end than the prestige that attaches to ruling over conspicuous production. The point that all these workers practice their trades in Troy not for their own livelihood but to serve and glorify the military aristocracy is driven home by Lydgate, who, omitting all the more humble and useful occupations from Guido's exhaustive catalog, includes only those that make jewelry, fine cloth, and military equipment (2.711–30).[44] Finally, with Troy rebuilt and its labor force installed, Priam commands a "Gret multitude, what of ȝong & olde" (2.780) from the surrounding country to immigrate to Troy. What lies behind the scene's positive representation of human labor, then, is not the power of labor itself but its subjection and instrumentalization by authority. Having the structure of a creationary command, "Let there be a city and it was," Priam's rebuilding of Troy elides the difficulties and economic contingencies of work. Like the massive golden bejeweled statue of Jupiter that Priam has made for his palace (2.1008–37), it submerges the agency of the worker within the person of the ruler.[45]

The Cooke MS, as an attempt to give a craft its own history, diverges from the generic norms of medieval historiography and its general concealment of the world of work. And as a progressive history of work, one that locates the crafts in the world *ab origine* and defines them not as the accompaniment of sin but as a divinely ordained means of making "diuers thingys to goddis plesans and al-so for our ese and profyt" (lines 23–25), the Cooke MS is antithetical to medieval primitivism. But despite the novelty and generic rarity of the work, it is also very traditional. Rather than creating anything like an original identity for masons and masonry, the Cooke MS assembles its history out of canonical sacred and secular historical narratives while carefully pruning from them anything potentially detrimental to the honor of the craft. It fashions not an autonomous cultural identity for masons but one that is grafted onto the authoritative and illustrious identities of the prophets, philosophers, saints, and rulers whose involvement with and patronage of masonry constitute the majority of its episodes. Similarly, the Articles and Points contained in the Cooke MS, which lay down regulations concerning masters and journeymen, both assert the right of masons to independent government and uphold the "profit of the lord" as the guiding principle of labor relations. The text, though clearly an "expression of the conscience and pride of the craft," still follows the logic of imitation and association according to which mercantile and artisanal elites defined and displayed social status, as instanced by their use of livery, coats of arms, and heraldic seals.[46] Like the rare form of armorial seal that combined depictions of a predatory animal with tools of a trade, the Cooke MS defends both the respectability of production and the legitimacy of the nonlaboring class.

The Cooke MS, dated to c. 1430, is the later of two manuscripts, known as the "Constitutions of Masonry," that contain overlapping histories and regulations of masonry, the other being the Regius MS (British Museum Bibl. Reg. 17 A1) of c. 1390. I have chosen to focus on the Cooke MS both because its history is the more elaborate of the two and because its author, as will be seen, was more closely attuned to the interests of masons themselves and more interested in their history. As their editors have demonstrated, the intersecting contents of the MSS argues for the existence of an earlier written version of the history and regulations of masonry.[47] The manuscripts themselves also speak of such a version or versions, referring to "chargys . . . as we haue seyn hem writen in latyn & frensche bothe" and "olde bokys of masonry."[48] The presumed original of the Cooke and Regius MSS contained both the history and articles of masonry, a blending of material that, insofar as its historical portion is largely the history of the articles themselves, reflects less a historical interest in masonry per se than a desire to authorize its regulation through history.

In reworking and expanding their presumed original, the Cooke and Regius MSS take very different paths. The Cooke author adds considerably to the history of the presumed original and announces his historiographical intention from the start: "I schalle schewe you some that is to sey ho and in what wyse the sciens of Gemetry firste be-ganne and who wer þe founders therof and of othur craftis mo as hit is notid in the bybille and in othur stories" (28–35). By contrast, the Regius author develops the regulatory dimension of the original in the direction of moral and religious instruction. The Cooke MS is more interested in the nature and prestige of masonry, the Regius MS in how masons should behave and believe. Where the Cooke MS emphasizes masonry's affiliations with intellectual and aristocratic culture, the Regius author stresses the obedience of masons to ecclesiastical and secular authority, the two general themes of its concluding extracts from John Mirk's *Instructions* and the *Urbanitas* poem (577–794). The divergence of these interests is clearest in the different ways the texts handle the two subjects that both apparently add to their original: the seven liberal arts and the tower of Babel.

Together with an account of the Four Crowned Martyrs, the Regius MS treats the building of the tower of Babel and Euclid's founding of the seven liberal arts as moral exempla that argue against excessive pride in one's craft and for the ordering of material work to spiritual values. Borrowing the story of the Four Crowned Martyrs from "þe legent of scantorum [sic]" (531)—probably a reference to Jacobus de Voragine's *Legenda aurea*—the Regius author emphasizes, more than does Jacobus, both the martyrs' exceptional skill (501–5) and their steadfast love of God (511–16).[49] In doing so, he capitalizes on the deeper significance of the Four Crowned Martyrs, namely that they are not only martyrs who happened to be masons but exemplars of the proper negotiation of the love of craft and the love of God. By dramatizing a crisis of choice between individual genius and "god and alle hys lore" (513), the story of the Four Crowned Martyrs both exposes and neutralizes the idolatrous potential of human making.[50] The Regius author's handling of the tower of Babel episode similarly foregrounds the power of craft only to underscore its inferiority to the power of God. While the tower is represented in traditional terms as a prideful work that mistakenly asserts the autonomy of human, earthly achievement, the Regius author adjusts the story for a masonic audience by emphasizing the tower's technological nature and purpose. The tower is described as the most perfect stonework masons are capable of: "playne werke of lyme & ston / As any mon schulde loke vppon" (539–40)—a clear warning against pride in the technical mastery of masonry.[51] Likewise, the purpose of the tower is defined, not according to Genesis 11.4 as a doomed attempt to attain the heavens and fame, but as an illicit achievement of engineering that would forever protect man from divine punishment: "Kyng nabogodnosor let hyt make / To gret strenþe for monnus sake / Þaȝgh suche a flod [as Noah's flood] a-ȝayn schulde come / Ouer þe werke hyt schulde not nome" (543–46).[52] The Regius author concludes his series of masonic moral exempla by portraying Euclid as kind of prophet of the arts who "Taȝghte þe craft of gemetri wondur wyde . . . [and] dyuers craftes mony mo / Þroȝgh hye grace of crist yn heuen" (552–55). Thus originating in God, the arts are also a way back to God, for "Whose vseþ hem wel he may han heuen" (576).[53] The moral purpose of all these stories is summed up in a direct address to masons to abandon "Pride & couetyse" (577), an exhortation that leads smoothly to the extracts from John Mirk's *Instructions* in which the Regius author, changing Mirk's text from third to second person, urges masons to attend church devoutly.

The Cooke MS treats the seven liberal arts and the building of the tower of Babel quite differently and in ways that are expressive of its more general alignment of masonry with intellectual and political authority. Far from insisting on the superiority of the liberal arts to the mechanical, the Cooke author is interested in the liberal arts as basic categories of knowledge that encompass all theoretical and practical disciplines, all discourse and labor. In keeping with the humanist tradition of locating the origin of the historically pagan liberal arts in God, the liberal arts are introduced under the general rubric of "wittys and connynge of dyuers thyngys and craftys" that God has given to man (16–19).[54] The Cooke author recognizes the liberal arts as forms of knowledge conceptually distinct from the mechanical arts or crafts, insofar as he groups them together and defines them individually (45–76), yet he shows no real interest in them as disciplines unto themselves. Befitting the double meaning of ME *craft* as either speculative or practical art, the distinction between science and craft is both maintained and repeatedly blurred. The "vii liberal sciens" are those "by the wiche . . . alle sciens and craftis in the worlde were fyrst founde" (41–44). The liberal arts are "vii sciens or craftys" (83–84). Geometry did not precede masonry, but simultaneously the "sciens of Gemetry and masonry [was] . . . occupied and contreuyed for a sciens and for a crafte" (191–94). Masonry is both a "crafte" (344) and a "sciens" (416). In short, the Cooke MS brings together the two branches of knowledge traditionally defined as separate, *theoretica* and *practica,* and thus anticipates the "new alliance of technē and praxis" that Pamela O. Long shows to have later "led to openly purveyed treatises on the mechanical arts" in the fifteenth and sixteenth centuries.[55]

Within this general association of theoretical and practical, pride of place is given to geometry, which the Cooke author boldly presents as both the "causer of alle" the arts and "the sciens þat alle resonable menn lyue by" (45, 127–28). Predictably, these arguments work to the credit and prestige of masonry as the most geometric of crafts: "amonge alle þe craftys of þe worlde of mannes crafte masonry hath the most notabilite and moste parte of þis sciens [of] Gemetry" (132–37). In other words, masonry is not only associated with the liberal arts but granted the unique position of being the craft most associated with the art from which all arts, liberal and mechanical, spring. However, this striking argument is put forth in a rather confused manner, and the author's high opinion of geometry and his rationalization of it remain unclarified. The primacy of geometry is first defined in terms of causation (45), but precisely how geometry causes the other liberal arts is not explained. After the definitions of each of the liberal arts (45–76), geometry's primacy is rephrased: "as I seyde by-fore ther ben vii liberalle scyens þat is to sey vii sciens or craftys that ben fre in hem selfe the whiche vii lyuen onle by Gemetry" (81–86). What the author means by *lyuen* becomes clearer in the following argument, one of "many . . . probacions" of geometry's primacy the author claims he could produce if time permitted (125–30):

Gemetria is i-seyd of geo þat is in gru. [Greek] erthe. and metrona þat is to sey mesure. And thus is þis nam of Gemetria compovnyd and is seyd the mesure of þe erthe. Mervile ye not that I seyd that alle sciens lyuen alle only by the sciens of Gemetry. For there is none artificialle ne hon[d-]crafte that is wroȝthe by manys hond bot hit is wrouȝght by Gemetry. and a notabulle cause. for if a man worche with his hondis he worchyth with summe maner tole and þer is none instrument of materialle thyngis in this worlde but hit come of þe kynde of erthe and to erthe hit wole turne a-yen. And ther is none instrument þat is to sey a tole to wirche with but hit hath some proporcion more ore lasse. And proporcion is mesure [and] the tole er the instrument is erthe. And Gemetry is said the mesure of erthe wherefore I may sey þat men lyuen alle by Gemetrye. For alle men here in this worlde lyue by þe laboure of here hondys. (94–124)

The logic of this argument is hardly unassailable. Attempting to demonstrate the geometric nature of all the arts, it makes its case only for the mechanical arts and then glosses over the discrepancy by asserting that everyone is a manual laborer. Nevertheless, the Cooke author does succeed in asserting the material nature of all forms of human labor. And insofar as all human work is characterized by the use of tools, his argument carries weight. The primacy of geometry is worked out, not in terms of a correlation between geometry and the formal principles of the other arts, but in terms of a materialist conception of the arts as so many species of manual labor that rely upon geometry peripherally through their tools. By praising the geometric component of artisanal work, the author effectively reduces all the arts to handicrafts, just as geometry itself is etymologically reduced to practical measurement and design. And by asserting that all the arts "live" by geometry insofar as all men live by "þe laboure of here hondys," the Cooke author conceptualizes the arts not only materially, as forms of production, but also occupationally, as forms of economic practice. In this scheme there is little room for the liberal arts as liberal in the sense of being enabled by their practitioners' freedom from the necessity of earning a livelihood.[56] Dialectic and husbandry are both occupational estates within which individuals make a living. The plowman behind his plow and the spectacled philosopher behind his desk are both manual workers.[57]

The text's definition of the divine origin of the arts and its argument for the primacy of geometry prepare the way for a narrative of masonry's historical origins that relies, not on an evolutionary model of graduated development out of material conditions, but on a model of invention and transmission whereby masonry is represented as entering the world *in toto* and fostered through history by a series of persons who mediate between its origin and its social practice. Here the argument for geometry's primacy is transformed into the demonstration of its temporal priority. With Cain's building of the city of Enoch (Gen. 4.17), "the first Cite þat euer was made" (183–84), the "sciens of Gemetry and masonri [was] fyrst occupied and contreuyd for a sciens and for a crafte and so we may sey þat it was cause & fundacion of alle craftys and sciens" (191–97). This identification of geometry and masonry as constituting a single art is a consistent feature of the history, as when it is claimed that Euclid taught the Egyptians "the crafte [of] masonry and yaf hit þe name of Gemetry by cavse of þe partynge of þe grounde þat he had taught to þe peple in the time of þe makyng of þe wallys and diches a-for-sayd to clawse owt þe watyr [of the Nile]" (508–16). Masonry is thus both ennobled through association with the liberal art of geometry—"masonry hath the most notabilite and moste parte of þis sciens [of] Gemetry" (135–37)—and presented as identical to it. Similarly, the transmitters and patrons of geometry/masonry are persons who lend their authority *to* masonry as well as persons whose only claim to fame, as far as the Cooke author is concerned, is being, or being associated with, masons. Though many of masonry's transmitters are of recognized philosophical, religious, or political authority—Euclid, Abraham, David, Solomon, Charles II (Charles the Bald?), St. Alban, Athelstan— several are not: Cain, Jabal, Nimrod.

In locating masonry's origins in biblical history, the Cooke author appropriates to masonry's honor events and persons of Genesis that were conventionally read in ways that reflected negatively on the nature and status of work and the worker. The material progress charted in Genesis's fourth chapter, as George Boas points out, "could be read as implying a primitivistic moral: the original city-builder was also the first murderer, and the loss of the easy a-technic life of the first pair in Paradise was followed by a progressive development of the arts by their posterity."[58] Though both primitivist and antiprimitivist attitudes were current during the Middle Ages, primitivist views of early man held sway among classical, patristic, and medieval authors. Indeed, "the primitivistic thesis," as James Dean has shown, "received fullest expression in legendary histories written in England in the thirteenth and fourteenth centuries, particularly those influenced by Comestor's *Historia scholastica*."[59] Both the primitivist association of labor and technology with moral corruption implicit in Genesis and any association of labor with human sinfulness or social subjection are ostentatiously avoided by the Cooke author. Not only is the Fall not mentioned, but the world is portrayed as still conforming to the intention of the Creator, who made "alle thyngis for to be abedient & soget to man" (11–12). Neither is there any reference to the labor of Adam and Eve, the *locus classicus* of labor as suffering. Cain is not a murderer, or a fugitive, or the progenitor of the peasantry, or the founder of the Earthly City. Rather, he is simply "Adamis sone" (185) and the first employer of the first master mason, Jabal (Gen 4.20).[60] Similarly, the text elides Lamech's relation to Cain—"[in the] age of adam by-fore noes flode þer was a mann þat was clepyd lameth" (161–63)—in the interest of praising the material progress of his progeny, made possible, of course, by the invention of geometry. The inventions of the antediluvian age are exhaustively described: the privatization of land and herds (204–13), music and musical instruments (213–26), smithcraft and metal working (239–45), weaving, spinning, and knitting (245–55). Finally, all of this knowledge and technology is objectified and preserved from any taint of moral corruption in a version of the legend of the two pillars. Foreseeing that "god wolde take vengans for synne oþer by fyre or watire" (256–59), Lamech's sons inscribe on two stone pillars (one of marble that cannot burn and one of "lacerus" [a corruption of Lat. *lateres,* bricks] that cannot sink) "alle þe sciens & crafte[s] þat alle þey had founde" (282–85). After the Flood the pillars are discovered by Pythagoras and Hermes, who "tought forthe þe sciens þat thei fonde þer y-wryten" (325–26).[61]

    This commitment to masonry's historical prestige even leads the Cooke author, in contrast to the moralism of the Regius MS, to rewrite the story of the tower of Babel as an honorable and foundational episode in the history of masonry, one that portrays Nimrod not in the usual medieval fashion as a proud tyrant but as a great teacher and patron of masonry: "And this same Nembroth be-gan þe towre of babilon and he taught to his werkemen þe crafte of mesnri and he had with hym mony masonys mo þan xl. þousand. And he louyd & cheresched them welle" (342–49).[62] Furthermore, the Cooke MS's Nimrod, before sending his masons off to build the city of Nineveh, first organizes masonry, granting it "a charge profitable for you & me" (388–89). These charges, claims the Cooke author (418–24), are the ultimate original of the Articles and Points contained in the latter portion of the MS. The episode thus establishes three fundamental characteristics of medieval masons: their self-government, their itinerancy, and their close association with the aristocracy, above all with the Crown through impressment. As the editors of the Cooke MS have argued, it was the interrelated development of these three aspects of masonry that ultimately led to the production of the Cooke MS itself.[63] The building of the tower of Babel thus proved irresistible to the Cooke author, both as a reflection of contemporary masons' own mastery of raising stonework toward the heavens and as a historical moment into which the historical forces behind his own composition could be projected.

The Cooke MS, then, represents an aggressive defense of the value and noble origins of masonry. If, as it has been generally assumed, the text was composed by a cleric, he was a cleric attuned to the interests of masons, one who wrote for them and at their behest, who did not mind turning biblical history into an advertisement for the honor of masonry, and who was relatively unpracticed in the art of textual composition. On the other hand, the possibility that the Cooke author was himself a mason should not be discounted, as there were certainly master masons around 1400 capable of composing such a text. The wealth and status that could attach to master masons, and the consequent potential for their education and ownership of books, is evidenced by the prestigious career of Henry Yevele (c. 1320–1400), the London master mason to three kings who died in possession of numerous properties and who worked on, among other things, Westminster and other royal palaces (Eltham, Sheen, Bayard's Castle in London), the Tower of London, the effigied tomb of Richard II, John of Gaunt's palace the Savoy, and the tomb of the Duchess Blanche.[64] The value of literacy to master masons is demonstrated by the royal writs directed to them and numerous building contracts.[65] As organizers of labor, master masons were not too far removed socially from the merchant class, concerning which Thrupp demonstrates that, at least in London, "all the men read English and . . . most of them had some training in Latin."[66] And Lon R. Shelby has argued that "from the fourteenth century onwards a good many, if not most, master masons would have enjoyed at least a primary education, in which they acquired the rudiments of reading in English."[67] The conversational and frequently awkward tone of the Cooke MS is consistent with a relatively uneducated author, perhaps a mason who could read but not write, who employed a minor cleric as amanuensis and collaborator, the mason supplying an older French version of his customs and the cleric supplying his ability to write as well as to fortify the history with references to authorities, all of which are inaccurate.[68]

A more important issue than the author's identity is the deeper question of why late medieval English masonry should develop and articulate such a historical identity. What is it about the social organization of masonry and the nature of the craft itself that fostered an interest in and consciousness of its origins? The answer lies, I suggest, in a combination of three characteristics that distinguished masonry from the majority of medieval trades: the close association of masonry with the ruling classes, the itinerancy of masons, and the relatively permanent and hence historic nature of their products.

Masonry stood apart from other medieval crafts "as the towers of a cathedral or the battlements of a castle stand out above the houses huddled about their base; it belonged to a different order and a different scale."[69] Physically and economically, the work of masons formed a special category of medieval work. Stone building (castles, palaces, churches, and public works) was the exception, not the rule, and was carried out mostly by the aristocratic and ecclesiastical elites, who alone "could command the great resources necessary for buying huge quantities of stone or leasing extensive quarries, providing timber, tiles, lime, irons of various kinds, lead and glass, and for paying the wages of artificers and workmen by the score, and sometimes by the hundred."[70] The work of masons, though not directed to the production of exchange values, was accordingly organized in ways that bear comparison to the capitalist factory.[71] Masons were both subjected in their economic dependence upon employers and distinguished from other wage laborers by their conspicuous production. So while masons could not claim economic self-sufficiency they could identify with the significant status of their employers. Accordingly, the Cooke MS emphasizes the gentle status of masons and constructs for them a postdiluvian aristocratic origin. Euclid, after learning geometry from

Abraham, teaches the sons of Egyptian lords "þat had no lyflode . . . a sciens þat they schylle lyue ther-by ientelmanly" (482–95). Master masons
were originally "þe ch[i]lderen of grete lordis" (666–67). Others "þat were
lasse of witte schold not be callyd seruante ner sogette but felaus ffor no-
bilite of here gentylle blode" (684–88). A master shall not take an apprentice "that is bore of bonde blode" (767), not only because of potential
conflict with the lord, but because masonry "toke begynynge of grete lordis children frely begetyn" (779–80). These real and imagined associations with the aristocracy likely encouraged medieval masonry's historical
self-consciousness, specifically, its development of an occupational genealogy that mirrored the political genealogies of its patrons.

It is equally probable that itinerancy led masons toward historical
identity as a compensation for their relative lack of regional identity. Impressment brought masons from diverse regions to work as a community
for extended periods of time. The impressment for work on Winsdor Castle in 1360–62, for example, gathered masons from the wide area enclosed
by Devon, Hereford, Salop, Derby, Lancashire, Yorkshire, and Notting-
hamshire.[72] Though masons could not express their occupational solidarity
in local or geographical terms, they could overcome their regional heterogeneity through history, by defining masons as a historical category, and
by emphasizing their national identity (Cooke MS, 602–42).[73]

Last, the permanence and historical aura of stone building certainly
fostered a consciousness of masonry's history. Looking at the work of his
predecessors, the mason could see more deeply and clearly than any other
worker into his occupation's past. The late medieval landscape was dotted
with buildings already old in their day, and "most surviving building accounts in the north [of Europe] before the sixteenth century are for renovation and repair of old buildings, not new constructions."[74] As evidenced
by the Anglo-Saxon poem *The Ruin,* in which the speaker remembers the
long-vanished "waldendwyrhtan" or master builders, and by the Middle
English poem *Saint Erkenwald,* in which the renovation of St. Paul's un-
covers England's pagan past, the historical presence of wrought stone
could capture the historical imagination, then as now. In this sense, it is
hardly coincidental that masonry is both the only medieval craft to nar-
rate its own history and the medieval craft most fully studied by modern
historians.

GOWER'S HISTORY OF WORK AND BOURGEOIS *BESINESSE*

Gower turns his attention to the history of work in *Confessio amantis* 4.2363–700, in which Genius, as part of his discourse on sloth, recounts the inventors of the various arts. Having argued the moral and material necessity of laboring according to one's station in life (4.2293–94) and the value of *besinesse* in general, Genius introduces this history as a commemoration of exemplars of industry on whose achievements contemporary life depends:

> For we, which are now alyve,
> Of hem that besi whylom were,
> Als wel in Scole as elleswhere,
> Mowe every day ensample take,
> That if it were now to make
> Thing which that thei ferst founden oute,
> It scholde noght be broght aboute.
> Here lyves thanne were longe,
> Here wittes grete, here mihtes stronge,
> Here hertes ful of besinesse,
> Whereof the worldes redinesse
> In bodi bothe and in corage
> Stant evere upon his avantage.
>   (4.2346–58)

The distinction between mental and material labor—here introduced by "Als wel in Scole as elleswhere"—is a principal feature of Gower's work history, and the Latin verse with which he prefaces it clearly expresses the poet's higher esteem for the latter:

> Expedit in manibus labor, vt de cotidianis
>   Actibus ac vita viuere possit homo.
> Set qui doctrine causa fert mente labores,
>   Preualet et merita perpetuata parat.
>   (4.vii)[75]

Material labor is thus valued as temporal, earthly, and merely useful, whereas mental labor is valued intrinsically as enacting and producing transcendental value. Both are forms of work, but intellectual labor, dependant upon the support of its physical counterpart, rises above it in honor and marks it as quotidian. Thus privileging intellectual over physical work, Gower treats of the mechanical arts' origins summarily (4.2396–2456) and devotes many more lines to alchemy (4.2457–2632) and letters and language (4.2633–71). His identification of exemplary industry with invention is itself characteristic of this preference. Narrating material progress as a series of discrete inventions, Gower elides its social and economic contexts and credits it to individual genius rather than laboring humanity as a whole.

But as much as Gower's opinion of the superiority of intellectual labor is unmistakable, so does his work history avoid the direct claim of this superiority, which is appropriately confined to the Latin quatrain. Gower does not, in the classical fashion, represent the intellectual disciplines as liberal in the sense of being enabled by their practitioners' freedom from the necessity of earning a living. Virtuous *otium* has no place in his scheme. Neither does the poet make any gesture toward the material dependence of the mental upon the manual laborer. Indeed, he says nothing at all concerning their social and economic relationship. Rather, intellectual work is portrayed simply as a natural species of labor, as a way of life whose purpose and legitimacy are as self-evident as the plowman's.

Before recording the inventors of the various arts, Genius provides a brief portrait of the origins of material and mental labor. Though historically vague, this passage sets forth Gower's own ideas about the history of work and makes his treatment of it more than a repetition of medieval traditions:

Bot er the time that men siewe,
And that the labour forth it broghte,
Ther was no corn, thogh men it soghte,
In non of al the fieldes oute;
And er the wisdom cam aboute
Of hem that ferst the bokes write,
This mai wel every wys man wite,

Ther was gret labour ek also.
Thus was non ydel of the tuo,
That on the plogh hath undertake
With labour which the hond hath take,
That other tok to studie and muse,
As he which wolde noght refuse
The labour of hise wittes alle.
And in this wise it is befalle,
Of labour which that thei begunne
We be now tawht of that we kunne:
Here besinesse is yit so seene,
That it stant evere alyche greene;
Al be it so the bodi deie,
The name of hem schal nevere aweie.

(4.2374–94)

Imagining a time before agriculture when men were in need of it, Gower directly opposes the idea of a Golden Age when the earth was innately bountiful—compare Chaucer's "Yit nas the ground nat wounded with the plough, / But corn up-sprong, unsowe of mannes hond" (*Form Age,* lines 9–10)—and thus represents work's history progressively rather than primitivistically. Gower's "gret labour" is not the accompaniment of the world's physical and moral decline but man's practical and creative response to natural conditions. The superiority of former times is a central theme of the *Confessio* and of Gower's poetry in general, but this passage reinforces the fact that his overbearing nostalgia for "A worthi world, a noble, a riche, / To which non after schal be liche" (Pro. 633–34) is generally not primitivist. Gower's characteristic use of the past is to evoke not a simpler and purer time before contemporary institutions but a time when they were more perfect, above all a time when the orders of society, keeping to their proper places and functions, harmoniously served each other and the common good.[76]

Gower's history of work subjects the origins of the arts to a similarly unrealistic idealization. While portraying the development of the arts as progress, it confines progress to the process of individual invention and thus leaves no room for progress as an extended development, as occupying historical duration. Much less does it entertain the possibility that the arts have undergone improvements since their invention. As Gower's organic and harmonious society occupies an unspecified and unspecifiable "tempus preteritum . . . beatum" (Pro. ii) when "the lif of man [was] in helthe" (Pro. 96), so his inventors occupy a vague and bygone time when men, long-lived and of superior strength and wit, were ideally equipped to discover the arts. A combination of biblical and classical personages and euhemerized deities, Gower's inventors are grouped together without any thought to time and place or to the interdependence of the arts. "Jadahel [Jabal] . . . A tente of cloth with corde and stake / He sette up ferst and dede it make" (4.2427–32), but "The craft Minerve of wolle fond / And made cloth hire oghne hond" (4.2435–36). "Philosophres wise" were first to get metal "out of Myne / And after forto trie and fyne" (4.2453–56), but "Tubal in Iren and Stel / Fond ferst the forge and wroghte it wel" (4.2425–26). Material progress, through the commemoration of "The name of hem [that] schal nevere aweie," becomes a list of names.[77]

But the most conspicuously problematic feature of Gower's history of work is the socioeconomic unreality of its division of the first intellectuals from the first laborers. As if they could live, not only not on bread, but on thought alone, Gower's first intellectuals "tok to studie and muse" without any apparent dependence upon the labor of those not so inclined. By eliding any sense of a material relation between intellectual and laborer and any sense of their division as the result of a social process, Gower portrays this division of labor, and the service of the latter to the former that it requires, as unquestionable. In the beginning, some men did not refuse the labor of their hands while others did not refuse the labor of their minds. Neither can claim priority. In their common rejection of idleness, "the Norrice / in mannes kinde of every vice" (4.1087–88), both are morally responsible, and in their common exercise of natural dispositions both enact an intrinsic and ordained order. However, that Gower chooses to represent manual labor as an objective necessity—"Ther was no corn, thogh men it soghte"—but mental labor as a subjective necessity—"As he which wolde noght refuse / The labour of hise wittes alle"—is conspicuous. Where plowing is work that has to be done by man in general, study is work that is desired by individual men. The difference is correlative to that expressed by the prefatory Latin quatrain cited above, in which manual labor is denoted objectively ("manibus labor"), mental labor is located in an individual subject ("Set qui . . ."), and the former is presented as a precluded option for the educated reader. Gower thus grants intellectual work a privileged position within the relation of natural disposition or talent to the division of labor. The intellectual's disposition toward his work is a matter of self-consciousness and choice, and through work he exercises powers, individual powers, that distinguish him from other men. The fitness of the physical laborer to his work, on the other hand, is not positively defined but implicitly characterized as a matter of default. Rather than acting upon individual talent, the manual laborer acts upon common necessity. More than being specially fit for his work, he is not fit for anything else.

The ideological significance of Gower's history of work is manifold. In contrast to the Cooke MS, which grafts the history of craft onto the history of the liberal arts and thus asserts its comparable status against the conventions of disdain for manual labor and laborer, Gower upholds the historical separability of mental and manual work and thereby the propriety of traditional social boundaries between them and the superior status of the former. Gower's representation of the autonomy of mental and manual work instances his general tendency to view society topographically and his devotion to the morality of order, hierarchy, and place.[78] Gower does not figure original mental and manual labor as functionally and socially separate for the express purpose of arguing that the intellectual may legitimately live off the labor of others or that laborers should not concern themselves with intellectual matters. Rather, the rhetorical force of this separation lies in the way it is presented without explanation or argument and thus makes such implications automatic—as automatic as the superior worthiness of the intellectual work through which the special class of men to which the poet belongs find "merita perpetuata," as natural as the existence of another class of people "who seek food *for us* by the sweat of their heavy toil" (*Vox clamantis,* 5.561).[79]

Yet Gower's history of work is more than an occasion for the poet to uphold, once again, the rightful order of things, and it is motivated by more than reverence for the industry of the past. Bearing a complex relation to the larger themes of book 4, his excursion into the history of work both fulfills and goes beyond the purposes that its position in the *Confessio* assigns to it. On the simplest level, Genius's inventory of inventors is a series of counterexamples to sloth. But he arrives at this commemoration through a winding discourse that touches upon labor in a variety of senses.

The labor theme, though present from the beginning of book 4 in terms of both effort in general and love's labor (all that a lover suffers and does to win his beloved), arises more specifically out of Genius's discourse on prowess (4.2014–44), which leads, after a series of exempla (Hercules, Pantasilee, Philemenis, Eneas) to the claim that a lover's success depends upon his *travail:* "who that is bold / And dar travaile and undertake / The cause of love, he schal be take / The rathere unto loves grace" (4.2191–94). In this context, labor is above all military and heroic, an act that "longeth to manhede" (4.2033), one that defines "Hou love and armes ben aqueinted" (4.2137). Concluding his treatment of prowess with the observation that "wommen loven worthinesse / Of manhode and of gentilesse" (4.2197–98), Genius is then prompted by Amans to define *gentilesse.* In agreement with Dante, the Wife of Bath, and Jean de Meun's Nature, Genius explains that true *gentilesse* derives not from wealth or lineage but from "vertu set in the corage" (4.2261) and that it is not simply an internal disposition but a principle of action "Whereof a man the vice eschuieth, / Withoute Slowthe and vertu suieth" (4.2273–74). Having thus defined *gentilesse* essentially as the love and practice of virtue, Genius turns to consider the relation of virtue to both courtly and spiritual love, and it is here that Gower's interest in labor, both as effort in general and as vocational action, becomes more insistent. First, Genius recognizes the inefficacy of virtue without wealth in "loves court" (4.2279)—"The povere vertu schal noght spiede, / Wher that the riche vice woweth / For sielde it is that love alloweth / The gentil man withoute good" (2280–83)—and the superior value of virtue and wealth combined—"Bot if a man of bothe tuo / Be riche and vertuous also, / Thanne is he wel the more worth" (4.2285–87)—only to point out that neither is efficacious without *besinesse:* "Bot yit to putte himselve forth / He moste don his besinesse, / For nowther good ne gentilesse / Mai helpen hem which ydel be" (4.2288–91). Second, working according to one's station in life is recommended generally as a means of improving one's condition: "who that wole in his degre / Travaile so as it belongeth, / It happeth ofte that he fongeth / Worschipe and ese bothe tuo" (4.2292–95). Last, labor is recommended even more generally as being consonant with love as "the vertu moral" (4.2321) that "above alle othre [virtues] is hed" (4.2326). Where "Slowthe is evere to despise" and thus, as a kind of loveless rejection of life itself, "accordeth noght to man" (4.2331–33), labor is the proper expression of virtuous rationality: "For he that wit and reson kan, / It sit him wel that he travaile / Upon som thing which mighte availe" (4.2335–37).

Gower's history of work thus comes at the end of a complex thematic progression that defines and values labor in diverse ways. Though not overtly structured, this progression follows definable patterns. To begin with, it traces labor both through the social hierarchy and with increasing social generality, from the heroic acts of the military aristocracy, to the *besinesse* of the rich and virtuous "In loves court," to the self-improving work of those in any estate, and last, to the morally necessary *travail* of every individual. Coupled with this increasing generality is an increasing vagueness of the described purpose of work, from valorous deeds as the means of winning a lady, to putting oneself forth more generally to find success in love, to working within one's estate as a means of attaining "Worschipe and ese," and finally, to working, almost for the good of working itself, "Upon som thing which mighte availe." The crux of this progression, which traces the value and necessity of labor from courtly to noncourtly contexts, is Genius's non-class-specific definition of *gentilesse*. As a virtuous disposition that is achievable "Als wel to povere as to the riche" (4.2234) and that eschews idleness, this definition frees the labor theme from its confinement in the romance world of "love and arms."

Gower's history of work, in its complex thematic context, is more revealing of a developed and identifiable attitude toward work than criticism of it has shown.[80] Though Gower's treatment of the value of work is not direct but rather embedded in other themes, notably *gentilesse* and intellectual labor, this indirection must itself be brought into question as a feature of Gower's work mentality. Specifically, why does Gower have Genius discourse upon virtuous *gentilesse* in book 4 under the rubric of sloth? Why does the discussion of *gentilesse* raise the issue of occupational, wealth-producing work? And last, why does Gower, having touched upon the practical value of work, immediately diminish this value by placing it beneath the intrinsic value of intellectual labor as something distinct from and superior to the business of earning a living?

The answer to these related questions lies in the fact that Gower's whole approach to work, in its simultaneous valorization of industry and subordination of it to higher noneconomic values, is characteristically bourgeois. In other words, his attitude is conflicted in a manner appropriate to the work mentality of that class who, more than any other, both appreciated the material and social value of work and sought nonworker and especially aristocratic identity and status. Gower's life records show that he moved "in the same two worlds as Chaucer, the upper middle class society of the franklin, merchant, and lawyer, and the aristocratic society of a trusted retainer in a noble household."[81] Gower's poetry similarly reveals an appreciation of both aristocratic and commercial values. As Fisher observes of the *Mirour de l'omme,* Gower's "aristocratic prejudice came to be tempered by other influences, and his treatment of the lesser estates shows the respect for wealth, trade, and the business boosted nationalism which Marxist philosophy has come to find typical of a rising bourgeoisie. . . . [O]n the one hand he subsumes so much that is most characteristic of the medieval mind, while on the other hand his understanding of the function of the entrepreneur and his spirited defense of the reward due risk capital read like something out of Adam Smith."[82] What lies behind the indirectness of Gower's valuation of work in *Confessio*'s book 4 is a negotiation of these contrary impulses. This indirectness communicates, on the one hand, the uneasiness of bourgeois occupational identity and, on the other, a class pride in the profitability of *indirect* labor. If Gower channels, as Gregory M. Sadlek has suggested, "the voice of a new work ethic," it is because of the ideological conflicts of his own voice, just as his favorite word for work, *besinesse,* comes to signify merchant-class occupational activity not simply because it is a "positive" term appropriate to nonproductive, commercial work but because it is more obviously a way of moralizing such work in a way that covers its negativity.[83] As Prudence, exposing this logic nicely, says in Chaucer's *Tale of Melibee:* "ye sholde alwey doon youre *bisynesse* to gete yow richesses, so that ye gete hem with good conscience" (VII.1631–32).

Genius's discourse on *gentilesse* exemplifies what Lee Patterson has called "the quintessential bourgeois strategy" of promoting "an aristocratic value whose full force can be made available only when it is detached from its social origin."[84] But in separating nobility from its conventional ties to birth and wealth, Genius's familiar argument also disassociates nobility from the leisure that birth and wealth make possible and thus encompasses, albeit indirectly, both a critique of privileged idleness and a validation of the means by which wealth is earned rather than inherited. By defining true nobility not only generally to mean virtue but specifically to mean virtue as action, it sets *gentilesse* against inactivity as a fault most

proper to false nobility, to those who possess only "the name of gentilesse"
(4.2207). That there is nothing arbitrary about Gower's location of his
treatment of *gentilesse* under the rubric of Sloth is all the more evident in
the context of other definitions of nobility as virtue. In the *Roman de la
Rose,* Nature both emphasizes the availability of nobility to "those who
cultivate the earth or live by their labor" and specifies that "whoever turns
his desire toward nobility must guard against pride and laziness."[85] In
Gentilesse, Chaucer similarly opposes *gentilesse* and sloth: "The firste
stok, fader of gentilesse . . . loved besinesse, / Ayeinst the vyce of slouthe"
(lines 1–11). And in the *Wife of Bath's Tale,* the loathly lady succinctly defines *gentilesse* as action: "he is gentil that dooth gentil dedis" (III.1170).
While these texts make *gentilesse* both unavailable to the idle and acces-
sible to the industrious, Gower goes further than any of them in drawing
connections between gentility and work and in doing so exposes both the
ideological value of the bourgeois concept of *gentilesse* and its origination
in a class-specific work mentality.

Behind Genius's discourse on *gentilesse* lies, as an unutterable truth,
the material and social fact that work, education, and social behavior in
general could create gentle status.[86] This is suggested, first, by the total
direction of Genius's discourse, which is to bring *gentilesse* and labor
into proximity and ultimately discredit the genealogies of false nobility
founded on the unstable "fortune of richesse" (4.2208) in favor of a genealogy of culture heroes founded on virtuous industry. Second, couched in
the moral issue of what constitutes true *gentilesse* are echoes of an appreciation for social mobility. On the one hand, in a statement that bears comparison to the fact that "the gentry . . . did not so much rise (though some
did) during the later middle ages as fall from the nobility which their an-
cestors had enjoyed in common with all landowners,"[87] Gower is here interested in the loss of wealth and station: "lacke of vertu lacketh grace, /
Wherof richesse in many place, / When men best wene forto stonde / Al
sodeinly goth out of honde" (4.2257–60). On the other, Gower praises the
self-promoting value of work: "who that wole in his degre / Travaile so as
it belongeth, / It happeth ofte that he fongeth / Worschipe and ese bothe
tuo" (4.2292–95). That these representations of social mobility are made
so as not to infringe upon the hierarchy that gives social mobility significance, that they recommend virtue and labor as a means of retaining and
increasing one's status and wealth ("worschipe and ese") without calling

into question the boundary between *gentil* and non*gentil,* gets to the heart of the paradoxical nature of bourgeois work mentality.

To uphold and transgress traditional social boundaries, to engage in commerce and disengage from commercial identity, to work at an occupation in order to be free of it—these conflicted modes of action are central to the cultural situation of medieval England's merchant class, a class that, more than cultivating its own economic identity and ideology, conceptualized itself through "the materials of other cultural formations— primarily aristocratic but also clerical—and lacked a [cultural] center of its own."[88] Gower's treatment of labor in *Confessio*'s book 4 is similarly conflicted. First, his association of *gentilesse* with labor as a means of improving one's condition exposes the inherent doubleness of the bourgeois concept of *gentilesse*—its simultaneous negation of conventional nobility and assertion of the availability of noble status through action—a doubleness that bears out the merchant class's commitment to a status order defined by aristocratic values and its desire to accommodate its own economically motivated labor (the antithesis of conventional nobility) to those values. Second, the increasing vagueness with which Genius describes the purpose of work outside courtly contexts, insofar as it negates the social dishonor of having to work by locating work's value beyond the socioeconomic and defining it in individual, subjective terms, discloses the weakness of bourgeois occupational identity. Last, Gower's historical separation of mental from manual labor, as a legitimization of forms of work that are not materially productive, exemplifies the characteristically bourgeois fusion of a desire for freedom from economic necessity with a vocational commitment to nonmanual occupations (mercantile, legal, etc.) as the means of earning such freedom.[89]

The complexity of Gower's treatment of labor in *Confessio*'s book 4 is thus intelligible, not only as an association of themes or a copresence of "various ideologically colored voices," but more directly as an expression of a class-specific attitude toward work. As voiced by Gower, this attitude comprises both positive and negative conceptions of work. Gower neither associates labor with sinfulness nor displays any nostalgia for a mythic time before labor. Nor does he express disdain for labor as intrinsically degrading.[90] Instead, he offers a progressive account of the history of work and identifies labor as both a universal necessity and an expression of virtue. In these terms, Gower's attitude toward work is positive and stands against status mentality and its disqualification of labor as a sign of weakness and inferiority. At the same time, Gower's attitude toward work is bound up with status concerns in ways that betray its class origin. Gower's representation of the virtuousness of *besinesse*, however significant in its own terms as part of the moral discourse of the *Confessio*, bears social meaning. As corroborated by Genius's discourse on *gentilesse*, it constitutes an attempt, not merely to defend the honor of work, but to define it in terms that are adaptable to aristocratic values. In turn, material production occupies an ambiguous position in Gower's scheme. As much as Gower honors labor as a necessary good—"'as the briddes to the flihte / Ben made, so the man is bore / To labour,' which is noght forbore / To hem that thenken forto thryve" (4.2345)—so does he diminish the honorableness of the most necessary form of labor through which "vivere possit homo." This ambiguity derives, not only from Gower's vocational commitment to intellectual work as a discipline that is both as socially and morally responsible as and superior to physical labor, but more generally from the merchant-class commitment to occupations that are both overtly economic and superior in status to the most common and essential forms of economic work.

CHAUCER'S *FORMER AGE* AND THE LIMITS OF PRIMITIVISM

Chaucer's *Former Age* is one of the more eloquent expressions of medieval primitivism. Chaucer's version of the Golden Age both synthesizes and goes beyond its medieval tradition, reshaping a constellation of canonical sources—principally passages from Ovid's *Metamorphoses,* Boethius's *Consolation,* and the *Roman de la Rose*—into a lyric whole. The originality of the *Former Age* is apparent on many levels. First, Chaucer's retelling of the myth, in comparison to its sources, is noticeably lacking in didactic or philosophic purpose. It points the reader less to an *understanding* of the loss of the Golden Age and to a course of action based in such understanding than to the simple and tragic *fact* of its loss: "Allas, allas, now may men wepe and crye!" (60). In each of Chaucer's sources the Golden Age figures as part of a larger narrative and fulfills specific discursive functions. In the *Metamorphoses* the Golden Age is represented, first, as an episode in the historical movement of the poem "ab origine mundi ad mea . . . tempora" (1.3–4), and second, within Pythagorus's discourse to Numa Pompilius (15.75–478), as a time of exemplary vegetarianism.[91] In the *Consolation,* Boethius's metrum on the Golden Age, prefaced by Lady Philosophy's discourse on the emphemerality of riches—"Fortune ne schal nevere maken that swiche thynges ben thyne that nature of thynges hath maked foryne fro the" (*Boece* 2.prs.71–73)—and the naturalness of moderation—"[with] fewe thynges and with ful litel thynges nature halt hir apayed" (*Boece* 2.prs.78–80)—serves above all to illustrate man's ideal virtuous relation to material goods, a relation that is presented as exemplary for the individual and society: "I wolde that our tymes sholde torne ayen to the oolde maneris!" (*Boece* 2.m5.28–30). And in the *Roman de la Rose,* the Golden Age, described at length by Ami (lines 8355–454), functions primarily as a lost paradisiacal time of equality and pure love between the sexes that both warns against selfishness in love and points up the necessity of employing to one's advantage the material contingencies of romantic love in the imperfect present.[92] In contrast to these sources, Chaucer's version of the Golden Age is neither a model for reform nor a means of counsel. As John Norton-Smith observes, Chaucer's "sombre enumeration of the insane principles of modern life allows no positive moral position."[93] And as A. V. C. Schmidt notes, "[T]he myth of the Golden Age as Chaucer gives it has no explanatory force and—I presume—no explanatory intention."[94]

The *Former Age* also surpasses its sources in the realism and detail with which it describes contemporary society, especially its technology. Ovid, Boethius, and Jean de Meun to varying degrees all describe the Golden Age in terms of features of contemporary society that it lacked, but Chaucer's use of such description outdoes his sources' in number and kind. Several of Chaucer's references to contemporary technologies— "the quern and ek the melle" (4), "the morter" (15), "mader, welde, or wood" (17), "coyn" (20), "toures" (23), "paleis-chaumbres" (41), "bleched shete" (45), "the hauberk and the plate" (49), and "taylage by . . . tyrannye" (54)—have no direct match in his sources, and as Andrew Galloway points out, such "divergences . . . suggest contemporary meanings at every point."[95] Thus the naming of both mill and handmill evokes the seigneurial right to license mills and tallage their use and peasant resistance to it through the use of handmills.[96] The naming of specific dyestuffs ("mader," "welde," and "wood"), as L. O. Purdon demonstrates, evokes the industrial abuses of dyers and their conflicts with foreign traders.[97] And as John Norton-Smith has argued, Chaucer's references to oppressive taxation and to Nimrod as a tyrant "desirous / To regne" (58–59) suggest the tyranny of Richard II in his final years.[98]

Last, the *Former Age* is noticeably more interested than its sources in impeaching contemporary modes of life. Dominated by the description of what the former age was not, the poem says less about what used to be than what now unfortunately is.[99] The poem's ideal past is less an identifiable historical age intelligible in its own terms than a negation of contemporary technology and corruption. In its critical bent, the *Former Age* is closer in meaning and tone to its Boethian source than to the accounts of Ovid and Jean de Meun. Like Boethius, Chaucer concentrates on describing the Golden Age negatively or in terms of characteristics it lacked. Like Boethius, Chaucer rejects the soft primitivism of Ovid, according to which ancient man, blessed with "eternal springtime" and "streams of milk and nectar" (1.107–11), lived an untroubled life of natural luxury. And like Boethius, Chaucer rejects the mythic foundations of the Golden Age and its loss. Where Ovid explains the loss of the Golden Age as the passing of the world's rule from Saturn to Jupiter and depicts the advent of labor and technology as a necessary response to Jupiter's institution of seasonal change, Boethius portrays the demise of the first age as caused by man, emphasizing the greed-inducing power of gold and gems: "What was he that first dalf up the gobbettes or the weyghtes of gold covered undir erthe and the precyous stones that wolden han be hydd? He dalf up precious periles" (*Boece* 2.m5.33–37).[100] So Chaucer, using the same figure (27–32), represents the world's decline as a manmade and technological historical process, despite the closing reference to "Jupiter the likerous" (56). But Chaucer's opposition of ideal past and imperfect present is more extreme and its indictment of contemporary society more total than Boethius's. For the *Former Age,* going against the grain of all sacred and secular historiography, speaks of a time when "hertes were *al* oon" (47) and the people were "voyd of *alle* vyce" (50). And this radical idealization of the past is counterbalanced in the poem's conclusion by an unbelievable pessimism about the present: "For in oure dayes *nis but* covetyse, / Doublenesse, and tresoun, and envye, / Poyson, manslawhtre, and modre in sondry wyse" (61–63).

Recognizing these original features of the *Former Age* as direct signs of its intention, critics have generally regarded the poem as a serious, critical, and emotional response to its times. For John Norton-Smith, "the poem is a bitterly detailed and accurate study of a violent acquisitive society," the product "of a mind too dispirited and embittered to imagine that public morality might be improved by an application of moral principles."[101] A. V. C. Schmidt similarly speaks of "the poem's air of *gravitas*," its "mood of deep pessimism that find[s] no parallel elsewhere in Chaucer's work," and its "intensity of tone and a total absence of irony which are . . . an inescapable sign of the author's *ernest*."[102] And A. J. Minnis calls the *Former Age* "the bleakest poem [Chaucer] ever wrote."[103] By these accounts, the *Former Age* is above all self-expression, a document of felt experience, and its voice is unequivocally the poet's own.[104] Lacking irony and a mediating persona, the poem communicates a feeling for the tragedy of historical decline that demands sympathy and respect.

But the *Former Age* is not without its ironies, and neither its voice nor its logic is as unambiguous as these studies suggest. Situating the *Former Age* in "a contemporary context of discussion about the decadent nature of contemporary uses of knowledge," Andrew Galloway identifies the principal irony of the poem as its narrator's complicity in the corruption he describes: "The intellectual innocence of the former age is implicitly contrasted not only to the present as a whole but also to the narrator's heavy burden of technical and vocational knowledge which unfolds at every occasion, and which includes his knowledge of how to wield rhetoric, producing a pervasive, self-indicting irony that has not sufficiently been appreciated."[105] For Galloway, the self-indicting irony of the narrator does not so much alter the meaning of the poem (as explicated by Norton-Smith, Schmidt, et al.) as enlarge it, widening its subject to include not simply the postlapsarian world but "post-lapsarian consciousness" (537). The narrator of the *Former Age,* by emphasizing the ignorance of the former age and "making modern practical or technical knowledge the measure of historical change," and by displaying his own knowledge and decadence vis-à-vis mankind's original simplicity, "both describes and embodies" such consciousness (537), a consciousness not only of the moral complications of modern practical knowledge but of one's own immersion, as an historical individual, in those complications. Galloway thus adds "darkly self-conscious" (549) to the established array of adjectives applicable to the *Former Age* ("serious," "passionate," "embittered," et al.).

But if the speaker of the *Former Age* is a person who shares in the corruption he decries, if his point of view originates not from a position of moral and historical objectivity but from within the decadence of his age, does the *Former Age* also call into question the legitimacy of its own representation of history? Is it possible that Chaucer's primitivist lyric interrogates primitivism and frames its historical narrative as just that, a way of understanding past and present that is subject not only to historical reality but to the complexity of motivations that mark the individual, in this case the nostalgic individual, as a subject of history? Answering "yes" to these questions, I will argue that the *Former Age*, more than being Chaucer's critical response to contemporary civilization, is his critical examination of primitivism and nostalgia in general. The *Former Age* does not satirize primitivism in the sarcastic mode of Prudentius's *Contra orationem Symmachi*.[106] Rather, the effective strategy of the poem is to both lure its reader into sympathy with its nostalgia and make him question that sympathy. Taking the logic of primitivist nostalgia to its illogical conclusions, the *Former Age* exposes it to be a misunderstanding of history, a false memory that stands in the way of historical understanding and begs more questions than it answers. While my reading of the poem thus revises previous criticism, it neither questions Chaucer's commitment to the moral values the poem espouses nor precludes the possibility of his belief in the superiority of former times. Rather, it insists only on two points: first, that the *Former Age*, more than demonstrating such commitment and belief, expresses Chaucer's skepticism of the primitivist principle—that vice originates in technological and economic development—as a means of understanding either history or contemporary society; and second, that Chaucer was suspicious of nostalgia, both as a mode of historical understanding and as a psychological condition.

Those features of the *Former Age* that most define its originality—its didactic openness, contemporary resonances, and intensity of tone—also foreground its subjectivity, the sense that behind the poem there is not only a literary tradition but the experience of a contemporary individual. As long as we can understand these features as elements of design rather than accidents of self-expression, they point to Chaucer's interest in primitivist nostalgia as an objectifiable mentality. That primitivism and nostalgia would have interested Chaucer as topics for poetry is not remarkable given their currency in the late fourteenth century. As James Dean's studies of the idea of *senectus mundi* demonstrate, the superiority of times past is a pervasive theme of the literature of the period. Nostalgia, of course, could take many forms—political, religious, moral—but primitivism, as a desire to return to a simpler mode of production, as nostalgia concerned with the ends and means of work, is particularly in evidence. Representations of the Golden Age and biblical history aside, there are also more complex and intriguing signs of primitivist and nostalgic attitudes toward work in the late fourteenth century. Wyclif worried over the vice-inducing effects of labor and the arts and attempted to draw a firm distinction between necessary and unnecessary work. In a sermon on Mary and Martha, for example, he describes the active life of worldly work as morally endangered by the surplus value it creates: "Þe secound liif . . . is clepid actif liif, whanne men travailen for worldli goodis and kepen hem in riȝtwisnesse. And þis is hard, but it is possible; and alȝatis ȝif coveitise be left; for Crist techiþ bi Matheu þat men shulden not be besie aboute her fode and hilyng, but bisynesse shulde be for hevene, þat shulde be eende of mannes traveile. And exces of þes goodis lettiþ ofte tymes þis eende."[107] And in his treatise on the nature of Edenic life, *De statu innocencie,* Wyclif emphasized that man, had he not sinned, would not have used any liberal or mechanical art, yet would have naturally possessed theoretical knowledge of all of them.[108] Reflecting Wyclif's teaching, the last of the Lollards' *Twelve Conclusions,* which were presented to Parliament and posted on the doors of Westminster Abbey and St. Paul's in 1395, demanded that "alle manere craftis nout nedeful to man . . . schulde ben distroyd for þe encres of vertu."[109] And in accordance with this contempt for superfluity, many Lollards cultivated an aesthetic of material simplicity by wearing clothing typical of common laborers.[110]

Where Wyclif and his adherents wanted to pare down the material life of society in the interests of righteousness, the ruling classes sought to pare down the material life of the worker in their own interest. The abortive Statutes of Laborers and sumptuary laws of the later fourteenth century, which sought a return to a "better" time by pinning wages to pre-plague levels and cracking down on socially inordinate consumption, are essentially legislations of nostalgia. That the economic changes stimulated by the Black Death stirred nostalgia, particularly nostalgia for a time when the third estate was more obedient, simple, and content with less, is most clearly seen in the works of John Gower. Gower's nostalgia and aggravated sense of present-day corruption are not on the whole primitivist, but his attitude toward laborers expressed itself in primitivist terms: "In olden days the workers were not accustomed to eat wheat bread; instead their bread was made from other grains or from beans. And they likewise drank only water. And they feasted on cheese and milk and but rarely on anything else. Their clothing was of gray material. At that time the world was well-ordained for people of their estate."[111] And while Gower has much to say about the corruption of all estates and occupations, he gives priority to the viciousness of the laborer, claiming that even if all others "had preserved honesty, Fraud would still be alive, for the common little people who are called laborers keep it alive in their way" (*Mirour de l'omme*, 26425ff).

Excluding the *Former Age,* Chaucer's works show little commitment to either nostalgia or primitivism. This is not to say that his poetry does not at times appeal to the past's embodiment of imperiled values. *Lak of Stedfastnesse,* the closest thing to a corollary to the *Former Age* that Chaucer produced, firmly opposes a past when "the world was so stedfast and stable / That mannes word was obligacioun" (1–2) to a present "turned up-so-doun / . . . for mede and wilfulnesse" (5–6). And like the *Former Age,* its critique of modern corruption is uncompromising:

> Trouthe is put doun, resoun is holden fable,
> Vertu hath now no dominacioun;
> Pitee exyled, no man is merciable.
> Through covetyse is blent discrecioun.
> The world hath mad a permutacioun
> Fro right to wrong, fro trouthe to fikelnesse,
> That al is lost for lak of stedfastnesse.
>   (*Sted* 15–21)

But the trajectories of *Lak of Stedfastnesse* and the *Former Age* are fundamentally divergent. In *Lak of Stedfastnesse,* reverence for the past does not extend to the imagination of an ideal way of life and does not express any preference for social and technological simplicity. The poem shows no trace of primitivism or any implication that the world's return to *stedfast-*

nesse is impossible within the context of contemporary institutions. Nor is *Lak of Stedfastnesse* at all nostalgic, as long as by "nostalgia" we mean not merely a belief in the superiority of former times but an attitude or experience characterized by longing for a lost past or place. Instead, *Lak of Stedfastnesse* is both concerned with human morality as an independent, subjective condition and committed more to addressing the problem of contemporary vice than to yearning for a bygone age. To the question of why the present world is "turned up-so-doun" the poem offers a conclusive, albeit simple, answer: it is due to the "lust that folk have in dissensioun" (9) and to their "wilful wrecchednesse" (13), in other words, to the waywardness of human nature itself. And in marked contrast to the conclusion of the *Former Age, Lak of Stedfastnesse* ends on a note of hope in the possibility of moral reform, imploring King Richard to "Shew forth thy swerd of castigacioun, / Dred God, do law, love trouthe and worthinesse / And wed thy folk agein to stedfastnesse" (26–28).

The focus of *Lak of Stedfastnesse* on historical decay as a feature of human nature rather than human institutions is exemplary of the shape of Chaucer's interest in the past as a locus of value. As James Dean recognizes in his analysis of the *senectus mundi* topos in Chaucer's work, this focus distinguishes Chaucer from his poetic contemporaries: "If Langland and Gower perceived corruption throughout the estates, human institutions, and individuals, Chaucer seems to have regarded mundane decay especially as a decline of virtue, a lack of commitment to *trouthe* and *gentilesse,* and a coarsening of human relationships."[112] Accordingly, Chaucer's other lyric apology for an ancient virtue, *Gentilesse,* follows the same rhetorical and didactic strategy as *Lak of Stedfastnesse.* It locates *gentilesse* in the past, not in a gesture of longing *for* the past, but to elicit an imitation *of* the past. The originality of *gentilesse* both authenticates the poem's denouncement of false nobility and underscores the viability of true nobility, that *gentilesse,* having existed before, is now achievable through imitation of its origin, "The first stok, fader of gentilesse" (1). Like *Lak of Stedfastnesse, Gentilesse* is neither nostalgic or primitivist. Indeed, by identifying the origin of human virtue with work—"This firste stok . . . loved besinesse, / Ayeinst the vyce of slouthe" (8–11)—*Gentilesse* opposes the primitivist identification of the origins of vice and labor that forms the crux of the *Former Age:* "But cursed was the tyme, I dare wel seye, / That men first dide hir swety bysinesse . . ." (27–28).[113]

In neither of these moral ballades is the unfavorable comparison of present to past a thematic endpoint. Instead, they offer complementary models of moral reform. Where *Lak of Stedfastnesse* imagines the reform of society from without, as it were, through the moral leadership of the king and his enforcement of justice throughout his realm, *Gentilesse* imagines reform as beginning from within, in the individual pursuit of virtue. Moreover, both poems exhibit a clear diffidence with regard to the actuality of their ideal pasts. Where *Lak of Stedfastnesse* evokes a vague "somtyme" (1) when the world was steadfast, *Gentilesse* hesitates to name "The firste stok, fader of gentilesse" (1). Each poem begins by conjuring a past whose identity we are forced to supply. In doing so, Chaucer both privileges the rhetorical over the historical value of the ideal past and foregrounds his reader's *imagination* of that past. That Henry Scogan interpreted "The firste stok" (*Gent* 1) as signifying God only points up the difficulty of locating the "fader of gentilesse" in history.[114] Though *Lak of Stedfastnesse* and *Gentilesse* obscure the question of the historicity of their ideal pasts behind their more pressing concerns for present matters, they nonetheless point to Chaucer's suspicion of the reality of pure origins.

The difficulty of aligning the mentality defined by the *Former Age* with Chaucer himself increases when we consider its thematic connections to the *Canterbury Tales,* in which the idealization of the past and lament for historical decline are associated, correctly, with clerical culture. In contrast to the nonprimitivist utopias in the tradition of the Land of Cockaynge, which are rooted in medieval popular culture, the representation of the Golden Age and the imagination of Eden as a primitivist utopia were almost exclusively clerical endeavors.[115] This reflects the deep connection between the idealization of the past and spiritual contempt for the world.[116] The most serious and elaborate medieval representation of the Golden Age was produced by Bernard of Cluny, a Benedictine monk of the twelfth century.

> Perdita secula moribus aemula praevaluerunt,
> Sunt sine nomine, qui sine crimine vivere quaerunt.
> Aurea secula pacis et oscula deperiere;
> Secula perfida, secula foetida sunt modo vere.
> Secula foetida, non voco sordida; sed voco sordem.[117]

Through a multitude of such antitheses, Bernard's *De contemptu mundi* defines past and present as inverse images of each other. And as these lines demonstrate, its contempt for the present holds sway over its reverence for the past. For Bernard and the tradition he represents, the past is little more than the accuser of the present. Transmuted from an historical to a rhetorical value, the past effectively ceases to be understood as what was and becomes simply an image of what is not. All questions as to the *process* of historical decline are buried beneath the *fact* of historical decline, a fact that itself appears as less an object of knowledge than a rhetorical posture—saying that the Golden Age has perished becomes just another way of saying that the present age is corrupt.[118] Within this framework, the poet-monk figures himself as a consciousness that oscillates between contempt and lament: "Talia mordeo, talia rideo, non sine fletu" (2.540) [I attack such things, I ridicule such things, but not without weeping]. And as his grief for the world surpasses the boundary of his representation—"While writing my poem, I weep to tell so many evils; in my poem I am unable to reveal so many disgraces" (2.962–63)—so his ridicule of the world exceeds reason: "the bad deeds of men are more pious, even more pleasing to the Lord that the good deeds of women" (2.519–20).

An individual of Bernard of Cluny's temperament may not be among the pilgrims of the *Canterbury Tales,* but there are reflections of the tradition he represents in the Clerk and the Monk. The *Clerk's Tale,* as Dean points out, is "framed by human mortality and transience, a significant feature of literature *de contemptu mundi.*"[119] And the *Tales* come closest to referring to the Golden Age when the Clerk, to explain that he has told his tale "nat for that wyves sholde / Folwen Grisilde as in humylitee . . . But for that every wight, in his degree, / Sholde be constant in adversitee / As was Grisilde" (*ClT* IV.1142–47), says that "This world is nat so strong, it is no nay, / As it hath been in olde tymes yoore" (*ClT* IV.1139–40). The didactic function of the *Clerk's Tale* is thus underwritten by the Clerk's awareness of the instability of life on both the individual and the historical level. The Clerk's ideal of "vertuous suffraunce" (1162) is founded upon a model of human life, not as series of objective accomplishments, but as a path of spiritual resistance to forces outside one's control. And both Griselda's moral exemplarity and her literal implausibility are constituted by her association with an irretrievable past.[120] Like the Golden Age, she is a virtuous ideal that is realistically untenable.

The *Monk's Tale* does not directly address the myth of the Golden Age, but its parallels with the *Former Age* are nonetheless compelling. First, the Monk himself is portrayed in the *General Prologue* in terms of historical decline. The Monk's love of hunting, disregard for the Benedictine Rule, and distaste for both intellectual and manual labor are indexed as examples of his modernity: "This ilke Monk leet olde thynges pace, / And heeld after the newe world the space" (*GP* I.175–76). There are also significant generic continuities between the *Monk's Tale* and the *Former Age*. Like the Monk's exempla, the *Former Age* is essentially tragic. The *Monk's Tale* traces the movement from "wele to wo" on the level of individual history, and the *Former Age* does so on the level of collective history. In fact, the *Monk's Tale* establishes a continuity between these two levels of decline, one that likewise rests upon a negative representation of labor, in its portrait of Adam:

> Hadde nevere worldly man so heigh degree
> As Adam, til he for mysgovernaunce
> Was dryven out of hys hye properitee
> To labour, and to helle, and to meschaunce.
> (*MkT* VII.2011–14)

As the *Former Age* ends in irresolution and hopelessness, so the Monk's tragedies follow individual lives to the point where "ther nas no remedie / To brynge hem out of hir adversitee" (*MkT* VII.1993–94). In accordance with Boethius's characterization of tragedy as a form of lament—"What other thynge bywaylen the cryinges of tragedyes but oonly the dedes of Fortune . . .?" (*Boece* II.pr2.67–68)—the *Monk's Tale* and the *Former Age* are both narrated from within a mood of grief: "Allas, allas, now may men wepe and crye!" (*Form Age* 60); "I wol biwaille in manere of tragedie . . ." (*MkT* VII.1991, cf. 2077–78, 2377, 2663, 2687, 2762). In other words, the Host's dissatisfied response to the *Monk's Tale,* through which Chaucer identifies the futility of the Monk's histories with his act of telling them, could apply as well to the *Former Age:* "no remedie / It is for to biwaille ne compleyne / That it is doon, and als it is a peyne, / As ye han seyd, to heere of hevynesse" (*NPPro* VII.2784–87). Last, the *Monk's Tale,* befitting the high style of tragedy, is the only portion of the *Tales* written in the same complex *ababbcbc* rhyme scheme as the *Former Age.*

That the *Tales* associate the idealization of the past and lament for historical decline with clerical culture and thereby investigate their social contexts supports the possibility that the narrator of the *Former Age* is as much a subject of the poem as the loss of the Golden Age, that Chaucer's composition of his most nostalgic poem was mediated by his interest in representing a nostalgic persona. The *Clerk's Tale* reveals Chaucer's interest in how the idealization of the past may produce models of virtue that are both exemplary and unrealistic, how belief in the world's moral decline both urges a return to past virtue and consigns virtue to the past. And by representing the inseparability of nostalgia for a golden past from contempt for the present world, the *Clerk's Tale* also investigates the subjectivity of the idealization of the past. As the Clerk's reverence for Griselda is bound to his sense that "Grisilde is deed, and eek hire pacience" (*ClT* IV.1177), so the *Former Age*'s imagination of a "lambish peple, voyd of alle vyce" (*Form Age* 50) is inextricable from its narrator's despair over the present.

The *Monk's Tale* sheds a complementary light on the *Former Age*. Where the *Clerk's Tale* investigates the limits of idealization, the *Monk's Tale* shows Chaucer's scrutiny of the other principal feature of the *Former Age*—lament for the futility of history. By ascribing such lament to a speaker who is himself described as embodying historical decline, the *Monk's Tale* provides an analogy for the narrator of the *Former Age* as someone who shares in the corruption he decries. Moreover, Chaucer constructs the tale-teller relation of the *Monk's Tale* in ways that question the motivation, rather than support the authority, of its lament. That the Monk, an "outridere" (GP 166), tells tales that are stockpiled in his cell (*MkT* VII.1972)—the locus of escape from the world of Fortune—makes his commitment to the moral purpose of his tragedies suspect, and his tale is burdened with narratorial ignorance and diffidence.[121] More importantly, the Monk, revealing Chaucer's interest in the psychological contexts of lament for historical tragedy, seems to suffer from a combination of sadness, dullness, and sloth that is *acedia*. His representation in the *Tales* begins with his lack off interest in work (*GP* 184–88) and ends with his lack of interest in play: "'Nay,' quod this Monk, 'I have no lust to pleye. / Now let another telle, as I have told'" (VII.2806–7). That the Monk's habitual condition is sad and slothful is also suggested by the Host, who invites the Monk to tell a tale with words that presume his cheerlessness and reticence toward the tale-telling game: "'My lord, the Monk,' quod he, 'be myrie of cheere . . . Ryde forth, myn owene lord, brek nat oure game'" (VII.1924–27). In short, the Monk embodies a bodily and spiritual hevynesse that expresses itself in the "hevynesse" of his tale (VII.2769, 2786) and threatens its hearers with "disese," "peyne," and ultimately, "sleep" (VII.2771, 2786, 2797).

The Former Age not only retells the myth of the Golden Age but retells it in a way that foregrounds both the act of retelling and the question of its motivation. This is evident first of all from the phrase "the former age" (2), which, draining the ideal past of historical specificity, reveals it to be more an object of desire than an object of knowledge. In naming man's idyllic past as "former" (2) rather than "first" or "golden," Chaucer "ignores the labels of Ovid and Jean de Meung, translating strictly Boethius's prior aetas, where the comparative form of the adjective (following Ciceronian use) signifies 'first.'"[122] That Chaucer understood this use of the comparative is clear in his translation of Boethius's Consolation: "Blisful was the first age of men" (Boece, 2.m5.1). Why this alteration? Norton-Smith notes that "'former' only signifies 'first' in a succession of two states . . . removing from the reader's mind the usual Ovidian or classical notion of the four ages with a successive decline in moral law" (120). Enlarging this observation to encompass the author's intention that his reader recognize this difference, we may see that Chaucer's former emblematizes both the dehistoricization of the past by nostalgic consciousness and the failure of such consciousness to understand history as process and duration. Underscoring the fact that the "blisful lyf" (1) of the poem occupies a time that is not real and definite but rather unidentifiable and simply past, "the former age" (2) traces the backward look of nostalgia toward a past that is not so much already there as constructed in the act of looking back. It casts a shadow of historical vagueness over the poem and thus brings the truthfulness of the historical representation it introduces under suspicion. And by organizing time into before and after, then and now, Chaucer's former signals the polarized periodization that nostalgia delivers upon the continuum of history, its reduction of historical process to an unintelligible rupture between antiquity and modernity.

The problematical, subjective nature of the Former Age's version of history, its participation in what David Aers has identified as "a factor Chaucer's art constantly foregrounds—the shaping presence of the knower and his interests in construing what is known," emerges more generally in the poem's narrative movement.[123] It is a movement characterized by recursiveness rather than resolution. As the speaker revolves between reverence for the past and contempt for the present, he enacts a hermeneutical circle that comes to rest not in an understanding of their relation but in the aporia of their irreconcilable opposition. This movement both takes place within and is mirrored by the overt formal and thematic structure that Chaucer gives to the poem, a structure that criticism of the *Former Age* has not sufficiently appreciated. Composed of eight eight-line stanzas (one of which, whether through scribal error or as an intentional emblem of the loss of perfection, is missing a line), *The Former Age* exhibits a stanzaic pattern of 3-2-3. The first three and the last three stanzas are each concerned with describing the former age both in terms of what it was and in terms of what it was not. Fittingly, the two central stanzas address the nature of the transition from the former to the present age. The first three and the last three stanzas also follow a parallel progression: the first two stanzas of each group describe the former age both positively and negatively, whereas the final stanza of each describes it only negatively. In total, then, the *Former Age* is framed by the repetition of a movement away from the *assertion* of the ideal past toward the *negation* of the present, a positive-to-negative movement that mirrors the total movement of the poem from "A blisful lyf, a paisable, and a swete" (1) to "Poyson, manslawhtre, and modre in sondry wyse" (63).

The structure of the *Former Age* both underwrites the "dispirited and embittered" tone of the poem and solidifies the impression that its cultural primitivism is not a legitimate form of historical knowledge but, in the words of Lovejoy and Boas, "the discontent of the civilized with civilization."[124] The tendency of the poem's speaker to move away from the direct description of the former age toward cataloging, even to the point of redundancy, the technologies and practices of which the former age was innocent stages an ascendancy of despair for the present over longing for the past. In other words, the *Former Age* not only expresses nostalgia but enacts a breakdown of nostalgia into despair. As Fred Davis has explained, nostalgic experience is constituted by "an inner dialogue between past and present" in which "it is *always* the adoration of the past that triumphs over lamentations for the present. Indeed, this is the whole point of the dialogue; for to permit present woes to douse the warm glow from the past is to succumb to melancholy or, worse yet, depression."[125] In the first three-stanza movement of the poem, the potential for the speaker's description of the golden past to devolve into bitter denunciation of all things modern is both registered and held in check, as the third stanza focuses entirely on subsequent technological and economic practices, yet remains, through its repetition of the "No . . . knew" clause, a description of the former age's innocent simplicity. In the final three stanzas, however, the rhetorical method of *oppositio* is broken by an eruption of direct commentary on the modern age: "For in oure dayes nis but covetyse, / Doublenesse, and tresoun, and envye, / Poyson, manslawhtre, and mordre in sondry wyse" (61–63). James Dean has remarked how the final line of the poem "is star-tling for its hypermetricality (it is something like an Alexandrine), as the text seems to strain with the violence of modern-day human sins."[126] More immediately, the text strains with the passion of the speaker's indictment of modern society as nothing but vicious, a passion whose excess is regis-tered as a failure of artistic control.

More important than the tonal meaning of the *Former Age*'s struc-ture, however, is the logical progression it helps to define. The first three stanzas focus on the atechnic, noncommercial, and laborless character of the former age. The next two, which form the discursive crux of the poem, argue, first, that sorrow and vice began with the "swety bysinesse" of seeking metal and gems, and second, that the creation of wealth—"bagges . . . and fat vitaile" (38)—is the efficient cause of war, that destruc-tion and violence would not be were it not for production and the peaceful arts. Finally, the last three stanzas return to describing former age life, but with a new and radical emphasis on its harmony and moral purity, as op-posed to later tyranny and cupidity, which are personified by Nimrod and Jupiter, respectively. On the surface, this three-part progression is or-dered and rational. We are told first of the *external* condition of primitive society, of the customary practices through which it sustained itself, in short, of its material relation to the natural world. Then we are told how a change in this relation, the first labor of seeking out metal and gems, brought about an *internal* change in human character: "Allas, than sprong up al the cursednesse / Of covetyse, that first our sorwe broughte" (31–32). Last, we are told of the cataclysmic nature of this change: spiri-tual unity—"Hir hertes were al oon withoute galles" (47)—is replaced with "Doublenesse, and tresoun, and envye" (62); atechnic simplicity gives way to "sondry wyse," or diverse techniques, of "Poyson, manslawhtre, and mordre" (63). On closer inspection, however, it becomes clear that the discursive order of the *Former Age* conceals a nest of problems and that the assurance of its closing call for universal lament masks a hermeneutical failure. At the heart of this failure is the explanatory inadequacy of its account of the downfall of the former age. If primitive life was so "blisful," why did men bother to labor in the first place? If original man was so "voyd of alle vyce," why did he strive after gold and gems?

The *Former Age* begs these questions first of all through its representation of labor. Where Genesis defines labor as one of the effects of the Fall, the *Former Age* identifies labor as a cause of its "Fall" and in doing so expresses a radically negative conception of work.[127] This negativity manifests itself not only in the phrase "hir swety bysinesse" (28), which seems to look disdainfully on labor as the degrading activity of someone else, but more clearly in the poem's depiction of work as transgression and violence against the natural order. Work enters the world of the *Former Age* not as a response to necessity, or as a means of producing material goods, or as an act of human ingenuity, but simply as the difficult means of acquiring what is naturally hidden: "metal, lurkinge in derknesse" and gems "in the rivers" (29–30). Original labor, rather than creating value, is a disclosing of false value that becomes the means of excess and decadence. More so than its Boethian source, the *Former Age* portrays the waywardness of original work as simultaneously the waywardness of the first act of work and the wayward *auri sacra fames* that its object awakens in the worker. Boethius's metrum ends with an unanswerable question that emphasizes the difficulty of understanding exactly how the Golden Age came to an end: "What was he that first dalf up the gobbettes or the weyghtes of gold covered undir erthe and the precyous stones that wolden han be hydd?" (*Boece*, 2.m5.33–36). And even if this question does allow us to understand the beginning of the end of primitive life as the discovery of a rare and glittering object that kindled in man an "anguysschous love of havynge" (*Boece*, 2.m5.30–31), Boethius makes no claim for this discovery being the singular historical origin of subsequent corruption. What matters for Boethius is the imagination of the former age as a model of virtue, not the mechanism of its demise. The *Former Age,* on the other hand, isolates the laborious pursuit of gold as the calamitous event at the source of modernity and speaks of it in the language of the Fall: "Allas, than sprong up al the cursednesse / Of coveytyse, that first our sorwe broghte" (31–32). And by defining this event both as the origin of later greed and as an act that presumes the greed of its agent, the poem threatens its own idealization of primitive man as morally pure and content with what the earth naturally gave him.

I am suggesting, then, that Chaucer intended the *Former Age*'s story of the double origin of labor and greed to be implausible, for it to appear as an inadequate imagination of work's origin that constitutes, instead of historical understanding, a projection into the past of the speaker's negative, Diogenean attitude toward work and his monocular perspective on its nature. Accordingly, it is precisely at this logical crux of the poem that Chaucer records both its subjectivity—"But cursed was the tyme, *I dare wel seye*" (27)—and its authority, the Cynic philosopher Diogenes, a dubious model of virtue, much less of Chaucerian value, when one considers his ambiguous representation in the Middle Ages.[128] Consumed with contempt for *coveytyse*, the speaker of the *Former Age* is incapable of seeing work as anything other than the pursuit of riches. Confusing production with the cause of violence, he conceptualizes labor as transgression. The extremity of his negative attitude toward work is summed up best in his representation of agriculture, which turns production into destruction: "Yit nas the ground nat *wounded* with the plough" (9). That agriculture, the most necessary of the arts catalogued in the poem, is the only art to be subjected to such heavy-handed rhetoric only points up the narrator's blindness to the necessary, productive, and beneficial aspects of human labor. Moreover, it prepares us to understand the inadequacy of his account of the origin of labor as its elision of the role of necessity in technological development.

Mater artium necessitas. This proverbial principle was the common property of both the primitivist and antiprimitivist traditions of the Middle Ages. Origen argued that "God, wishing to exercise human understanding in every respect, that it might not remain fallow and ignorant of the arts, created man in want, so that by his very want he might be forced to invent arts, some for food, others for shelter."[129] Isidore of Seville describes labor as the means of preserving something of Eden "in maledictae hujus terrae" (*De ordine creaturarum*, PL 83.940). Hugh of St. Victor illustrates his view of necessity as the providential catalyst of the arts with another proverb: "Ingeniosa fames omnes excuderit artes" (*Didascalicon* 1.10,

PL 176:748). Hunger is also identified as the prime mover of material prog-ress in the prologue to the widely read *Saturae* of Persius: "magister artis ingenique largitor venter."[130] And Dante, though he doubts the historical reality of the Golden Age (*Purgatorio* 28.139–44), revises Ovid's soft pri-mitivism by describing primitive man's hunger and thirst: "Lo secol primo quant'oro fu bello; / fè savorose con fame le ghiande, / e nettare con sete ogni ruscello" (*Purgatorio* 22.148–50). In Virgil's *Georgics,* Jupiter insti-tutes the hostility of nature "so that man, by reflecting on his need, might devise the various arts little by little" (1.133–34), and this same text's "labor omnia vicit improbus" (1.145–46), in a present tense form, also became proverbial. So in Ovid's *Metamorphoses* the first forms of labor, building shelter and growing food, arise in response to Jupiter's institution of sea-sonal change (1.113–24). And in the *Roman de la Rose,* Jean de Meun re-peats the principle as part of Genius's lament for the world's decline: "Thus have the arts sprung up, for all things are conquered by labor and hard poverty; through these things people exist in great care. For difficulties incite people's ingenuity because of the pain they find in them."[131]

The *Former Age*'s elision of necessity as a cause of work is effectively recorded in the first movement of the poem, above all in its description of the former people's diet: "They eten mast, hawes, and swich pounage, / And dronken water of the colde welle. . . . corn up-sprong, unsowe of mannes hond, / The which they gnodded and eete nat half ynough" (7–11). Galloway argues that equation of early man's food with pig fodder "re-veals the historical distance and decadence" of the speaker and "'gnod-den,' a wittily vulgar verb that Chaucer uses only here, describing some primitive technique of rubbing or grinding, or perhaps simply gnawing corn straight from the stalk, illuminates the distance that the modern con-sciousness recounting this golden age possesses from such earlier modes of production and consumption."[132] In a complementary way, Schmidt in-terprets "eete nat half ynough" (11) as a wry ellipsis that points to modern corruption: "not half enough [by our modern civilized standards—which are, needless to say, decadent]."[133] A common effect of these readings is to remove the elements of hardship from the former age and resolve their contradiction with its idealization by consigning them to the narrator's voice, to save the Golden Age, as it were, from the poet who speaks of it. But the literal and more obvious meanings of these phrases constitute a real and significant intrusion of harsh realism upon the "blisful lyf" of the former age. *Pounage* (or *pannage*) refers to the acorns and other things swine find to eat in the forest. The phrase "swich pounage" thus produces the discordant image of the "blissed folk" of the former age as pigs rooting about the woods for food.[134] Since *pannage tyme* was in the late fall, the phrase also echoes the approach of winter, with its scarcity of food—an association underscored in representations of the Labors of the Months, where November's labor is the knocking down of acorns for swine. The phrase "eete nat half ynough," by suggesting that primitive man could not find enough to eat, more directly characterizes the former age as a time of need. It is not easy to dismiss these echoes of bare necessity as rhetorical accidents. Their impropriety as terms of idealization could easily have been avoided. They are supported by the poem's rejection of the soft primitivism of Ovid. And their signification of necessity is reinforced by their juxtaposition with the fundamental human technologies of fire, agriculture, and milling (6, 9, 12).[135]

Contrary to its own account of the origin of work and its representation of primitive life as intrinsically satisfying, the *Former Age* thus introduces the question of necessity and so suggests a counternarrative of technological development as originating in need rather than greed. Together with the poem's consistent emphasis on the technical *ignorance* of primitive society, its discordant allusions to the harshness of primitive life form a kind of shadow version of the Golden Age that forces an interpretive choice: either commit to the speaker's nostalgia or remain open to the possibility that the innocence and happiness of the former age are the creation of nostalgia, a fictive covering for a form of life that might very well have been simply primitive. Indeed, by suggesting the scarcity of food in primitive times and describing it as pig fodder, the *Former Age* echoes the *anti*primitivist tradition of portraying atechnic society as impoverished and beastlike. This tradition, as the several antiprimitivist texts gathered by Lovejoy and Boas show, offered an opposite perspective on the same material conditions of life represented by primitivism. As Diodorus Siculus wrote, "The men who were born in the beginning lived, they say, an undisciplined and brutish life, each going off to feed by himself upon the tenderest herbs and the fruits that grew wild upon the trees. . . . The first men, therefore, led a miserable existence, none of the things which are useful for life having yet been discovered: they had no clothing, were unacquainted with the use of fire and dwellings, and knew nothing at all of the cultivation of food."[36] A comparable description of the harshness of primitive life and its improvement by intelligent labor, based on Isidore of Seville's *Etymologies,* occurs in Ranulf Higden's account of the origin of building in the *Polychronicon:* "Men were first naked and vnarmed, nouȝt siker aȝenst bestes, noþer aȝenst men, and hadde no place to fonge hem, and to kepe hem fro colde and fro hete; þan by besynesse of kynde witte þey beþouȝt hem of buldynge, þerfore þey bulde hem smale cootes and cabans, and waf ham and heled hem wiþ smalle twigges and wiþ reed, þat hire lyf myȝte be þe more saaf."[37] And in Macrobius's *Commentary on the Dream of Scipio,* which Chaucer almost certainly read in its entirety, there is a similar passage.[38] Presenting the evidence against the eternity of the world, Macrobius asks,

> Who would readily admit that that the world has always existed, when credible histories show that the cultivation and improvement and even the invention itself of many things are recent, and when antiquity remembers or relates that men were originally rough and in their wild carelessness not much different from the savagery of the beasts, and when there is a tradition that they did not eat the same food as we, but first were nourished by acorns and berries, and only later hoped to derive sustenance from the furrows? And since we think this to have been the beginnings of things and of the human race itself, how can we believe the ages first to have been golden, and that then nature, degenerating through the baser metals, debased the later ages with iron?[139]

By inscribing such a realist perspective within the *Former Age*'s idealization of primitive life—how *could* the former age have been golden?—Chaucer allows us to see, not so much the error of believing that primitive life was blissful, peaceful, and sweet, but the arbitrariness of such belief. By allowing representational contradiction in his idealization of human prehistory, he entertains skepticism of it.[140] The significance of the poem's allusions to the harshness of primitive life lies less in their potential antiprimitivism then in their *compatibility* with the speaker's contempt for economic and technological development as forces of corruption, a

compatibility against which his idealization of the former age and his account of the double origin of work and greed appear fanciful and overde-
termined. There is no contradiction, of course, in maintaining both that
work and technology arose naturally of necessity and that they precipitate
vice, that human history is marked, not by a fall from virtuous simplicity,
but by a movement from animality to corruption. In fact, this is precisely
the viewpoint that Macrobius exemplifies. Commenting, in the same chapter cited above, on the periodic destruction and renascence of civiliza-
tions, he writes,

> [S]o it happens that in a civilized world there are uncivilized men
> ignorant of culture. . . . [T]hey wander about the earth until, relin-
> quishing little by little the roughness of their roaming, wild life,
> they naturally form communities and associations; at first, there is
> among them the simplicity of yet being ignorant of wrong and in-
> experienced in cunning, and to this early period is given the name
> "Golden Age." Thereafter, the more experience moves them towards
> material development and the arts, the more easily does rivalry
> creep into their spirits. Though beneficial at first, this rivalry imper-
> ceptibly turns into envy, and from this is born all that the human
> race undergoes in subsequent ages.[141]

Macrobius thus provides a significant counterpoint to the *Former Age*.
Where the *Former Age* idealizes primitive life as virtuous and pleasurable,
Macrobius perceives it as simply primitive. Where the *Former Age* defines
corruption as a cataclysm, Macrobius understands it as an imperceptible
process. Where the *Former Age* condemns civilization as unnatural and
unnecessary, Macrobius describes its natural evolution, its wickedness,
and its usefulness.[142] And where the *Former Age* repeats the legend of the
Golden Age, Macrobius depicts an historical reality to which men have
retrospectively given the name "Golden Age."

Against the possibility of such a reasonable account of the nature of
primitive society and the material progress that brings it to an end, the
Former Age presents its glorification of the past as suspicious, as a symp-
tom of nostalgia rather than knowledge. In turn, the inseparability of the
speaker's idealization of the past from his contempt for the present is confirmed in the final movement of the poem. Bound together by proportion-

ally hyperbolic language, his juxtaposition of past and present here falls prey to a relativization whose totality and finality are manifested through a series of superlatives. The blessed folk of the past now sleep in *"parfit quiete"* (44); their hearts are *"al* oon" (47); *"Everich of hem"* (48) is faithful; they are void of *"alle* vyce" (50). Correlatively, the present *"nis but"* (61) greed, duplicity, and so on. The *Former Age* thus dramatizes primitivist nostalgia as a rudimentary form of existential historicism, as described by Fredric Jameson: "For existential historicism . . . the experience of history is a contact between an individual subject in the present and a cultural object in the past. Each pole of this experience is thereby at once open to complete relativization. . . . It is this threat of infinite relativization which the more properly ideological presuppositions of existential historicism are then called upon to limit and to conjure. These consist . . . in a certain psychology of human nature, or better still, in a certain anthropology."[143] But where existential historicism thus produces a past that confirms its presuppositions about human nature and society, the *Former Age*'s total relativization of past and present threatens its anthropology and urges us to question its ideology. Just as the breakdown of the speaker's nostalgia into despair in the final lines of the poem unveils his contempt for the present as the origin of his idealization of the past, so the glorification of the past in the poem's final movement discloses nostalgia as the source of primitivism. For by representing the virtuous past as wholly incommensurable with the vicious present, the *Former Age* destabilizes the intelligibility of its own explanation, and the possibility of any explanation, for the loss of the former age. Like all other dreams of a golden past, the *Former Age* succeeds in representing what could only have been if human nature were not what it is, what could never have been. But unlike most other such dreams, it shows us that it does so.

To understand the *Former Age* as Chaucer's reductio ad absurdum of primitivist nostalgia only enlarges, rather than restricts, both the polemical and the tragic meanings of the poem. For neither is limited to the simple fact of modern-day corruption but rather includes its modern perceiver. More specifically, by representing primitive life as a form of ignorance, the *Former Age* rebuts the Wycliffian identification of material simplicity with superior knowledge. And by bringing the Gowerian indictment of the worker as the cause of corruption to its logical end in an indictment of civilization itself, the *Former Age* counters the selfish, self-preserving nostalgia of the ruling class. Looking past these polemical implications, the tragedy of the *Former Age* resides not only in its representation of the interdependence of work and violence but in its representation of a consciousness that mistakes this interdependence for identity and in doing so misunderstands the nature of both.

Chaucer's *Former Age* thus takes the question of work's meaning to a hermeneutic level beyond that of the previous two texts discussed in this chapter. The imagination of work's origins produced in the Cooke MS and Gower's history of work is more clearly the product of particular social and ideological perspectives. The authors implicitly make the case for their versions of the history of work and connect them unambiguously to the values they espouse. The voice of the *Former Age* is not so easily related to social and ideological identity. Rather, it seems to speak out of the opposite of identity, a condition of alienation. The poem represents a world in which authentic work, work without complicity in the world's violence and greed, is not only unavailable but unimaginable. Like all nostalgia, its imagination of a world before work has the character of a failing fantasy, the fictional construction of an impossible world. But this nostalgia, born from an overwhelming sense of the meaningless of human work, also evokes its subject as a being who longs for meaningful work.

"My Werk"

Chaucer and the Subject of *Swink*

In late medieval England, work became a subject for literature in ways that it had never been before.[1] This new interest is most evident in the best poetry of the period, in *Piers Plowman*'s spiritual heroization of labor and in the *Canterbury Tales*'s representation of "a society in which work as a social experience conditions personality and the standpoint from which an individual views the world."[2] And this interest, insofar as we may generalize it, is especially an interest in the subjective dimension of work, in the space between occupation and the individual.

The literary discovery of the worker as a subject took shape around the problem of the motive for work, which was articulated most generally in terms of the distinction between those who want to work and those who do not. The distinction was particularly striking in the late fourteenth century, having had new life breathed into it by the postplague labor shortage and the successive attempts by government to control wages, which took aim, in the language of the Statute of Laborers of 1351, "against the malice of servants who were idle and unwilling to serve after the pestilence without taking outrageous wages . . . [and who] completely disregard the said ordinance in the interests of their own ease and greed."[3] Together with the Revolt of 1381, these developments made it increasingly difficult to ignore that the third estate was a body of individuals whose work was motivated by subjective economic interests. Where the political organization of artisans and agriculturalists in 1381 gave witness to workers' ideological self-consciousness, the reorganization of the workforce with respect to its increased bargaining power gave witness to their economic self-consciousness. The unwillingness of laborers to work for pre-plague wages was particularly conspicuous in the context of traditional social theory, which highlighted society's functional interdependence and defined work objectively as service. John Gower, a vociferous spokesman for the principle that the business of the third estate was to "seek food for us by the sweat of their heavy toil" (*Vox clamantis*, 5.561),[4] was shocked that the peasantry should desire anything else. His description of the "common little people" in the *Mirour de l'omme* exemplifies how the new mobility and self-determination of laborers provoked their characterization as idle, greedy, arrogant, and inordinately consumptive:

> They perform little labor, but they expect to get high wages without deserving them—three time as much as their labor is worth. . . . But custom and old usages have now been turned upside down. This is well known to whoever has work to do, and it is the thing that hurts the most. For I find not one laborer in the market wherever I may go, for all are unwilling to work. . . . Vagabond laborers see the world in need of their services and labor, and they are arrogant because there are so few of them. They do not behave at all like their forefathers, for I myself have seen the day when many submitted to service who are now unwilling to do so. . . . For this the poor lesser folk (who should stick to their work) demand to be better fed than the one who has hired them. Moreover, they clothe themselves in fine colors and handsome attire, whereas they were formerly clothed (without pride and without conspiracy) in sackcloth. (lines 26425ff)[5]

In short, the traditional model of society as an organic functional hierarchy was running up against the fact that work is deeply motivated on the individual level by desires for wealth and status and that, however significant its objective values, work is above all the means of earning a living. This conflict, a conflict between the objective and subjective ends of work, made questions about why people work and why they should work all the more interesting and significant. The issue of what motivates work was an important subject of the "series of contrasting and often competing discourses" that emerged around the "'problem' of labor" in the fourteenth century.[6] More specifically, anxieties about the self-interest of workers provided a rich context for sophisticated representations of work's connection to the self, of its intrinsic subjective meaning.

Medieval ideas about work as a subjective value were anchored to the principle that work is necessary to avoid the perils of idleness, and it was in this context that late medieval authors began to address this issue. The increased significance of the work-idleness distinction in the literature of the period is evident first of all in a broadening of the concept of sloth to include specifically occupational laziness. This development is well documented in Siegfried Wenzel's study of the subject.[7] As the discussion of sloth moved from scholastic to pastoral and devotional contexts (manuals of confession, handbooks for preachers, works of religious instruction), the sin of sloth came to be thought of in increasingly practical terms: "The shift from a state of mind (taedium) to external behavior (ydelnesse in servitio Dei) pervades and informs the entire popular image of acedia, which emphasizes, not the emotional disorientation of disgust for the divine good, but rather the numerous observable faults which derive from such a state" (88). These faults continued to be understood as neglect of spiritual duties and good works, but "toward the end of the Middle Ages the sin of acedia came to include failure in the performance of worldly duties and activities" (91). Sloth, as a religious and moral concept, took on new economic meanings. More and more it was defined in opposition not only to good works but to work in general and was associated with "such faults as eating the fruit of other men's labor undeservedly, of wasting one's youth in idleness instead of learning a profitable trade, of failing to make the proper effort to earn one's bread, or of . . . neglect in the obligations of one's status or profession" (90–91). This deepening of sloth's material significance is encapsulated in the word wastour, which in the fourteenth century began to be used to mean specifically an idle, unproductive consumer (MED, s.v. "wastour n.," 2). And in John Bromyard's Summa praedicantium, the slothful are strikingly portrayed as outside both the divine and socioeconomic order: "God has ordained three classes of men. . . . And all the aforesaid who maintain their own status are of the family of God. The Devil, however, finds a certain class, namely, the slothful, who belong to no Order. They neither labour with the rustics, nor travel about with the merchants, nor fight with the knights, nor pray and chant with the clergy. Therefore they shall go with their own Abbot, of whose Order they are, namely, the Devil, where no order exists but horror eternal."[8]

But it is in the poetry of the late fourteenth century that the ethical and economic meanings of work and idleness were most interwoven. As we have already seen, Gower's treatment of sloth in the *Confessio amantis* produced a discourse on the value of work in which a non-class-specific definition of nobility, a belief in the superiority of intellectual over manual labor, and a concern with social advancement are combined in a characteristically bourgeois manner. In the *Mirour de l'omme,* Gower had emphasized the necessity of commerce and the moral legitimacy of profit seeking.[9] Similarly in the *Confessio,* the drift of his representation of *besinesse* as a moral necessity, befitting the specifically commercial meaning the word would later develop, is toward a merchant class work ethic in which the wealth- and status-producing value of work is both acknowledged and uneasily subsumed within its ethical meaning. Gower voices an occupational ethic whose ideal agent is busy, virtuous, and rich, and whose personal right to the wealth he gains through work is rationalized not in terms of the use value or objective nature of his work but in terms of the moral merit he accrues by working busily and avoiding idleness.

Langland's representation of the moral and material meanings of work and idleness is more consistent and developed than Gower's. First of all, Langland moves well beyond the principle that the moral value of work resides in its negation of idleness. The weakness of this principle is that it lends moral value to work only as activity and says nothing of the means and ends of work itself. Langland erects the moral meaning of work on a firmer foundation by identifying it with production and physical labor. Likewise, he solidifies the economic meaning of idleness by identifying it with consumption and an unwillingness to work. For Gower, the moral value of manual labor is largely extrinsic to it. It has little to do with the nature or purpose of production, which he views as merely the bodily means of serving bodily needs. It is only a subjective benefit that accompanies the act of production, primarily the benefit of avoiding idleness. Only with regard to intellectual pursuits, through which one earns "merita perpetuata" (*Confessio amantis* 4.vii), does Gower unite the moral value of work with the nature of work itself. Langland, on the other hand,

makes manual labor the norm of responsible action. Productive labor is itself a moral act, and the legitimacy of other forms of work are defined in
terms of their commensurable service of the common good.[10]

Langland's commitment to the intrinsic virtue and nobility of work
enables him to develop a rich account of work as a subjective necessity.
Work is more than a material, social, and moral *responsibility* of Langland's individual, it is also an *expression* of individual nature. One of the
clearer signs of this theme in the B-text occurs as part of Hunger's argument for labor as a universal obligation: "Kynde Wit wolde that ech
a wight wroghte, / Or in [te]chynge or in [telllynge or travaillynge in
preieres— / Contemplatif lif or Actif lif, Crist wolde men wroghte"
(B.6.247–49). Here Langland posits a kind of work instinct, a natural understanding of the material and spiritual necessity of work and a propor-
tionate inborn desire for work that parallels divine will. As Louise M.
Bishop explains, "The connection of subjectivity and labor, then, is created: the individual hears, through Kind Wit, the divine call to labor."[11] So
Piers the Plowman, as the ideal worker at the center of Langland's vision
of socioreligious reform, embodies not simply the acceptance of labor as a
responsibility but an active will to work. So "trewe tidy men," says Wit,
are those "that travaille *desiren*" (B.9.105).

Piers Plowman addresses the subjective necessity of work more directly in B.19.229–56, where the varieties of occupational skills are defined as forms of knowledge infused in individuals by grace. The passage
is concerned with the subjective dimension of work in several aspects.
First, it defines labor skills as essential, inborn attributes of individuals.
Like Plato's *Republic* (2.370b), it imagines the social division of labor as
founded upon a natural division of occupational talents and thus posits a
vital link between work and the person. Second, it emphasizes the subjective side of work by representing its varieties not only as tasks but as forms
of knowledge. The emphasis is particularly telling with regard to manual
labor—"And some he [Grace] taughte to tilie, to dyche and to thecche, / To
wynne with hir liflode bi loore of his techynge" (B.19.239–40)—so that
even menial tasks are regarded as operations of intelligence, as acts of
knowing subjects. Last, the passage gives occupational identity a salvific
function. As James Simpson explains, Langland "reimagines the 'craftes'
of labour as the product of an apostolic spirit, springing from the new
formed Church. Labour, or works, can now find a place in the scheme of

salvation, since Christ has instituted an order in which salvation does not depend wholly on grace."[12] By representing worldly work as an exercise of God-given talents that leads the individual back to God, Langland here anticipates Protestant conceptions of the calling, as well as the specifically secular, occupational meanings that *calling* and *vocation,* as new terms for work as an individual pursuit with subjective extra-economic significance, would attain in the sixteenth century. Likewise, in the portion of the C-text known as the *apologia,* Langland's citation of *"In eadem vocacione in qua vocasti estis* [1 Cor. 7.20]" (C.5.43a) attributes a more than clerical meaning to *vocatio,* being parallel to the general meaning *labour* carries in its preceding lines, in which Will defends his vocation as an exercise of natural talent: "And yf y be labour sholde lyuen and lyflode deseruen, / That laboure þat y lerned beste þerwith lyuen y sholde" (C.5.41–42).[13]

And it is in the *apologia* (C.5.1–104) that Langland's interest in the subjective dimension of work emerges most clearly. Being a conversation between the poet, Reason, and Conscience, the *apologia* dramatizes Langland's understanding of Kind Wit's call to labor. Most importantly, the *apologia* addresses the complex, historically contingent process whereby this call is heard and imperfectly lived out in the world. Not only does it synthesize the central themes of Langland's interest in work—the priority of manual labor, the relation of socioeconomic function to individual talent, and the salvific value of work—but, in the mode of occupational autobiography, it wrestles directly with their subjective experience. The *apologia*'s waking vision opens with the poet's perception of a fundamental conflict between the necessity of work and his idleness, a perception made acute by harvest season, a time of intense shared labor:

> For as y cam by Conscience with Resoun y mette
> In an hot heruest whenne y hade myn hele
> And lymes to labory with and louede wel fare
> And no dede to do but to drynke and slepe.
>   (lines 6–9)

It opens, in other words, with a powerful recognition of the priority of labor, of productive physical work as the norm against which Will must justify his own nonmanual work, both with respect to social justice, as a "craft þat to þe commune nedeth" (20), and with respect to spiritual justice, as a good work that merits heavenly reward: *"Reddet unicuique iuxta opera sua* [Matt. 16.27]" (32a). In attempting to make this justification, Will puts forth many arguments: that he is physically unfit for manual labor (22–25); that he is predisposed by education and talent to a clerical life (35–43a); that he earns his living legitimately through prayer (44–52), a practice that is ambiguously a form of both labor (45) and begging (51); that he is exempt from common labor on the basis of his clerical and social status (53–81); that he knows inwardly—"in my conscience" (83)—the work that Christ wants him to do; that prayers and penance are the "leuest labour þat oure lord pleseth" (85); and finally that man does not live by bread alone (86–88).[14] With regard to Langland's construction of himself as a subject of work, the most fascinating feature of these arguments of vocational self-justification is their simultaneous multiplicity and insufficiency. For by this feature Langland presents himself as both deeply committed to justifying his work and incapable of doing so. By the end of the *apologia,* in which Will folds before Conscience's objection that his way of life is "no sad parfitnesse" (90), his multistoried rebuttal of Reason appears less a construction of an unassailable vocational identity than an exhaustion of his resources of vocational self-construction. Yet despite this failure, Will does not make any concrete vow to change his way of life. Rather, he promises to "bigynne a tyme / That alle tymes of my tyme to profit shal turne" (100–101), a new beginning that will *capitalize* on his past waywardness and whose newness is undercut by Conscience's final injunction that he "contynue" (104) his way of life. The *apologia* is thus paradoxically constituted, as Donaldson says, by Langland's "inability to justify himself either for writing or for begging, and his perfectly obvious intention to go right on doing both so long as they are necessary to his search for Truth."[15] And as Langland's vocational meditation concludes with Conscience's justification of this intention, so does it validate Will's simplest and most impertinent defense of his work: "Forthy rebuke me ryhte nauhte, Resoun, y ȝow praye, / For in my conscience y knowe what Crist wolde y wrouhte" (82–83). In the end, the *apologia* thus proves to be a radical defense of the subjective significance of work. To generalize its claims, it insists that an individual's work may elude objective, rational justification and yet be known subjectively, through conscience, to be both licit and necessary. Correlatively, the *apologia* represents work as motivated by purposes that extend beyond both its exchange value and its use value. It allegorizes an introspection whereby its author, "Romynge in remembraunce" (11), discovers within himself an instinctive will for self-fulfillment through his work that is irreducible, even to his own rational-ization of that work. Beginning with the poet-cleric's alienation from the productive, purposeful world of material labor, the *apologia* ends with alienation's opposite, with his renewed and deepened identification with the labor he has chosen and been called to.

Piers Plowman is clearly the work of the period to which the issue of work is most thematically central, but the most developed literary investi-gation of the subjective dimension of work belongs to Chaucer's *Canter-bury Tales.* Of all medieval texts, the *Tales* are uniquely organized around occupations and ordered toward representing individuals within them. On the one hand, Chaucer's pilgrims, in keeping with the assumptions of estates satire, figure the inseparability of professional and personal iden-tity, of work and the individual. The portraits of the *General Prologue* are above all occupational portraits. They represent not so much people who happen to have occupations but people *as* occupations. The consistent em-phasis in the *Prologue* upon professional knowledge and skill, as Jill Mann says, "contributes relatively little to our sense of the individual psychology of the pilgrims, but it contributes a great deal to our sense of their working lives."[16] Similarly, Traugott Lawler has shown how Chaucer's depiction of "the generality of professions, and of professionalism itself, provides a constant limitation on individuality."[17] On the other hand, the *Tales* move beyond the estates conception of occupational identity and investigate the separability of persons from their work. Chaucer's pilgrims are not simply different sorts of workers but subjects of different sorts of work. As Lee Patterson, emphasizing the pilgrims' appropriation of the narratorial voice in the *Prologue,* explains, "To an extraordinary degree, Chaucer allows the members of the various estates to define themselves, a procedure that in effect undermines their definition as estates. Rather than being represen-tatives of social functions, . . . the pilgrims become individuals who have been assigned those functions, men and women enacting externally im-posed roles toward which each has his or her own kind of relationship."[18] The pilgrims *inhabit* their occupations, just as their bodies inhabit the clothes that display their professional identities. Indeed, the attention given to "array" (*GP* 41) in the *Prologue* not only signifies the importance of dress as a social marker but points more deeply to the distinction between persons and their work in that clothing is both worn and taken off—a separability of occupational identity from the self of which the sign of the Tabard Inn is a fitting emblem.

The *Tales* articulate, within this general emphasis on the junctions and disjunctions between persons and professions, a spectrum of relationships between individuals and their work. How does Chaucer represent work's significance to the individual above and beyond its material ends, its intrinsic significance? Earlier I summarized the predominant ways medieval culture articulated the subjective necessity of work, namely by representing work as a moral benefit, as a divinely instituted and specifically human act, as a participation in God's creativity, and as a remedy for man's fallen nature. The *Tales* do not address these issues comprehensively or systematically, but they come closest to doing so in Fragment VIII, comprising the Second Nun's and Canon's Yeoman's tales.

The thematic bond between the *Second Nun's Tale* and the *Canon's Yeoman's Tale* has been the subject of much criticism.[19] The importance of work to this bond has also been recognized. As Joseph Grennen has argued, the Canon's Yeoman's version of alchemy, in relation to the Second Nun's narrative, appears as "a perversion of religious ideals such as zeal and perseverance, and as a profane parody of the divine work of Creation," and at the lexical level the emphasis on the word *werk* in the two tales "is a way of keeping attention centered on the existence of an evil as well as a good Work, and evil as well as good works."[20] The contrasts between Cecilia's good works and the work of alchemy (whether the failing alchemy of the Canon or the alchemical illusions of the Yeoman's tale) may be multiplied indefinitely. Where Cecilia's "lastynge besinesse" (*SNT* 98) effects the permanent results of conversion, salvation, and the establishment of her church, the ceaseless work of alchemy is fruitless: "oure labour is in veyn" (*CYT* 777). Where Cecilia works to build a community around the sharing of faith, the Canon and his Yeoman sever their relationship over alchemy's secrecy, and the second Canon's trickery depends upon and causes division: "He wente his wey, and never the preest hym sy / After that day" (*CYT* 1381). Where the sweet odor of Cecilia and Valerian's supernatural crowns spreads spiritual transformation—"The sweete smel that in myn herte I fynde / Hath chaunged me al in another kynde" (*SNT* 251–52)—alchemy physically deforms its practitioner—"I am so used in the fyr to blowe / That it hath chaunged my colour" (*CYT* 666–67)—who in turn pollutes others: "His savour is so rammysh and so hoot / That though a man from hem a mile be, / The savour wole infecte hym" (*CYT* 887–89). And so on.

Such objective differences between Cecilia's good works and alchemy may work to the discredit of the latter, but they are only part of a more complex relationship between the meanings of work in the two tales, one that cannot be brought within the frame of moral approbation and proscription. The narratives of the Second Nun and the Canon's Yeoman present us not only with different types of work but with differently constructed subjects and subjective meanings of work. Indeed, the more or less self-motivated and marginally productive character of all the forms of work represented in Fragment VIII—the Second Nun's "feithful bisynesse" (*SNT* 24) of translation, Cecilia's "good werkynge" (*SNT* 116), the Canon's "craft" (*CYT* 619), the Yeoman's "labour" (*CYT* 713), and the second Canon's "sleightes" (*CYT* 976)—suggests that they were brought together by Chaucer precisely as a way of speaking about work's subjective dimension. All of the work in Fragment VIII is more inspired than constrained, answering less to material necessity and the responsibility for useful production than to individual desire. The Second Nun's translation of St. Cecilia's life may be useful, but it hardly fulfills her own criticism of idleness as devouring "al that othere swynke" (*SNT* 21). Instead of understanding her translation as useful production, she values it as a *re*production—"I do no diligence / This ilke storie subtilly to endite, / For bothe have I the wordes and sentence / Of hym that . . . The storie wroot" (79–83)—that fulfills wholly subjective ends, namely, avoiding idleness (22–25) and escaping damnation: "So for to werken yif me wit and space, / That I be quit fro thennes that most derk is!" (64–65). Correlatively, the second Canon's trickery may earn him a significant profit, but it is motivated above all by the joy he finds in his fraudulent and imaginative craft: "this chanoun, roote of al trecherie, / That everemoore delit hath and gladnesse— / . . . How Cristes peple he may to meschief brynge" (CYT 1069–72). In a proportional manner, the Yeoman's tale indulges in the processes of work and narration, though in a characteristically conflicted way: "It weerieth me to telle of his falsnesse, / And natheless yet wol I it expresse, / To th'entente that men may be war therby, / And for noon oother cause, trewely" (1304–7). By raising the possibility of an "oother cause" for his tale, these lines bring into question rather than fix both the Yeoman's and our own interest in his technical representations, especially as they replicate the recurring turns in his discourse whereby, having arrived at a condemnation of alchemy, he launches again into detailing its techniques (750, 784, 852, 862, 898). Moreover, they bring into view the both comforting and dangerous fact that there are pleasures in the processes of work, purely technical pleasures, that transcend its objective purpose, however moral or immoral it may be.

The central result of Chaucer's investigation of work's subjective dimension in Fragment VIII, I will argue, is a strong defense of work as a subjective necessity, as an intrinsic requirement of the human person. The Second Nun and the Canon's Yeoman provide very different perspectives on the nature of this necessity, and the relationship of the latter to the former is essentially corrective. In the *Second Nun's Tale*, Chaucer shows the limits of the conventional, especially monastic, valorization of work as the negation of idleness. By understanding the intrinsic value of work in wholly subjective and moral terms, the Second Nun paradoxically reifies work and denies it any substantive connection to the self. As she values work primarily as busyness, as a way to avoid oneself or escape what one would be while not working, so she seeks to erase her own agency from her work of translation, and so her tale's heroine is a self-effacing instrument of a higher power praised above all for the ceaselessness of her working, "lyk a bisy bee" (195). Where the *Second Nun's Tale* is thus burdened by the threat of a reduction of work to mere busyness and colored by the loss of subjectivity, the *Canon's Yeoman's Tale* investigates a form of work that is wholly motivated by its own nature and that seeks self-fulfillment instead of self-effacement. That the Yeoman shows alchemy to not only fail but achieve the opposite of its ends—poverty instead of wealth, foolishness instead of wisdom, multiplicity instead of unity, alienation instead of fulfillment—only deepens the significance of its quest. For as the departure of the Canon dramatizes, the promise of alchemy is stronger than its disappointments. And the Yeoman, by exhibiting the scars of alchemy's failure, above all his loss of subjectivity through fruitless toil—"I am nat wont in no mirour to prie, / But swynke sore and lerne multiplie" (668–69)—simultaneously gives witness to the essentially human longing for self-fulfilling and self-objectifying work.

The discourse on idleness with which the Second Nun begins her tale both reiterates the monastic theory of labor and suggests the limitations of that theory. "Idleness is the enemy of the soul. Therefore, the brothers should be occupied according to schedule in either manual labor or holy reading."[21] So says Benedict's *Rule,* and the argument was used to explain the work of monks and nuns alike throughout the Middle Ages. A passage in the *Ancrene Wisse,* closer in imagery to the Second Nun's discourse, highlights work's defensive power: "As St. Jerome teaches, do not ever be long or lightly altogether idle, not doing anything; for immediately the fiend offers his work to her who does not labour at God's work and whispers to her at once. For while he sees her busy, he thinks like this, 'I'd come near her now for nothing; she cannot pay attention to listen to my lore.'"[22] According to the wealth of the house to which she belonged, a nun's work might be more or less practical, but whatever its objective value its principal purpose was subjective: to protect the worker from temptation.[23] Yet work also entailed its own temptations. As a this-worldly and wealth-producing act, it threatened the spiritual focus of the convent. And as an exercise of personal talents, it courted individualism. The potential for the personal abuse of labor in nunneries is demonstrated, for example, by the flagrantly anti-Benedictine practice of allowing individual nuns to retain profits of their work.[24] Nuns' regulations sought to protect their labor from these threats by depersonalizing it, namely by not allowing nuns to choose their work or to work on anything of their own and by enjoining them to work in a spirit of religious devotion.[25]

The limitations of this theory of labor are twofold. First, it entails a paradoxical understanding of the subjective meaning of work. It defines the value of work subjectively by identifying it with the morally safe state of occupation it puts the worker in. At the same time, it constrains the subjective value of work by disallowing any specifically personal relation to one's work. Second, it introduces a significant degree of arbitrariness into the concept of work. By valuing work as not-idleness, it encourages a confusion of work with simple busyness. The cultural waning of English nunneries in the late medieval period, marked above all by the decline of learning and labor, most likely exacerbated these limitations. As nunneries grew in wealth they relied more and more on hired servants to perform the manual labor they required, with the result that nuns could combat idleness in increasingly less practical ways.[26] In turn, the more labor gave way to the broader category of not-idleness as the measure of legitimate occupation, the more arbitrary and open to personal preferences their work became.

The Second Nun's prologue exhibits the pressures of a consciousness that is both committed to the monastic work ethic and burdened by its limitations. The Second Nun celebrates the virtues of *bisynesse* but struggles to understand it as something of more lasting and more than personal value than mere occupation, as *werk*. She is personally committed to and interested in her *werk* of translation but can justify it only as *bisynesse*. These pressures are first of all evident in her discourse on idleness. Where monastic regulations defined *labor*—manual and intellectual—as the means of combating idleness, the Second Nun defines it as *bisynesse:*

> The ministre and the norice unto vices
> Which that men clepe in Englissh Ydelnesse,
> That porter of the gate is of delices,
> To eschue, and by hire contrarie hire oppresse—
> That is to seyn, by leveful bisynesse—
> We oghten we to doon al oure entente,
> Lest that the feend thurgh ydelnesse us hente.
>
> (1–7)

This syntactically tortured and almost scholastic stanza defines the proper method of negating idleness in the widest possible terms, as any lawful means of keeping busy. Basically, "leveful bisynesse" is a negative definition of this method, one that emphasizes not the positive, intrinsic value of idleness's opposite but simply its opposition to idleness and lack of interference with any other principles. The Second Nun thus begins by valuing work—though she has not yet called it that—in entirely subjective terms: more than doing something useful, what matters is keeping busy; and more than just keeping busy, what matters is keeping busy *ceaselessly*, with "al oure entente," because the Devil "*Continuelly* us waiteth to biclappe" (8–9). And this commitment to busyness is mirrored in the Second Nun's reverence for St. Cecilia, whose "lastynge bisynesse" (98) she ceaselessly praises (116, 124, 195, 342, 538). But as her discourse on idleness develops, it reaches out increasingly toward the objective nature of work. First, the polysemy of "Wel oghte us werche and ydelnesse withstonde" (14) brings up the concept of working well, of doing good work or working skillfully. The usefulness of work is then implied through the uselessness of idleness, "Of which ther nevere comth no good n'encrees" (18). Finally, the necessary and productive nature of work is explicitly valued in the closing description of sloth, which "holdeth [idleness] in a lees / Oonly to slepe, and for to ete and drynke, / And to devouren al that othere swynke" (19–21). Rhetorically, the sum effect of the Second Nun's exposition is to justify busyness as labor, as a means not only of avoiding idleness but of satisfying the common responsibility for useful and productive work. It appears as a statement caught between subjective and objective meanings of work, at once committed to work purely as a process of self-improvement and cognizant of, but incapable of commitment to, work as useful production.

The conflicted structure of the Second Nun's attitude toward the nature of her work appears more generally in the way she both displays and resigns her agency as a worker. On the one hand, the Second Nun's prologue, which is full of first-person pronouns, makes it very clear that her tale is *her* work—"my werk" (77, 84)—and that she has chosen it for specific and mostly personal reasons, above all to eschew idleness (22) and ensure her salvation (66). Likewise, she exhibits that she is translating. The references to "Englissh" within the etymologies of Cecilia's name (87, 106) may be more or less necessary, but the other reference—"Which that men clepe in Englissh Ydelnesse" (2)—is gratuitous and serves only to foreground the Second Nun's knowledge of Latin, a knowledge that she could rightfully be proud of given its rarity among nuns at the time.[27] On the other hand, the Second Nun denies the self-motivated and personal character of her work and presents herself, like the Lord's "owene thral Cecile" (196), as an unskilled servant. She prays to Mary for "wit and space" (65) and "help" (77) to complete her work. She apologizes for her lack of literary skill ("Foryeve me that I do no diligence / This ilke storie subtilly to endite," 79–80), renounces any claim to her tale as her product ("For bothe have I the wordes and sentence / Of hym that . . . The storie wroot," 81–83), and somewhat paradoxically asks the reader "that ye wole my werk amende" (84).

It is commonly assumed that the inappropriateness of the Second Nun's narrative to a pilgrim-narrator, above all its references to its ex-

plicitly textual form (25, 30, 32, 80–84, 94, 124), was not intended by
Chaucer but rather owes to its being an unrevised version of the "lyf . . . of
Seynt Cecile" mentioned in the *Legend of Good Women* as an independent composition (F 426, G 416), though there is no separate evidence that
the Second Nun's prologue belonged to this earlier work.[28] At the same
time, while the Second Nun's tale is attributed to her in all MSS of the
Tales only in the rubrics, the thematic appropriateness of her tale, as a hagiographical and devotional work, is both clear in itself and reinforced by
the verbal and thematic parallels between the prologues of the Second
Nun and the Prioress, whose "chapeleyne" (*GP* 164) she is. According to
the orthodox opinion of the day, especially Boniface VIII's decree *Periculoso,* which made unqualified enclosure of nuns universal church law
(grave illness excepted), neither the Prioress or her secretary should even
be on pilgrimage.[29] In compensation for this transgression, and more generally in keeping with their vocation, both the Prioress and the Second
Nun approach their tales with devotional solemnity. Like the Second Nun,
the Prioress prefaces her tale by praising the Virgin Mary and begging her
help (*PrT* 467–73), belittling her own skill (482–87), and defining her tale
as work: "To telle a storie I wol do my labour" (463). The last of these parallels is particularly important, as it reinforces Chaucer's interest in the attitudes of the monastic pilgrims (the Prioress, the Second Nun, and the
Monk) toward the labor ethic of their vocation and the playing out of
those attitudes on a pilgrimage that not only brings each of them "out of
his cloystre" (*GP* 181) but asks them "to talen and to pleye" (*GP* 772), activities under threat of censure by the principle "ydelnesse is the thurrok
of alle wikked and vileyns thoghtes, and of alle jangles, trufles, and of alle
ordure" (*ParsT* 714).

Immediately following the portraits of the Prioress and the Second
Nun in the *General Prologue,* the issue of monastic work is directly raised
in the portrait of the Monk:

> What sholde he studie and make hymselven wood,
> Upon a book in cloystre alwey to poure,
> Or swynken with his handes, and laboure,
> As Austyn bit? How shal the world be served?
>   (*GP* 184–87)

Borrowing the voice of the narrator, the Monk here both shows his familiarity with the authoritative argument for the manual labor of monks (Augustine's *De opere monachorum*) and points to its limitations. Unlike the
labor of lay persons, who, as Langland says, "werche and wynne and the
world sustene" (*PPl* B.9.109), a monk's labor was not to serve the world
but to sustain and perfect himself.[30] "The virtue of the monk." as Ovitt explains, "was restraint and self-effacement in spite of achievement . . . [and]
[m]onasticism . . . saw significance in the process of labor, not its products."[31] While the Monk's rejection of labor reveals his disillusionment
with the monastic life as spiritual service of the world, from a material
point of view his rhetorical question, which critiques the isolated and self-
serving character of monasticism, has real significance: monastic work is
not aimed at serving the world and constrains rather than encourages
commitment to work's objective usefulness. "Work was worship, but it
was also a material precondition to prayer and a distraction easily surren-
dered."[32] That the uncloistered Monk does not serve the world but rather
enjoys it in extravagant aristocratic fashion—"Of prikyng and of huntyng
for the hare / Was al his lust, for no cost wolde he spare" (*GP* 191–92)—
does not cancel the significance of his objection, which is underscored by
the poet-narrator's agreement, "I seyde his opinion was good" (*GP* 183).
Rather, the Monk's patent depression and disconsolate demeanor, which
bespeak an inability truly to enjoy the world, appear dialectically related
to his vocational unfulfillment. He has, as he says, "no lust to pleye" (*NPT*
2806) because he does not, and has no lust to, work. The Monk, refusing
the spiritual alienation from world and self that monastic labor is devised
to engender, and fulfilling no other useful function, has become more
tragically alienated from both. And he expresses as much by telling a series of futile tales about futility.

In contrast to the Monk, the Second Nun's workmanlike approach to
her tale reflects her commitment to the monastic ideal of self-effacing
labor, a commitment that is in keeping with her depersonalized portrait: "Another Nonne with hire hadde she, / That was hir chapeleyne"
(*GP* 163–64). Of all the pilgrims, the Second Nun is the most purely vocational being brought within the view of the narrator, who never allows us
to hear her name or see her appearance. To a superior degree the Second
Nun *is* her tale—a self-objectification that is mirrored in the conclusion of

her narrative when Cecilia becomes "the chirche of Seint Cecile" (550).
Even the explicitly textual form of the Second Nun's, I suggest, is part of
this pattern. As a text rather than a spoken tale the Second Nun's narrative
constitutes the most extravagant resistance to the Host's invitation "to
talen and to pleye" staged in the *Tales*, a resistance to the pleasurable and
self-expressive nature of the tale-telling game that derives from the Second Nun's ascetic love of work and that aims to convert its audience from
idleness—"the porter of the gate . . . of delices"—to "leveful bisynesse."
This resistance, mirrored in Cecilia's resistance to authority, is fictionally
allowed to usurp the poet-narrator's power over *his* work. The *Second
Nun's Tale* is in a sense busywork: a tale celebrating busyness, translated
as an act of busyness, for the purpose of engendering busyness: "for to put
us fro swich ydelnesse . . . I have heer doon my feithful bisynesse" (22–24).
Yet beneath this almost frenetic display is hidden a natural desire for self-
expressive, creative, and thus to some degree nonmonastic work, and
more specifically a self-assertive wish for an authorship conventionally
unavailable to women. Graciously, albeit fictionally, Chaucer fulfills this
wish. Aside from the general fact that dramatic verisimilitude is not a rule
firmly applied in the *Tales*, there is at least one piece of strong evidence
outside the *Second Nun's Tale* that supports this interpretation of its explicitly textual form. Of all the links in the *Tales*, the link between the
Second Nun's Tale and the *Canon Yeoman's Tale*, which is itself the only
explicit evidence on which the unity of Fragment VIII rests, is the only
link that does not register the *spoken* nature of the tale it follows: "Whan
ended was the lyf of Seinte Cecile" (*CYT* 554). Of the Second Nun's productive self-effacement there is no better emblem.

That the *Canon's Yeoman's Tale* is going to be a very different type of
performance than the Second Nun's and that it will be say something very
different about the nature of work are immediately made clear with the
urgent entrance of the Canon and his Yeoman among the pilgrims. In contrast to his sparse, faceless portrait of the Second Nun, the narrator's
description of the approaching Canon is reminiscent of the fuller, characterizing portraits of the *General Prologue*. In fact the lateness and indefi-
niteness of the narrator's recognition of the Canon as such—"I demed
hym som chanoun for to be" (573)—reverses the descriptive order employed in the *Prologue* (*degree* first, then *array*) and privileges personal

over professional identity more than any other portrait in the *Tales*. The Canon and his Yeoman make their appearance not as particular types of workers but as particular men who are, in fact, working, and working their poor horses, very hard:

> His hakeney, that was al pomely grys,
> So swatte that it wonder was to see;
> It semed as he had priked miles three.
> The hors eek that his yeman rood upon
> So swatte that unnethe myghte it gon.
> (559–63)

From an unknown origin the Canon and his Yeoman thus emerge as a spectacle of purposeful labor, a display of exhausting teleological activity that stands out against the Second Nun's sense of *bisynesse* as its own purpose. The narrator's reaction to this spectacle—"But it was joye for to seen hym swete!" (579)—is likewise opposed to the Second Nun's work ethic, which values work ascetically as the negation and avoidance of comprehensively proscribed "delices" (3)—an asceticism mirrored in Cecilia's hair shirt (133). But this happy observation, which is but the first of an array of intersections between pleasure and work represented in the *Canon's Yeoman's Tale*, points to the possibility of there being joy in labor over and above its stress.

As the possibility of joy and fulfillment in work is inalienable from the potential for the worker's disappointment and alienation, so the Canon and his Yeoman embody contrary but deeply related perspectives on the nature of their craft. The most singular feature of the Canon, before the immoderate speech of the Yeoman sends him off "for verray sorwe and shame" (702), is his mirth: he is eager to ride in the "joly" (584) and "myrie compaignye" (586) of the pilgrims "For his desport" (592); "he loveth daliaunce" (592); and the Host finds him "ful jocunde" (596). Most importantly, the Canon is represented as combining an inexhaustible love of play with a rare proficiency for work:

> He kan of murthe and eek of jolitee
> Nat but ynough; also, sire, trusteth me,
> And ye hym knewe as wel as do I,

Ye wolde wondre how wel and craftily
He wolde werke, and that in sondry wyse.
                                    (600–604)

That the Canon's mirth and playfulness run deeper than mere conviviality and the fraudulent purposes it may serve is confirmed in the Yeoman's report of the indefatigable optimism and good cheer with which he confronts and accepts the interminable failures of his self-destructing art: "Be as be may, be ye no thyng amased; / As usage is, lat swepe the floor as swithe, / Plukke up youre hertes and beeth glad and blithe" (935–37). Overall, the Canon is defined as wholly committed to a form of work that he enjoys. On the one hand, his happiness is a deferred and false happiness, a fool's paradise defined by the pursuit of the fata morgana of alchemical success that, seeming always near, stirs fresh hope (868–74). It is a happiness not in achieving goals but in the apparent proximity of a goal that promises, as the hyperbolically defined joy of the duped priest in the Yeoman's tale shows, consummate happiness:

This sotted preest, who was gladder than he?
Was nevere brid gladder agayn the day,
Ne nyghtyngale, in the sesoun of May,
Was nevere noon that luste bet to synge;
Ne lady lustier in carolynge,
Or for to speke of love and wommanhede,
Ne knyght in armes to doon an hardy dede,
To stonden in grace of his lady deere,
Than hadde this priest this soory craft to leere.
                                    (1341–49)

And as the joy of alchemical success is here portrayed as superior to specifically courtly pleasures, we may see in the Canon's relish of alchemical work a kind of revolutionary zeal, a desire for the fatal combination of learning and labor—a fusion of the powers of the first and third estates— that will outmode the present social order.[33]

On the other hand, it is precisely the ever-failing nature of the alchemical search that underwrites its pleasure as a pleasure of pure process, an open-ended exercise of individual genius. The Yeoman in fact *credits* the failure of the Canon's work to his excess of intelligence, as if he possessed a meddling genius ill suited to both conventional pursuits and practical results, a will to outdo marred by a propensity to overdo:

> He is to wys, in feith, as I bileeve,
> That that is overdoon, it wol nat preeve
> Aright, as clerkes seyn; it is a vice.
> Wherfore in that I holde hym lewed and nyce.
> For whan a man hath over-greet a wit,
> Ful oft hym happeth to mysusen it.
>
>   (644–49)[34]

These lines may point up the ultimate unintelligibility and practical impossibility of alchemy, but more directly they say something about the kind of personality alchemy attracted and hence the nature of its attraction. This attraction was inextricably bound to the *practice* of alchemy, a practice that held its own despite its failure. As Lee Patterson explains, "Although alchemical study was incapable of making gold, it could produce alchemists; and although it was unable to change the material world, mastering its elaborate theory could change the self-identity of the alchemist. What alchemy provided, in short, was a way to be intellectual."[35] Hence the Yeoman's emphasis upon the sense of privileged wisdom the alchemical workshop generates: "Whan we been there as we shul exercise / Oure elvysshe craft, we semen wonder wyse, / Oure termes been so clergial and so queynte" (750–52); "And whan we been togidres everichoon, / Every man semeth a Salomon" (960–61). Hence also the second Canon's seductive instructions to the priest: "Taak in thyn hand, and put thyself therinne / Of this quyksilver an ounce, and heer bigynne, / In name of Crist, to wexe a philosofre" (1120–22). Yet as these lines show, the attractions of alchemy are not only intellectual but technological. Moreover, they concern the most basic human impulses for creative manual work, impulses displayed most clearly in the Yeoman's compulsive fascination with the particulars of alchemical craft and in the second Canon's promise to the priest: "thyne owene handes two / Shul werche al thyng which that shal heer be do" (1154–55). The *Canon's Yeoman's Tale* thus represents alchemy as promising the very opposite of alienation and figures the fulfillment of this promise, however spurious, in the Canon. Likewise, the

Canon's simultaneous love of both work and play, and his pursuit of a craft that is also, as the Yeoman recognizes, a "game" (708, 1402), points to the human longing for a form of work that transcends this distinction. That the Canon is willing, by borrowing gold under the false pretense of alchemical illusions (673–77), in effect to prostitute his craft to fund it only underscores the depth of this longing.

Being a recovering alchemist, the Yeoman occupies the privileged position of being at once inside and outside the alchemical quest, a position that authorizes his double representation of its attractions and its failures. As Peggy A. Knapp has observed, "[T]he analysis of the conditions of the Yeoman's work shows it to be the alienated labor of modernity: partial, out of touch with the product, poorly remunerated, in competition with his fellows, and intellectually ungraspable."[36] But the Yeoman is not simply alienated, for he has suffered these dissatisfactions not only as conditions of labor but as the tragic outcomes of a labor that consciously sought their very opposites. He is acutely aware of alchemy's failure not as its victim but as its conscious and willing participant. Accordingly, a central feature of the Yeoman's tale is that while it discredits the practice of alchemy it does not discredit its intentions. Rather than attacking alchemy as intrinsically wrong, the Yeoman reveals it to be effectively, rather than in principle, impossible. The problem with alchemy, in other words, is not that it is an evil work but that it *does not* work and so results in the loss of health, wealth, and happiness that is the overt target of the Yeoman's complaint (720–45, 879–82, 1402–25). Likewise, the ultimate cause of alchemy's failure, according to the Yeoman, is not man but God himself, who "Ne wil nat that the philosophres nevene / How that a man shal come unto this stoon" (1473–74).

As the Yeoman's double perspective on alchemy testifies to the self-consciousness of his experience of it, so does it establish the ultimate subject of his narrative to be not alchemy per se but the subject of alchemy, the individual complex of needs and desires that alchemy promises to, but cannot, fulfill. From the moment the Yeoman, in response to the Host's probing questions, begins to act as something more than a yeoman, as something more than, as the narrator initially observes, "ful of curteisye" (587), he begins to appear as a person, as a subject with something of his own to say. And he begins to emerge as a subject in direct relation to his acknowledgment of the loss of subjectivity that his labor entails: "I am nat wont in no mirour to prie, / But swynke soore and lerne multiplie" (668–69). Just as this bodily alienation previews the several forms of alienation he subsequently shows alchemy to cause, so his tale becomes the "mirror" through which he discovers, articulates, and struggles to overcome his divided state.[37] Or, to use a more appropriate metaphor, his tale becomes the vessel into which he pours himself and so effects his own transmutation, however incomplete, from vain toiler to creative human being. Accordingly, the Yeoman approaches this work of self-transformation with a playful delight in self-expression that usurps his master's intention to play and that is inversely proportional to his self-effacing and self-defeating labor: "'A!' quod the Yeman, 'heere shal arise game; / Al that I kan anon now wol I telle'" (703–4).

That the topic of alchemy would attract Chaucer as a means of investigating the subjective necessity of work is evident from the nature of alchemy itself. First, alchemy promised not only the transmutation of base metal into gold but various forms of self-transformation, both as means and as end. Alchemical writings often emphasized the alchemist's bodily, intellectual, and spiritual integrity as necessary preconditions for his successful work, preconditions that were significant personal achievements in themselves. The *Summa perfectionis* of Pseudo-Geber, a text that Chaucer most likely read, is particularly clear on this point.[38] To have any hope of success, the alchemist must, among other things, "have his organs in an integral condition" and "have natural ingenuity and a soul subtly searching the natural principles and foundations of nature"; he must possess "the highest scrutiny" and a "constant will to work"; he must "have a good temper and be little given to anger"; and finally, he must be "intent upon the end alone, since our art is reserved by the divine power, and He . . . extends it to and withdraws it from whomever He wills."[39] In these terms, the alchemical project sought to foster not only profound knowledge of its subject but self-conscious virtue and a critical knowledge of oneself. At the same time, this emphasis provided a ready-made set of ways to locate the blame for failure not only in technical error but in oneself. In the *Canon's Yeoman's Tale*, this dimension of the alchemical quest is reflected in the way the Canon, after his work explodes, quells the ensuing "greet strif" (931) of his workshop by both placing the blame on himself and assuming the responsibility for future success: "'Pees!' quod my lord, 'the nexte tyme I wol fynde / To brynge oure craft al in another plite, / And but I do, sires, lat me han the wite'" (951–53).

Alchemical writings also emphasized the self-transforming powers of both the elixir or philosopher's stone and alchemical gold itself. "With curious frequency, medieval sources speak of alchemy as useful for health as well as wealth. The elixir has medicinal properties ascribed to it, as do other alchemical concoctions."[40] Roger Bacon, outdoing Hugh of St. Victor's concept of the arts as the remedy for man's fallen condition, "goes so far as to say that alchemical gold, because it contains the four elements in an even better proportion than natural gold, can restore the human body to a condition of elemental quality like that of Adam and Eve and the resurrected at the end of time."[41] And in Morienus's *Testament of Alchemy*, similar notions of the preparatory and consequent self-transformations of the Great Work are combined in a way that raises its agents to the level of a spiritual elite: "No one will be able to perform or accomplish this thing . . . by means of any knowledge unless it be through affection and gentle humility, a perfect and true love. . . . And from among his servants, he [God] chose to select certain ones to seek after the knowledge he had established that rescues him who masters it from the wretchedness of this world and assures him riches to come."[42]

By stressing the superior sort of person an alchemist had to be and could become, alchemical texts also offered the prospect of a complete and consummate exercise of human powers. Alchemy, as Thomas Norton wrote, is "thende of worldly connynge."[43] It joined into one discipline the several hierarchically valued categories of medieval culture—theoretical and practical, contemplative and active, liberal and mechanical, sacred and secular—and so promised a kind of reintegration of the division of labor. Marx would dream of authentic labor as the pursuit of a society "where nobody has one exclusive sphere of activity but each can become accomplished in any branch he wishes" and where it is possible "to do one thing today and another tomorrow" according to preference.[44] So alchemy had long proposed a work that was formally comprehensive, interdisciplinary, and thus wholly gratifying. It said, in effect, that philosophy could be productive and that labor could be philosophical. Geber thus names the alchemist a "bone mentis artifex," a craftsman of good intellect, and exhorts him to "strive . . . with the greatest application of labor and with a lengthy spell of intense meditation."[45] Alchemy promised that wisdom could be materialized and that material acts could engender wisdom. So Geber thanks God that "[w]e have seen with our eye and touched with our hand the sought-for goal of this, with our magistery."[46] In sum, alchemy sought the realization of the positive principles on which Marx's analysis of alienated labor is predicated, namely that "free, conscious activity is man's species character"—freedom from material needs and responsibilities is itself a commonly cited requirement of alchemical work—and that through work man "duplicates himself not only, as in consciousness, intellectually, but also actively, in reality, and therefore he contemplates himself in a world that he has created."[47] In the Yeoman's tale, alchemy's hybrid and comprehensive character is most clearly expressed by the full range of words the he uses in speaking about it—*science, swynk, werk, art, labour, travaille, craft*—and by his description of his work as both physical and intellectual, to "swynke sore *and* lerne multiplie."

These fundamental characteristics of alchemy help to explain Chaucer's interest in alchemy as a site of alienation. Moreover, they illuminate his representation of alienation as a rupture between the theoretical and the practical, learning and labor, a rupture that is dramatized in the Yeoman's bitter divorce from the Canon: "For nevere heerafter wol I with hym meete / For peny ne for pound, I yow biheete" (706–7). Alchemical work has estranged the Yeoman not only from his health and wealth but, more significantly, from his own intelligence and understanding: "of my swynk yet blered is myn ye" (730). Just as alchemy has caused the Yeoman to experience a reduction of work to mere, fruitless labor, so has it engendered, through its intrinsic unintelligibility, his perception of himself as "a lewed man" (787). Accordingly, one of the greatest charms of the Yeoman's tale is the way it enacts his realization that his own supposed *lewednesse* is really the *lewednesse* of alchemy itself (838–51, 967–69, 1394–99, 1442–47) and thus his growing confidence in, and reclamation of, his own intelligence. The progress of this realization is demonstrated most clearly in the tremendous difference between the Yeoman's sense of his intellectual authority at the beginning and at the end of his tale. He starts by admitting that, despite his seven-year apprenticeship, he is "never the neer" (721) his former master's science. And he apologizes thereafter that his ignorance does not permit him to present the details of his craft in their proper order but only "as they come to mynde" (787); he presents his own alchemical knowledge as simply what his master taught him (819) and what he overheard (821). But by the end of his tale, it is very clear that the Yeoman's knowledge of alchemy extends well beyond the workshop, as he demonstrates, in an extravagant display of intertextual criticism that shows his familiarity with "What philosophres seyn in this mateere" (1427), that alchemy is untenable from alchemical sources themselves. Turning alchemy's secrecy on its head to prove its futility, the Yeoman thus manages to bring to conclusion—"Thanne conclude I thus" (1472)—his pursuit of an art that "kan nat conclude"(773).[48]

What most enables the Yeoman's recovery of himself, of course, is his tale proper, a tale that suggestively functions both as a conjuring and an exorcism of the falseness of alchemy and as a work of alchemical self-transformation. In his prologue, the Yeoman had introduced the possibility that his rehearsal of alchemical lore was sufficient "To reyse a feend" (861). Fictionally fulfilling this possibility, the Yeoman's tale both creates and takes revenge on—"On his falshede fayn wolde I me wreke" (1173)—"a feend" (984) who is a personification of alchemical lore. This is true in the obvious sense that the Canon-fiend poses as an alchemist and thus promises his dupe all the major promises of alchemy: secret knowledge (1051, 1139, 1370), philosophical status (1122), creative and profitable work (1154–55, 1212), consummate happiness (1286–87, 1341). But to understand the second Canon as a personification of alchemical lore also clarifies the more cryptic and hyperbolic statements the Yeoman makes of him, above all, that his falseness is infinite and beyond description and that "he abit nowhere" (1175). In his prologue, the Yeoman had portrayed the unending character of alchemical terminology in terms of writing: "To tellen al wolde passen any bible / That owher is" (856–57), where *bible* is used to mean "large book." And in his opening description of the false Canon the Yeoman uses a similar figure: "His sleightes and his infinite falsnesse / Ther koude no man writen, as I gesse, / Though that he myghte lyve a thousand yeer" (976–78). Whether or not Chaucer had in mind the possible pun on "chanoun" (972) and *canoun* (scripture, authoritative text), as in "Avycen / Wroot nevere in no canon" (*PardT* 889–90), these lines, by figuring the Canon's falseness as more than a thousand years of writing, wryly point to both the antiquity and the confused proliferation of alchemical texts. Likewise, the false Canon's sly, confusion-producing speech—"For in his termes he wol hym so wynde, / And speke his wordes in so sly a kynde, / Whanne he commune shal with any wight, / That he wol make hym doten anonright" (980–83)—clearly figures the fact that "Philosophres speken so mystily / In this craft than men kan nat come therby, / For any wit that men han now-a-dayes" (1394–96). In turn, when the Yeoman says that the fiendish Canon "is heere and there; / He is so variaunt, he abit nowhere" (1174), he portrays him as the elusiveness of alchemical understanding, an elusiveness that alchemical texts themselves frequently acknowledged, either as the elusiveness of their language—"O doubtful names which are like the true names, what errors and anguish you have provoked among men"—or as the mystical ubiquity of the philosopher's stone itself: "[O]ur Stone is cast out into the streets, raised aloft to the clouds, dwells in the air, is nourished in the river, sleeps upon the summit of mountains."[49] Last, the Yeoman's oath to the Host that his tale's Canon "kan an hundred foold moore subtiltee" (1091) than his former master neatly figures alchemy's endless outmatching of its students.

By personifying alchemical teaching as a fiend—an obfuscation that enacts alchemy's habit of personifying its substances—the Yeoman gives literary form to his enchantment by it and, more specifically, to his experience of alchemy's failure as the malevolent effect of a supernatural and undiscernable being: "Though that the feend noght in oure sighte hym shewe / I trowe he with us be, that ilke shrewe!" (916–17). Indeed, his representation of the Canon-fiend as a real being—"Ther is a chanoun of religioun / Among us" (972–73)—shows that he is still under alchemy's spell. But this procedure of personification, through which alchemical tradition is itself fictionalized, in turn becomes the means whereby the Yeoman recognizes the fictive character of the fiend that he believed to sabotage his work. In other words, the Yeoman's tale is a therapeutic work of self-disenchantment *only after which* he is capable of dealing with alchemy as texts (1428–80) and thus also capable of letting it go. And this process of disenchantment is clearly mirrored in his tale, in that the representation of the Canon's illusions affords the Yeoman an opportunity to demonstrate his craft knowledge as nonalchemical and thus as his own real knowledge, as well as to delight in its reality: "What, devel of helle, sholde it elles be! / Shaving of silver silver is, pardee!" (1238–39).

Where the Yeoman's tale thus appears as a conjuration and exorcism of the fiend of alchemical falsity, the Yeoman presents it as an alchemical work of self-transformation. He may have started his performance with a relish for play, but the deeper he gets into his confessional tale the more he finds it to be real work: "Of his falsnesse it dulleth me to ryme" (1092)—a dull and dulling work that recapitulates perfectly his experience of alchemical labor as simultaneously dazing, tiring, and discoloring. But the Yeoman also represents this work as retransmuting his "leden hewe" (728) to the color of gold:

Evere whan that I speke of his falshede,
For shame of hym my chekes wexen rede.
Algates they bigynnen for to glowe,
For reednesse have I noon, right wel I knowe,
In my visage; for fumes diverse
Of metals, whiche ye han herd me reherce,
Consumed and wasted han my reednesse.
                                (1094–1100)

And as the Yeoman hereafter does not let us forget the pain of his tale's labor—"It dulleth me whan that I of hym speke" (1172); "It weerieth me to telle of his falsnesse" (1304)—so are we to imagine this transformation as continuing throughout his tale. Nevertheless, the Yeoman here strikingly disclaims any lasting transformation, with all of its attractive implications, and by this is expressed his return to a deeper kind of health. For by disowning the self-transforming effect of his labor, the Yeoman renounces the solipsism of alchemy's promise of self-fulfilling and self-gratifying work. Work can and should be these things, but work can never be them when they are reduced, as alchemy effectively reduces them, to the aim of work itself. In these terms, Chaucer's Yeoman is anything but a sentimental spokesman for work's subjective necessity. Rather, he both reclaims the inherent suffering of work and claims its reward: "God sende every trewe man boote of his bale!" (1481).

Fragment VIII of the *Tales* stands out as Chaucer's most sustained representation of the human longing for meaningful work, for forms of creative and productive activity that are inherently fulfilling, both in terms of their process and in terms of what they achieve. Yet the power of this representation lies in the tensional space of failure, the gap between work and worker, that each tale opens up. In the *Second Nun's Tale*, it is the unresolved tension between the material and monastic meanings of work, between production and busyness, that gives witness to the Second Nun's desire for more than the latter, for authorship and a work of her own. That she writes within rather than against the ethic of her vocation only underscores and authenticates her desire for true, meaningful work. In the *Canon's Yeoman's Tale,* it is the failure of work, and the Yeoman's victory over it, that reveals the more stable, authentic motives that underwrite "that slidynge science" (732). Moreover, by finally relinquishing the fantasies of alchemy, though not their truth, the Yeoman elegantly emphasizes both the need for and the elusiveness of work's meaning. The richness of work's significance to the individual comes into focus through work's potentiality, through its ongoing, imperfect, and unfinished nature. Work is always work in progress and its meaning bound to work yet to be done, as figured by the last three work-filled days of Cecilia's life, the Yeoman's need for more productive and profitable employment, and the way the dramatic entrance of the Canon and Yeoman into the pilgrimage "revises" the project of the *Tales.* In Fragment VIII Chaucer thus explores versions of a tension in the nature of work introduced in the portrait of the Plowman, the pilgrim most defined in terms of work's intrinsic subjective value: "A trewe swynkere and a good was he, . . . / He wolde thresshe, and therto dyke and delve, / For Christes sake, for every povre wight, / Withouten hire, if it lay in his myght" (*GP* 531–38). Here also true work is an imperfectly realized ideal, a significance, that subsists in the human longing for it.

Notes

Introduction

1. Lines 1–4, in *Secular Lyrics of the XIVth and XVth Centuries,* ed. Rossel Hope Robbins (Oxford: Clarendon Press, 1956), 106–7. For an overview of the poem and its contexts, see Elizabeth Salter, "A Complaint against Blacksmiths," *Literature and History* 5 (1979): 194–215.

2. Lines 10–12, in "The Debate of the Carpenter's Tools," ed. Edward Wilson, *Review of English Studies* 38 (1987): 445–70. See also John W. Conlee, ed., *Middle English Debate Poetry: A Critical Anthology* (East Lansing, MI: Colleagues Press, 1991), 222–35.

3. Recent studies that address this problem include Steven Justice, *Writing and Rebellion: England in 1381* (Berkeley: University of California Press, 1994), and Stephen Knight, "The Voice of Labour in Fourteenth-Century English Literature," in *The Problem of Labour in Fourteenth-Century England,* ed. James Bothwell, P. J. P. Goldberg, and W. M. Ormrod (York: University of York, 2000), 101–22.

4. As Lisa H. Cooper observes, "[P]erhaps the most telling aspect of the poem is that the carpenter is the *Debate*'s subject, but not its protagonist. . . . [T]he curiously absent wright never appears to speak on his own behalf: the topic of his tools' and spouse's conversation, he is constituted only by what they have to say about him" ("'These Crafty Men': Figuring the Artisan in Late Medieval England" [PhD diss., Columbia University, 2003], 140).

5. For example: "Tubal cain fonde first smythes craft and grauynge, and whan Tubal cain wrouȝte in his smeþes craft, Tubal [Jubal] hadde grete likynge to hire þe hameres sowne, and he fonde proporciouns and acorde of melodye" (Ranulf

Higden, *Polychronicon*, ed. C. Babington and J. R. Lumby, 8 vols. [London: Long-man, 1865–86], 2.5, quoting Trevisa's translation). On the history of the legend, see James McKinnon, "Jubal vel Pythagoras, Quis Sit Inventor Musicae?" *Musical Quarterly* 64 (1978): 1–28, and Paul E. Beichner, *The Medieval Representative of Music: Jubal or Tubalcain?* (Notre Dame: University of Notre Dame, 1954).

6. For example, the gimlet promises, "I schall crepe fast into þe tymbyr, / And help my mayster within a stounde / To store his cofer with xx pounde" (20–2), whereas the grooping-iron worries, "Late vs not wy[r]ke to we suete / For cachyng of ouer gret hete. / For we may after cold to take; / Than on stroke may we no hake" (247–50).

7. Notably, Cooper, "'These Crafty Men,'" and Gregory M. Sadlek, *Idleness Working: The Discourse of Love's Labor from Ovid through Chaucer and Gower* (Washington, DC: Catholic University of America Press, 2004).

CHAPTER 1.   "Labour of Tonge"

1. Examples from late-twentieth-century histories of work are easy to find: "Work and life were of one piece, and, when there were no raids and wars, life was peaceful and cyclical, based on yearly rhythms of work in tune with the seasons" (Herbert Applebaum, *The Concept of Work: Ancient, Medieval, Modern* [Albany: State University of New York Press, 1992], 310); "Traditional craftsmen were per-suaded that work was good not necessarily because of the rewards it brought, but because the act of work itself permitted them to fulfill the principal social role the surrounding community had assigned to them" (Edward Shorter, "The History of Work in the West: An Overview," in *Work and Community in the West,* ed. Edward Shorter [New York: Harper and Row, 1973], 10); "[I]n the late Middle Ages labor, which was once a tool for cultivating individual and moral values and for sustain-ing a community's collective life, began to be controlled by the purveyors of 'mega-technics,' by managers and middlemen" (George Ovitt Jr., *The Restoration of Perfection: Labor and Technology in Medieval Culture* [New Brunswick: Rutgers University Press, 1987], 201–2); "Economic life and social life were one and the same thing. Work was not yet a means to an end—the end being money and the things it buys. Work was an end in itself, encompassing, of course, money and commodities, but engaged in as a part of a tradition, as a natural way of life" (Rob-ert L. Heilbroner, *The Worldly Philosophers,* 4th ed. [New York: Simon and Schus-ter, 1972], 14).

2. Witness, for example, André Gorz's description of economic rationaliza-tion: "[L]a rationalisation économique du travail n'a pas consisté simplement à ren-dre plus méthodiques et mieux adaptées à leur but des activités productives préexistantes. Ce fut une révolution, une subversion du mode de vie, des valeurs,

des rapports sociaux et à la nature, *l'invention* au plein sens du terme de quelque chose qui n'avait encore jamais existé. L'activité productive était coupée de son sens, des ses motivations et de son objet pour devenir le simple *moyen* de gagner un salaire. Elle cessait de faire partie de la vie pour devenir le *moyen* de 'gagner sa vie.' Le temps de travail et le temps de vivre étaient disjoints; le travail, ses outils, ses produits acquéraient une réalité séparée de celle du travailleur et relevaient de décisions étrangères. La satisfaction 'd'œuvrer' en commun et le plaisir de 'faire' étaient supprimés au profit des seules satisfactions que peut acheter l'argent" (*Métamorphoses du travail* [Paris: Galilée, 1991], 36).

3. See Karl Polanyi, *The Great Transformation* (Boston: Beacon Press, 1957); Ferdinand Tönnies, *Community and Society,* trans. Charles P. Loomis (New York: Harper and Row, 1963); Emile Durkheim, *The Division of Labour in Society* (Chicago: Free Press, 1933); Max Weber, *The Protestant Ethic and the Spirit of Capitalism,* trans. Talcott Parsons (New York: Charles Scribner's Sons, 1958), and *Economy and Society,* ed. Guenther Roth and Claus Wittich (Berkeley: University of California Press, 1968), 375–80; Karl Marx, *Economic and Philosophical Manuscripts of 1844,* trans. M. Milligan (New York: International Publishing, 1971). On Romanticism and the idealization of medieval life, see Alice Chandler, *A Dream of Order: The Medieval Ideal in Nineteenth-Century English Literature* (Lincoln: University of Nebraska Press, 1970).

4. Ruzena Ostrá, "Le champ conceptuel du travail en ancien français," *Etudes Romanes de Brno* 5 (1971): 43–44. Cf. "L'idée contemporaine du travail n'apparaît en fait qu'avec le capitalisme manufacturier. Jusque-lá, c'est-á-dire jusqu'au XVIIIe siécle, le terme de 'travail' (labor, Arbeit, lavoro) désignat la peine des serfs et des journaliers qui produisaient soit des biens de consommation, soit des services nécessaires à la vie et exigeant d'être renouvelés, jour après jour, sans jamais laisser d'acquis. Les artisans, en revanche . . . ne 'travaillaient' pas, ils 'œuvraient' et dans leur 'œuvre' ils pouvaient utiliser le 'travail' d'hommes de peine appelés à accomplir les tâches grossiéres, peu qualifiées" (Gorz, *Métamorphoses,* 28–29).

5. "Il n'y a pas de mot au Moyen Age pour désigner *le* travail (pas plus que dans l'Antiquité). Les hommes du Moyen Age n'avaient-ils donc pas une conception d'une unité des activités que nous appelons le travail?" (Jacques Le Goff, "Travail, techniques et artisans dans les systèmes de valeur du haut Moyen Age (Ve–Xe siècles)," in *Artigianato e tecnica nella società dell'alto medioevo occidentale,* Settimane di studio del Centro Italiano di Studi sull'Alto Medioevo 18 [Spoleto: Presso la sede del Centro, 1971], 240). The quotation in the text is from Jacques Le Goff, "Pour une etude du travail dans les ideologies et les mentalites du Moyen Age," in *Lavorare nel medio evo: rappresentazioni ed esempi dall'Italia dei secc. X–XVI* (Todi: Presso L'Academia Tudertina, 1983), 14. See also Le Goff, "Le travail dans les systèmes de valeur de l'occident médiéval," in Hamesse and Muraille-Samaran, *Le travail au Moyen Âge,* 9.

6. As recorded in the *OED*, the first use of *labour* to signify "physical exertion directed to the supply of the material wants of the community" or "the specific service rendered to production by the labourer and artisan" is Adam Smith's (*OED*, s.v. "labour n.," 2ab). About this new meaning Raymond Williams writes: "Where labour in its most general sense had meant all productive work, it now came to mean that element of production which in combination with capital and materials produced commodities. This new specialized use belongs directly to the systematized understanding of capitalist productive relations" (*Keywords: A Vocabulary of Culture and Society* [London: Croom Helm, 1976], 146).

7. Karl Marx, *Grundrisse*, trans. Martin Nicolaus (New York: Penguin, 1973), 105.

8. Ibid., 104.

9. R. Williams, *Keywords*, 178.

10. Marx, *Grundrisse*, 84.

11. For Max Weber also, indifference toward the content of work is a defining feature of capitalism: "It [one's duty in a calling] is an obligation which the individual is supposed to feel and does feel towards the content of his professional activity, *no matter in what it consists,* in particular no matter whether it appears on the surface as a utilization of his personal powers, or only of his material possessions (as capital)" (*Protestant Ethic*, 54, my italics).

12. S. Todd Lowry, *Ancient and Medieval Economic Ideas and Concepts of Social Justice*, ed. S. Todd Lowry and Barry Gordon (Leiden: Brill, 1998), 1.

13. In his proposal for future study of the work vocabularies of all periods and cultures, the anthropologist Maurice Godelier interprets Marx's comments on the general concept of labor to mean that it is "absurd to go looking for the idea of work in general in precapitalist societies" ("Work and Its Representations: A Research Proposal," *History Workshop* 10 [1982]: 166–67). This is misleading insofar as Marx distinguishes between two types of general conceptions of labor, one old and one new: "Labour seems a quite simple category. The conception of labour in this general form—as labour as such—is also immeasurably old. Nevertheless, when it is economically conceived in this simplicity, 'labour' is as modern a category as are the relations which create this simple abstraction" (*Grundrisse*, 103). But in correlating the economic abstraction *labor* with "indifference towards specific labours," the term of political economy with mentality, Marx, in describing work as previously "thinkable in particular form alone," appears to lose sight of the "immeasurably old" noneconomic conception of labor per se. In fact, Marx is dealing with three distinguishable general conceptions of work: the "immeasurably old" conception of work as a general category of productive activity (i.e., work as a type of activity), the purely economic abstraction first used by Adam Smith, and the individual version of that abstraction characterized by "indifference towards specific labours." The last, as a feature of mentality, links the previous two and constitutes

the basic, popular, modern conception of work—that which defines work as essentially employment, as the general category of remunerated activity.

14. Christopher Dyer similarly cautions against making "a strict separation between 'medieval and 'modern' attitudes towards work" ("Work Ethics in the Fourteenth Century," in *The Problem of Labour in Fourteenth Century England*, ed. James Bothwell, P. J. P. Goldberg, and W. M. Ormrod [York: York Medieval Press, 2000], 24).

15. The vocabulary of work has drawn significant attention, but little concerned with the late Middle Ages. Studies of antique terminology include Guido Keel, *Laborare und operari: Verwendungs- und Bedeutungsgeschichte zweier Verben für "arbeiten" im Lateinischen und Galloromanischen* (St. Gall: Schwald, 1942); Dieter Lau, *Der lateinische Begriff "Labor"* (Munich: Fink, 1975); and F. Gryglewicz, "La valeur morale du travail manuel dans la terminologie grecque de la Bible," *Biblica* 37 (1956): 314–37. Studies that give attention to medieval Latin terminology include Birgit van den Hoven, *Work in Ancient and Medieval Thought* (Amsterdam: J. C. Gieben, 1996); Peter Sternagel, *Die Artes mechanicae im Mittelalter* (Kallmung über Regensburg: Lassleben, 1966); Elspeth Whitney, *Paradise Restored: The Mechanical Arts from Antiquity through the Thirteenth Century* (Philadelphia: American Philosophical Society, 1990); Jacqueline Hamesse, "Le travail chez les auteurs philosophiques du 12e et du 13e siècle: Approche lexicographique," in *Le travail au Moyen Âge: Une approche interdisciplinaire*, ed. Jacqueline Hamesse and Colette Muraille-Samaran (Louvain-la-Neuve: Institut d'Études Médiévales de l'Université Catholique de Louvain, 1990): 115–27; Jacques Le Goff, "Le travail," 7–21, "Pour une etude du travail dans les ideologies et les mentalites du Moyen Age," in *Lavorare nel medio evo: rappresentazioni ed esempi dall'Italia dei secc. X–XVI* (Todi: Presso L'Academia Tudertina, 1983), 11–33, and "Travail, techniques et artisans," 239–66; P. Bonnerue, "*Opus* et *labor* dans les règles monastiques anciennes," *Studia Monastica* 35 (1993): 265–91. Studies of vernacular terminology include Elizabeth Baldwin Stevens Girsch, "A Semantic Analysis of Old English 'Craeft' and Related Words" (PhD diss., University of Toronto, 1989); Ruzena Ostrá, "Le champ conceptuel du travail dans les langues romanes," *Etudes Romanes de Brno* 3 (1967): 7–84, and "Le champ . . . en ancien français"; G. B. Pellegrini, "Terminologia agraria medievale in Italia," in *Agricoltura e mondo rurale in Occidente nell'alto Medioevo*, Settimane di studio del Centro Italiano di Studi sull'Alto Medioevo 13 (Spoleto: Presso la sede del Centro, 1966), 605–61, and "Tradizione e innovazione nella terminologia degli strumenti di lavoro," in *Artigianato e tecnica*, 329–408.

16. William of Nassyngton, "*Speculum vitae*," 5.77–78, *Englische Studien* 7 (1884): 469.

17. Throughout this chapter I use the substantive to refer generally to all forms of the word, unless context dictates otherwise.

18. *OED*, s.v. "work n.," 4. This, together with the definition of work as the product of such activity (definitions II.9, 10), is both the oldest and most current meaning of *work* offered by the *OED*. Ostrá relies on the definition of *travail* as "effort ordonné à la production d'une chose (oeuvre) utile" ("Le champ . . . en ancien français," 21, quoting P. Foulquié and R. Saint-Jean, *Dictionnaire de la langue philosophique* [Paris: Presses universitaires de France,1962]). This definition is superior insofar as it makes clear that our concept of work is inseparable from the idea of useful production, specifically the material production necessary to individual and society. But it is inferior in that it names useful production as the end of work as if it were the worker's prime motive, the subjective reason for effort and not simply the goal of effort as an objective process. The first end of work, rather, that which must be achieved even if useful production is not, is the satisfaction of the worker's basic needs, the gaining of his livelihood. With the understanding that the most necessary "means of gaining one's livelihood" are through useful production, the *OED*'s definition is here preferable.

19. "In the labour process . . . man's activity, with the help of the instruments of labour, effects an alteration, designed from the commencement, in the material worked upon. The process disappears in the product; the latter is a use value, Nature's material adapted by a change of form to the wants of man. Labour has incorporated itself with its subject: the former is materialized, the latter transformed" (Karl Marx, *Capital,* vol. 35 of *Collected Works* [New York: International Publishers, 1996], 190–91).

20. Hannah Arendt, *The Human Condition* (Chicago: University of Chicago Press, 1958), 8.

21. Marx, *Capital,* 1.3.7, p. 188.

22. Unless otherwise noted, I am relying on the *MED* for such information.

23. See Ernest Klein, *A Comprehensive Etymological Dictionary of the English Language,* 2 vols. (New York: Elsevier, 1966), s.v. "travail n."; P. Meyer, "L'etymologie du Prov. *trebalh,*" *Romania* 17 (1888): 421–24; Charles Du Fresne Du Cange, *Glossarium mediae et infimae Latinitatis,* 10 vols. (Graz, Austria: Akademische Druck-u. Verlagsanstalt, 1954), s.v. "trepalium."

24. "The sense-development has not followed the same course in French as in English. Thus English has not developed the simple sense 'work,' for which the OE word has lived on. On the other hand, French has not evolved the sense 'journey' = F. *voyager,* which appeared early in Anglo-Fr., and has become the main sense in English, and is differentiated by the spelling TRAVEL, while the more original senses, so far as they continue in use, retain the earlier spelling *travail*" (*OED*, s.v. "travail n.").

25. At least in the textual record. According to the *MED,* the meanings "work" and "to work" for *travail* and *travailen,* respectively, predate all other senses by a quarter century or more.

26. For example, Chaucer writes, "ye shul use the richesses whiche ye have geten by youre wit and by youre travaille"(*Mel* VII.1597). The complement of *wit, travaille* here emphasizes the exertion and effort, physical and otherwise, involved in work, its experience rather than its agency, which *wit* more overtly signifies. As expressive of effort, *travailen* is the natural opposite of idleness: "ʒwane he i-saiʒ ani idel Man þat louede glotonie / And ne trauailede nouʒt for is mete, he cleopede him 'frere flie'" (*The Early South-English Legendary from Bodleian MS. Laud Misc. 108*, ed. Carl Horstmann [London: 1887], 257). Yet *travailen* is a sufficiently general term that it may also denote production. Here it is used transitively to mean to bring something forth through labor: "We repyn & beryn awey þe frut nowʒ of here lore, þat þese goode men sewyn sum tyme & trauayleden wol sore" (*The South English Ministry and Passion*, ed. O. J. Pickering [Heidelberg: Carl Winter, 1984], lines 1505–6). Similarly, *travail* may denote the product of work itself: "Traueiles of þin hondes þou schalt ete" (*Book to a Mother*, ed. Adrian James McCarthy [Salzburg: Institut fur Anglistik und Amerikanistik, Salzburg, 1981], p. 91, line 5). However, uses of *travail* to signify work as production and work as product are rare and/or late. All the citations for *travail* meaning "The outcome, product, or result of toil or labour; a 'work'" that the *OED* provides are from the sixteenth and seventeenth centuries, a good indication of the rarity of such usage in Middle English, which should thus be considered to signify what ModE *effort*, as a substantive, does, namely the product of work as a product of effort rather than as a product of a productive process. Nor does *travail* signify livelihood or professional occupation per se, except where context lends it such meaning. Nor are the transitive senses of *travailen* especially concerned with the concept of work; they are focused instead on the causing of pain. Thus *travailen* may signify torture pure and simple: "Jesu! thow madist hem so meke, / Whan thow were to the deth travaylit, / To save the soulis that were seke" (*A Paraphrase on the Seven Penitential Psalms*, ed. William Henry Black [London: T. Richards, 1842], p. 53).

27. For example: "O bretherne, takeʒ of hou gret dampnacion it be to take frute of trauel wyth-outen trauele" (*Speculum Christiani*, ed. Gustaf Holmstedt [London: Oxford University Press, 1933], p. 170, lines 24–25); "Quat bote is to sette traueil / On thyng þat may not auail" (*Cursor mundi*, ed. Richard Morris [London: Kegan Paul, 1874–93], lines 89–90); "Ylkeone of vs schal resceyue his owne mede aftyr hys trauayle" (*The Pauline Epistles*, ed. M. J. Powell [London: K. Paul, 1916], 1 Cor. 3.8).

28. *Catholicon Anglicum*, ed. Sidney J. Herrtage (Oxford: Camden Society, 1882), 391.

29. John of Trevisa, *On the Properties of Things: John Trevisa's Translation of Bartholomaeus Anglicus "De Proprietatibus Rerum,"* gen. ed. M. C. Seymour (Oxford: Clarendon Press, 1975), 338. Lydgate, for example, uses the word in connection with both poetic and military labour: "It wer ydelnes / Me to preswme by

and by texpresse / Hir beute al, it wer a vayn travail"; "Was þat a dede of a manly kny3t?— / To slen a man forweried in fi3t, / Feynt of travail." (John Lydgate, *Siege of Thebes,* ed. Axel Erdmann, EETS, e.s., 108 [London: Kegan Paul, 1911], 4.2823, 2.5051.)

30. For example: "þere were philosofres þat trauaillede here wittes for to fynde and knowe cause of þinges and manere of lyuynge" (Ranulf Higden, *Polychronicon,* ed. C. Babington and J. R. Lumby, 8 vols. [London: Longman, 1865–86], 3.221, quoting Trevisa's translation); "þe herte resteþ efter þe trauayl of guode workes" (*Dan Michel's Ayenbite of Inwyt,* ed. Richard Morris [London: Oxford University Press, 1866], p. 251, line 12).

31. Malory, *Works,* 2nd ed., ed. Eugène Vinaver (Oxford: Oxford University Press, 1970), 56.

32. As expressed in his commentary on Gen. 2.15: "Non enim erat laboris afflictio, sed exhilaratio voluntatis, cum ea quae Deus creaverat, humani operis adjutorio laetius feraciusque provenirent" (Augustine, *De genesi ad litteram* 8.8, PL 34:379) [There was not the pain of labor, but instead the will's rejoicing, when those things which God had created came forth more gladly and more fruitfully through the help of human work]. On Augustine's view of work in general, see Rudolph Arbesmann, "The Attitude of Saint Augustine toward Labor," in *The Heritage of the Early Church,* ed. David Neiman and Margaret Schatkin (Rome: Pont. Institutum Studiorum Orientalium, 1973), 245–59; Biago Amata, "S. Agostino: *De opere monachorum:* Una concezione (antimanichea?) del lavoro," in *Spiritualità del lavoro nella catechesi dei padri del iii–iv secolo,* ed. Sergio Felici (Rome: Libreria Ateneo Salesiano, 1986), 59–78; and A. T. Geoghegan, *The Attitude towards Labor in Early Christianity and Ancient Culture* (Washington, DC: Catholic University Press, 1945), 201–12.

33. *The Holy Bible, Containing the Old and the New Testaments, with the Apocryphal Books, in the Earliest Versions Made from the Latin Vulgate by John Wycliffe and His Followers,* ed. Rev. Josiah Forshall, 4 vols. (Oxford: Oxford University Press, 1850), here cited from the early version. Note that "in thi werk," translating "in opere tuo," does not denote what will be a new state of being, whereas "in traueyls," translating "in laboribus," does. In Gen. 2.15 man is placed in paradise "ut operaretur, et custodiret illum," "that he shulde worche and kepe it" in Wyclif's version, whereas *labor* and *travail* appear first at 3.17 in each version, respectively. Cf. God's words to Adam in the Chester play *De creatione mundi et Adami et Evae:* "In thy worke waryed the earth shalbe, / And in great traveyle behoveth the / On earth to get thy lyving" (lines 326–28, in *English Mystery Plays,* ed. Peter Happé [New York: Penguin, 1979]).

34. Albert C. Baugh and Thomas Cable, *A History of the English Language,* 4th ed. (Eaglewood Cliffs, NJ: Prentice Hall, 1993), 173–75.

35. A glance at a couple conspicuous translations of the late fourteenth century reveals the preeminence of *travail* as an equivalent for *labor*. Of the eighteen occurrences of *labor-laborare-elaborare* in Boethius's *Consolation,* Chaucer renders fifteen with *travail-travailen*. For "apium . . . labor" (3.m1.5) he rightly supplies "Hony" (3.m1.5). For "Haec erit vobis requies laborum" (3.m10.4), Chaucer writes, "Her schal ben the reste of your labours" (3.m10.4–5), though nothing distinguishes this general use of *labour* from the bulk of the others. His other use of *labour,* however, does reveal a distinguishing feature. Translating "Ultimus caelum labor inreflexo / Sustulit collo pretiumque rursus / Ultimi caelum meruit laboris" (4.m7.29–31) with "and the laste of his labours was that he susteynede the hevene uppon his nekke unbowed; and he diservide eftsones the hevene to ben the pris of his laste travaile" (4.m7.58–62), Chaucer reveals the greater emphasis that *labour* places on the objective process of work, on the task itself, as opposed to the subjective emphasis of *travail,* here used to make clear that Hercules deserved reward not by virtue of the task he accomplished but by virtue of his resolute effort. Though *labor-laborare* occurs 188 times in the Vulgate, the Wycliffite Bible renders *labor* with *labour* only thrice in the early version and twice in the late.

36. A. Ernout and A. Meillet, *Dictionnaire etymologique de la langue latine: histoire des mots,* 4th ed. (Paris: Klincksieck, 1985), s.v. "labor n."

37. Boethius, *Cons.,* 4.m7.13, and Virgil, *Georg.,* 1.145–46, in *P. Vergili Maronis opera,* ed. R. A. B. Mynors (Oxford: Clarendon Press, 1969), respectively. On the Stoic conception of *ponos,* see van den Hoven, *Work,* 28–38.

38. As read from Ostrá, "Le champ . . . en ancien français," 35, table 1.

39. For example: "And yf y be labour sholde lyuen and lyflode deseruen, / That laboure þat y lerned beste þerwith lyuen y sholde" (William Langland, *Piers Plowman: the C-Text,* ed. Derek Pearsall [Exeter: University of Exeter Press, 1978], 5.42–43; "Aftir the labourous and swetyng that he had by dayes, his body with reste he wolde refresshe" (*The Book of the Foundation of St. Bartholomew's Church in London,* ed. N. Moore [London: Oxford University Press, 1923], p. 4, line 27); "ʒeildes til your creatur / þe tend part o your labour" (*Cursor mundi,* lines 1985–86).

40. For example, "And sche was labowryd wyth many fowle and horibyl thowtys" (*The Book of Margery Kempe,* ed. Lynn Staley [Kalamazoo, MI: Medieval Institute, 1996], lines 4201–2).

41. For example: "But that erthe, (be wel certeyn,) / Wher as sowe was thys greyn, / Was nat labouryd" (John Lydgate, *The Pilgrimage of the Life of Man,* ed. F. J. Furnivall [London: Roxburghe Club, 1905], lines 5395–97); "in an houre / He lest al that he mai laboure / The longe yer" (Gower, *CA* 4.969–71).

42. For example: "Bot thing which yifth ous mete and drinke / And doth the labourer to swinke / To tile lond and sette vines" (Gower, *CA* 4.2439–41); "It is one

of the principalle dedis of a prince to maynteyne, kepe, and avaunce labourage of the londe" (*The Boke of Noblesse,* ed. J. B. Nichols [London: Nichols, 1860], 69). As Latin *laborator* may specifically mean "a plowman," so with ME *labourer* (*MED,* s.v. "labourer n.," 1b). On the extensive agricultural associations of Latin *labor,* see J. F. Niermeyer and C. Van den Kieft, eds., *Mediae Latinitatis Lexicon Minus* (Leiden: PUB, 1976), s.v. "labor n.," 1, 2, 5, 6–9; s.v. "laborare v.," 2, 3, 5; etc.

43. *Labour's* orientation toward the process and the product of work, the greater breadth of its conceptual perspective as compared to the more narrow, subjective emphasis of *travail,* is evident in miniature by its relation to the work of procreation. Though both *labour* and *travail* may signify the labor of childbirth (*MED,* s.vv. "labouren v.," 3a, "labour n.," 4b, "travail n.," 3f, "travailen v.," 4ae, "travailour n.," c, "travailing ger.," 3c, *OED* s.vv. "labour n.," 6, "labour v," I.16, "travail," I.4), only *labouren* is also found signifying sexual intercourse (*MED,* s.v. "labouren v.," 1a, 4c): "Thus laboureth he til that the day gan dawe; / And thanne he taketh a sop in fyn clarre, / And upright in his bed thanne sitteth he" (Chaucer, *MerT* VI.1842–44); "'I trowe, certes, that oure goode man / Hath yow laboured sith the nyght bigan / That yow were nede to resten hastily.' And with that word he lough ful murily, / And of his owene thought he wax al reed" (Chaucer, *ShipT* VII.107–11). The suitability of *labouren* for such euphemistic use is a function both of its transitive senses "to spend labour upon" and "to impose labour upon" (*OED,* s.v. "labour v.," I.1 and I.9a; *MED,* s.v. "labouren v.," 4c, 5)—from the male perspective here represented the sexual act is both an exertion and the causing of the female to undergo exertion—and its agricultural associations. Cf. *Roman de la Rose,* ed. Ernest Langlois (Paris: Firmin Didot, 1914–24), lines 19701ff.

44. For example: "Hadde nevere worldly man so heigh degree / As Adam, til he for mysgovernaunce / Was dryven out of hys hye prosperitee / To labour, and to helle, and to meschaunce" (Chaucer, *MkT* VII.2011–14; Cf. Chaucer, *PardT* VI.505–7); "Than cam an aungil with a swerd, / And drof Adam into a disert; / Ther was Adam sore aferd, / For labour coude he werkyn non" (Thomas Wright, ed., *Middle English Lyrics and Ballads* [London: T. Richards, 1856], 2). Cf. "Il a mengé, donc il labourera [God judging Adam]" (*Du procès de paradis,* in *Le mistére du Viel Testament,* ed. James de Rothchild, 1.1539 [Paris: Firmin Didot, 1878–91], vol. 1).

45. *The Middle English Poem, "Erthe upon Erthe,"* ed. Hilda H. R. Murray (London: Kegan Paul, 1911), p. 23, lines 101–4.

46. For example, "on geswyncum ðu etst of ðære eorðan eallum dagum dines lifes" (*The Old English Version of the Heptateuch, Ælfric's Treatise on the Old and New Testament and His Preface to Genesis,* ed. S. J. Crawford, EETS, o.s., 160 [Oxford: Oxford University Press, 1969], 90).

47. Witness God's words to Adam in some paraphrases of Gen. 3.17: "And, Adam, for þou trowd not me, / wyn þou thy foyd with swynke and swett" (*A Mid-*

dle English Metrical Paraphrase of the Old Testament, ed. U. Ohlander [Stockholm: Almqvist and Wiksell, 1955]); "Of erth þou sal, wit suete and suinc, / Win þat þou sal ete and drinc" (Morris, *Cursor mundi,* lines 921–22).

48. Ælfric, *De temporibus anni,* ed. Heinrich Henel (London: Oxford University Press, 1942), 11.12.

49. Klein, *Comprehensive Etymological Dictionary,* s.v. "swink v." OE *swingan* is related to "OS., OHG. *swingan,* OFris. *swinga,* MLG., MHG. *swingen,* G. *schwingen,* 'to swing, swingle, oscillate', MDu. *swinghen,* 'to waver', Goth. *afswaggwjan,* 'to cause to swing'" (*Comp. Etym. Dict.,* s.v. "swing v").

50. Here are some examples. For work in general: "Of alle men on londe, / Mest swinkeþ þe bonde" (*The Minor Poems of the Vernon MS.,* ed. F. J. Furnivall [London: Kegan Paul, 1901], p. 769, lines 133–34). For work as effort: "ʒe moten rowen aʒein stream, wid muchel swinc breoken ford" (*The English Text of the Ancrene Riwle,* ed. J. R. R. Tolkien and N. R. Ker [London: Oxford University Press, 1962], p. 58, lines 17–18). For work as production: "And syn that slouthe hire holdeth in a lees / Oonly to slepe, and for to ete and drynke, / And to devouren al that othere swinke" (Chaucer, *SNT* VIII.19–21). For work as product: "His tithes payde he ful faire and wel / Bothe of his propre swynk and his catel" (Chaucer, *GP* I.539–40). Like *labouren, swinken* may also be used transitively to denote earning or achievement (*MED,* s.v. "swinken v.," 1d).

51. In Chaucer's works the number of occurrences of *travail, labour,* and *swink* are 75, 97, and 30, respectively; in Gower's *Confessio amantis,* 57, 25, 3; and in the B-text of *Piers Plowman,* 17, 31, 9. Cf. *Gesta Romanorum,* which has 9, 44, and 3. Counted (with help from Larry D. Benson, *A Glossarial Concordance to the Riverside Chaucer* [New York: Garland, 1993] and the *Corpus of Middle English Prose and Verse* (www.hti.umich.edu/c/cme/) from the Riverside Chaucer; *The Early English Versions of the Gesta Romanorum,* ed. Sydney Herrtage, EETS, e.s., 33 (London: Trubner, 1879); John Gower, *Complete Works of John Gower,* ed. G. C. Macaulay, 4 vols. (Oxford: Clarendon Press, 1899–1902); William Langland, *The Vision of Piers Plowman,* ed. A. V. C. Schmidt (New York: E. P. Dutton, 1978).

52. The *Catholicon Anglicum* and the *Promptorium parvulorum* have entries for *travail, labour,* and their derivatives but none for *swink* (*Catholicon Anglicum,* 206, 391; *Promptorium parvulorum,* ed. A. L. Mayhew [London: Kegan Paul, 1908], cols. 254, 272, 488, 489, 501). Nor does either of the Latin-English dictionaries, the *Ortus vocabulorum* or the *Medulla grammatice,* provide *swink* as an equivalent for *labor.* See *Ortus Vocabulorum, 1500* (Menston: Scholar Press, 1968), and Florent A. Tremblay, "The Latin-Middle English Glossary *Medulla Grammatice* B.M. Harl. MS.1738" (PhD diss., Catholic University of America, 1968).

53. The distinction between reported speech and authorial voice is sometimes blurred by the dramatic and poetic form of the *Tales.* But if we count the prologues as reported speech and the individual tales as authorial or more textual, we

see that *swink* occurs in reported speech 73 percent of the time, whereas *travail* and *labour* occur in reported speech only 26 percent and 24 percent of the time. The accuracy of this artificial representation is confirmed by measuring the colloquialness of these three terms by a different criterion: the frequency with which they are used in syntactical connection with a first-person subject or pronoun— that is, in a notably personal, more speechlike voice, as in "What! Thynk on God, as we doon, men that swynke" (Chaucer, *MilT* I.3491). Here also *swink* tops the list with 40 percent, followed by *labour* and *travail* at 18 percent and 13 percent, respectively. Ignoring the prologue-tale distinction and counting the frequency of direct quotation and personal voice combined yields *swink* (53 percent), *travail* (35 percent), *labour* (30 percent). All figures are calculated from Benson's *Glossarial Concordance*. The *Canterbury Tales* are peculiarly appropriate for this kind of counting because of "the lexical novelty of Chaucer's English, by turns traditionally aureate and traditionally colloquial" (Christopher Cannon, *The Making of Chaucer's English* [Cambridge: Cambridge University Press, 1998], 167). That *swink* appears with such greater frequency among *travail* and *labour* in Chaucer's works than in the *Confessio amantis* and *Piers Plowman* (see above) thus also attests to its colloquialness.

54. *MED*, s.v. "swinken v.," 1d, 1g, 3b, 3c; OED, s.v. "swink v.," 2a, 2b.

55. *MED*, s.vv. "labouren v.," 1c, 2b, 5a, 5b; "labour n.," 1d, 2c; "laboured adj."; "labourer n.," 2b; "labouring ger.," 1c; 2b; "travailen v.," 2ac; "bitravailen v.," a; "outtravailed ppl."

56. *MED*, s.vv. "travail n.," 1c, 1d; "travailen v.," 1ad, 3b; "labour n.," 3a.

57. Ælfric's text is quoted from Bruce Mitchell and Fred C. Robinson, *A Guide to Old English*, 5th ed. (Oxford: Blackwell, 1992), p. 183. Ælfric's oxherd, the work companion of the plowman, also exclaims, "ic swince þearle!" (29).

58. *OED*, s.v. "work v.," 3b. In *Cleanness*, for example, God is "þe Wyȝ þat wroȝt alle þinges" (5). *Goddes hond-werk* is also standard (*MED*, s.v. "hond-werk, n.," b). The equivalence of *werk*, *opus*, and their cognates is best illustrated in *Promptorium parvulorum*, 3 vols., ed. Albert Way (London: Camden Society, 1843–53), 3:522–23.

59. *MED*, s.v. "werken v.(1)," 5e. Likewise the noun may simply mean "physical exertion" (*MED*, s.v. "werk v.(1)," 6ad).

60. For example: "Mony a mery mason was made þer to wyrke" (*Saint Erkenwald*, ed. Clifford Peterson [Philadelphia: University of Pennsylvania Press, 1977], line 39); "Hir knyves were chaped noght with bras / But al with silver, wroght ful clene and wel" (Chaucer, *GP* I.366–67); "Sella forsothe gate Tubalcaym, that was an hamer smyth, and a smyth into alle werkis of bras and of yrun" (Forshall, *Holy Bible*, early version, Gen. 4.22); "Helpe for ought that may befall / To worke this shipp, chamber and hall" (Chester *Noah*, lines 49–50, in Happé, *English Mystery*

Plays). See also *OED*, s.vv. "work v.," 3, 4, 5, 6, 12; "work n.," 9, 10, 11, 12, 14, 17; "workman n.," 1a, 2a, 4; *MED*, s.vv. "werk n.(1)," 8a, 8b, 8c, 8d, 10c; "werken v.(1)," 7, 11.

61. Similarly, *werk* bears a strong association with the visual, literary, and musical arts. See *OED*, s.vv. "work n.," 14, 14; "work v.," 24b, 27b; *MED*, s.vv. "werk n.(1)," 10b, 10c; "werken v.(1)," 11d, 12b.

62. See *OED*, s.vv. "work v.," 1, 1b, 2, 3c; "work n.," 1, 3a.

63. In the Wakefield *Noah*, for example, Noah is both one of the few "that well has wroght" (98), being in the eyes of God "always well-wirkand" (120), and a good, though initially reluctant, worker who brings his task to providential completion in a spirit of devotion: "It is better wroght / Then I coude haif thoght. / Hym that made all of noght / I thank oonly" (285–88). Overall, the York *Building of the Ark* and the Wakefield *Noah* represent work as a redemptive force, at once an attribute of the postlapsarian burden and a means of alleviating that burden. Like "good works," work in the plays has both material and spiritual power. The craftsman simultaneously reestablishes divine order in the material world and participates spiritually in God's creativity. Dramatically, these ideas are present in the plays through the rejuvenation and pleasure that Noah finds in building the ark ("Five hundred winters I am of eld— / Methink these years as yesterday! / Full weak I was and all unwield, / My weariness is went away, / To work this work here in this field / All by myself I will assay," *Building of the Ark*, 91–96, cf. *Noah*, 276ff.), the coincidence of the ark's symbolic status and its well-craftedness (*Building of the Ark*, 73–86, 96–111; *Noah*, 118–38, 253–82), and the representation of God as Craftsman ("Myghtfull God veray, maker of all that is," *Noah*, 1; "they make me to repente / My werke I wroght so wele and trewe," *Building of the Ark*, 17–18), whereby Noah's service is characterized not only by obedience but by apprenticeship: "Thus shall I work it both more and min / Through teaching of God, master mine" (*Building of the Ark*, 103–4); "He that to me this craft has kenned, / He wis us with his worthy will" (*Building of the Ark*, 150–51). Quotations are from *York Mystery Plays: A Selection in Modern Spelling*, ed. Richard Beadle and Pamela M. King (Oxford: Clarendon Press, 1984), and *Early English Drama: An Anthology*, ed. John C. Coldeway (New York: Garland, 1993).

64. *OED*, s.v. "work v.," 26; see also 27 and "work n.," 4.

65. *OED*, s.v. "craft n.," 1; *MED*, s.v. "craft n.," 1.

66. *OED*, s.v. "craft n," 2; *MED*, s.v. "craft n.," 2.

67. This association is first of all evident in the verb *craften*, which is wholly transitive and very near in meaning to transitive *werken*: "In stede of Welle or wynche have a cisterne / And rayn of ever hous in it gouverne. / Let crafte hit up plesaunt as may suffice / Unto thi self" (*Palladius on Husbondrie*, ed. Barton Lodge [London: N. Trübner, 1879], 1.426–29). Similarly, the noun *craft* is used to denote

the productive technique and/or the exercise of an art or handicraft: "Colours comeþ of kynde or beþ y-made by crafte" (John of Trevisa, *On the Properties of Things*, 304). As technique can be understood subjectively or objectively, *craft* applies equally to the skill of productive work as an attribute of the workman—"þis is clepid a material place, for it is made bi mannes crafte of lyme, of tymbre & of stoon" (*The Lanterne of Liȝt*, ed. Lilian M. Swinburn, EETS, o.s., 151 [London: Kegan Paul, 1917] ch. 7, p. 36, lines 10–11)—and to the technique of productive work as something abstract and communicable: "The craft which thilke time was, / To worche in latoun and in bras, / He lerneth for his sustienance" (Gower, *CA* 2.1849–51). *Craft* is also used, alone or in the compound *craftwerk*, to denote the product of work: "These Maystres and these riche clerkes / That witti were of craffty wer-kes, / That this thyng schold vndirtake / And that crafft-werk to make . . ." (*The Laud Troy Book*, ed. J. Ernst Wulfing, EETS, o.s., 121–22 [New York: Kraus Reprint Co., 1972], lines 11143–46).

68. For example: "A prentys whilom dwelled in oure citee, / And of a craft of vitailliers was hee" (Chaucer, *CkT* I.4365–66).

69. "And al he [Grace] lered to be lele, and vch a craft loue oþere, / Ne no boest ne debaet be among hem alle. / 'Thouh somme be clenner then somme, ȝe sen wel,' quod Grace, / 'That all craft and connyng cam of my ȝefte'" (*PPl* C.21.250–53).

70. *MED* s.vv. "mechanic," a; "craft n," 5. On the origin of the term *artes mechanicae* and its difference from the classical *artes illiberales*, see Whitney, *Paradise Restored*, pp. 70–73.

71. Reginald Pecock, *Folewer to the Donet*, ed. Elsie Vaughan Hitchcock, EETS, o.s., 164 (Oxford: Oxford University Press, 1924), 52.

72. Chaucer's *Canon's Yeoman's Tale*, for example, frequently plays upon the double meanings of *craft* and *crafti*.

73. John Wyclif, *Select English Works*, ed. Thomas Arnold, 3 vols. (Oxford: Clarendon Press, 1869), 2:235; *Speculum Gy de Warewyke*, ed. Georgiana Lea Morrill, EETS, e.s., 75 (London: Kegan Paul, 1898), line 212, p. 11.

74. Hans-Georg Gadamer, *Truth and Method*, trans. Joel Weinsheimer and Donald G. Marshall, 2nd ed. (New York: Continuum, 1994), 429.

75. See Edward Sapir, *Selected Writings of Edward Sapir in Language, Culture, and Personality*, ed. David G. Mandelbaum (Berkeley: University of California Press, 1949), 3–32; Stephen Ullmann, *Semantics: An Introduction to the Science of Meaning* (Oxford: Basil Blackwell, 1970), 243–53; R. Williams, *Keywords*, 15–22; Anna Wierzbicka, *Understanding Cultures through Their Key Words* (Oxford: Oxford University Press, 1997), 1–31; Peggy Knapp, *Time-Bound Words: Semantic and Social Economies from Chaucer's England to Shakespeare's* (New York: St. Martin's Press, 2000), 1–12.

76. Sapir, *Selected Writings*, 27.

77. Malcolm Crick, *Explorations in Language and Meaning: Towards a Semantic Anthropology* (New York: John Wiley and Sons, 1976), 64.

78. Le Goff, "Le travail," 14.

79. See Joyce Tally Lionarons, "Magic, Machines, and Deception: Technology in the *Canterbury Tales*," *Chaucer Review* 27 (1993): 377–86; Andrew Galloway, "Chaucer's 'Former Age' and the Fourteenth-Century Anthropology of Craft: The Social Logic of a Premodernist Lyric," *ELH* 63 (1996): 535–53.

80. Such as that of Stephen Ullmann, *The Principles of Semantics* (Oxford: Basil Blackwell, 1957), 171–257.

81. Ibid., 186.

82. These developments are described in brief in Ullmann, *Semantics*, 243–53, and Ann-Marie Svensson, *Middle English Words for "Town": A Study of Changes in a Semantic Field* (Göteborg: Acta Universitatis Gothoburgensis, 1995), 5–11. Other studies of Middle English vocabulary that rely upon the field concept include Hans-Jürgen Diller, "Emotions in the English Lexicon: A Historical Study of a Lexical Field," in *English Historical Linguistics 1992*, ed. Francisco Moreno Fernández, Miguel Fuster, and Juan Jose Calvo, Current Issues in Linguistic Theory 113 (Amsterdam: Benjamins, 1994): 219–34; Nicola Pantaleo, "'Ase roser when it redes': Semantic Shifts and Cultural Overtones in the Middle English Colour Lexicon," in *English Historical Linguistics 1992*, 273–84; Bernhard Diensburg, "The Lexical Fields Boy/Girl—Servant—Child in Middle English," *Neuphilologische Mitteilungen* 86 (1985): 328–36.

83. Ullmann, *Semantics*, 245.

84. Maurice Godelier sees the development of the French work vocabulary as characterized by such a shift: "In summarizing the direction which the meanings of the words for work have taken in the last few centuries, we could say, with Lucien Febvre, that there has been a shift in meaning from words which first connoted painful activities bringing little merit to those who performed them, and even degraded them and placed them in a condition of social inferiority, while today the right to work, and the dignity of the worker, have positive meanings" ("Work and Its Representations," 166). Considering the longevity of *labeur, peine, besogne,* and the advent of *turbin,* all of which have significant associations with pain, difficulty, and degradation, this overstatement appears to be the mistaken result of considering *travail* in isolation. Godelier here refers to Lucien Febvre, "Travail: Évolution d'un mot et d'une idée," *Journal de Psychologie Normale et Pathologique* 41 (1948): 19–28.

85. Georges Matoré, *La methodé en lexicologie: Domaine français* (Paris: M. Didier, 1953), 68.

86. Wierzbicka, *Understanding Cultures*, 16.

87. R. Williams, *Keywords*, 12–13. Studies of Middle English words that adopt Williams's formulation include Richard Firth Green, *A Crisis of Truth: Literature*

and Law in Ricardian England (Philadelphia: University of Pennsylvania Press, 1999), 1–40, and Andrew Galloway, "The Making of a Social Ethic in Late Medieval England: From *Gratitudo* to 'Kyndenesse,'" *Journal of the History of Ideas* 55 (1994): 365–83.

88. C. S. Lewis, *Studies in Words*, 2nd ed. (Cambridge: Cambridge University Press, 1967), 1.

89. Knapp, *Time-Bound Words*, 6.

90. Obviously such diagrams can be fine tuned *ad infinitum*. The attempt here is to represent *dominant* meanings and associations, in other words usage, as represented by the *OED* and *MED*.

91. As Ostrá has pointed out, the work vocabulary of Old French is characterized by a similar division surrounding *laborer* and *ovrer*. Only the terms of the *laborer* group "comportent la notion de fatigue et de pénible, ainsi que la nuance d'affectivité négative qui en est complémentaire" ("Le champ . . . en ancien français," 35). Only the terms of the *ovrer* group "étaient susceptibles d'être utilisés pour designer le travail comme objet" (36) and "en nombreux contextes . . . ont une valeur nettement laudative, due sans doute à l'élément notionnel d'art présent dans leur noyau sémantique" (38). For Ostrá, the subsequent history of the French work vocabulary is characterized by the disintegration of this division: "Au cours de l'évolution depuis l'ancien français jusqu'à l'epoque contemporaine, des changements profonds se sont produits dans la structure du champ. Le plus frappant d'entre eux est sans doute l'avènement du verbe *travailler* qui, en ancien français, faisait à peine partie du champ, au centre de cette structure onomasiologique. Au bout de cette évolution longue et mouvementée, une structure unitaire a remplacé l'ancienne organisation dichotomique" (44). The English work vocabulary undergoes a similar evolution, with the significant difference that the word that achieves a central, unifying position comes from the center rather than the periphery of the medieval semantic field. *Swink* becomes obsolete; *travail* splits into *travail* and *travel*, with the former reapproaching its original denotation of pain and becoming roughly synonymous with *toil* and *drudgery; labour*—still serving to distinguish unskilled from skilled, and manual and nonmanual, work—becomes an economic category, but the deepest change concerns *work*. On the one hand, *work*, losing many of its uses as a term for action in general, becomes much more restrictedly a term for work. On the other hand, *work* (as a term for work), like French *travail*, becomes fully extensive in meaning—that is, readily capable of signifying work in all the aspects covered by other terms. Obviously this second change is not nearly as drastic as that which French *travail* undergoes—*werk* was already the most extensive, in both signification and association, of the Middle English terms—but *work* clearly comes to dominate the English work vocabulary in a way that *werk* did not. *Werken*'s transitive signification of production, which is at the heart of its artisanal associations, drops out of use (except in the past participle *wrought*).

This move away from occupational specificity is paralleled by the development, from the sixteenth century onwards, of *work*'s signification of effort in general (*OED*, s.v. "work n.," 4b.). Meanwhile, *work,* as both noun and intransitive verb, comes to signify primarily occupational action of any type.

92. "Au centre du champ, on a en ancien français les verbes *ovrer* et *laborer,* dont le premier met en valeur surtout le résultat (utile), tandis que le seconde se situe plutôt dans la perspective de l'effort. Hâtons-nous de dire, toutefois, que les deux expressions ont une valeur très générale, plus extensive en tout cas, que tous les autres verbes du champ. C'est à bon droit donc que nous les considérons tous deux comme constituant le centre du champ" (Ostrá, "Le champ . . . en ancien français," 21).

93. Ibid., 37–43. Prosper Boissonnade, *Le travail dans l'Europe chrètienne au Moyen Age: Ve–Xve siècles* (Paris: F. Alcan, 1921), 276. Cited from Ostrá, "Le champ . . . en ancien français," 38.

94. Van den Hoven, *Work,* 1–111.

95. "Alienation is a mirror-image of a work ethic: it reflects what is projected into it but the image is reversed. The concept of alienation emerges from a work ethic because of an inevitable recognition that men are not as involved in their work as the ethic demands" (P. D. Anthony, *The Ideology of Work* [London: Tavistock, 1977], 1, 305).

96. Ibid., 314.

97. Hendrik De Man, *Joy in Work,* trans. Eden and Cedar Paul (London: Allen and Unwin, 1929), 67.

98. "What distinguishes the worst architect from the best of bees is this, that the architect raises his structure in imagination before he erects it in reality" (Marx, *Capital,* 188). "Labour is . . . a process . . . in which man of his own accord starts, regulates, and controls the material reactions between himself and Nature. . . . By thus acting on the external world and changing it, he at the same time changes his own nature" (187). "The object of labour is . . . the objectification of man's species life: for he duplicates himself not only, as in consciousness, intellectually, but also actively, in reality, and therefore he contemplates himself in a world that he has created" (Marx, *Economic and Philosophical Manuscripts,* 77). Cf. "[T]hrough work man *not only transforms nature,* adapting it to his own needs, but he also *achieves fulfilment* as a human being and indeed, in a sense, becomes 'more a human being'" (Pope John Paul II, "Laborem exercens," in *The Priority of Labor,* ed. Gregory Baum [New York: Paulist Press, 1982]); "[Man] is, in his own apprehension, a centre of unfolding impulsive activity—'teleological' activity. He is an agent seeking in every act the accomplishment of some concrete, objective, impersonal end. By force of his being such an agent he is possessed of a taste for effective work, and a distaste for futile effort. He has a sense of the merit of serviceability or efficiency and of the demerit of futility, waste, or incapacity. This

aptitude or propensity may be called the instinct of workmanship" (Thorstein Veblen, *The Theory of the Leisure Class* [New York: Dover, 1994], 9).

99. The authority of Augustine's interpretation is evidenced, for example, by Aquinas's repetition of it (*Summa theologica* pt. 1, Q. 102, art. 3).

100. Michael Camille, "'When Adam Delved': Laboring on the Land in English Medieval Art," in *Agriculture in the Middle Ages*, ed. Del Sweeney (Philadelphia: University of Pennsylvania Press, 1995), 247–76.

101. Angelo di Barardino, ed., *Encyclopedia of the Early Church*, trans. Adrian Walford (New York: Oxford University Press, 1992), 469. This is essentially a Christian version of the Platonic stress on the intellective component of craft work: "The crafts such as building and carpentry which give us Matter in wrought forms, may be said, in that they draw on pattern, to take their principles from that realm and from the thinking There" (Plotinus, *Enneads*, trans. Stephen MacKenna [New York: Larson, 1992], 5.9.11). At the same time, Irenaeus's singling out of the hands as God-given instruments of work should not be overlooked. Man is here seen as physically composed for rational, purposive work. Cf. "Instead of these [horns and claws], he has reason and hands whereby he can make himself arms and clothes, and other necessaries of life, of infinite variety. Wherefore the hand is called by Aristotle (*De anima* 3.8), *the organ of organs*. Moreover this was more becoming to the rational nature, which is capable of conceiving an infinite number of things, so as to make for itself an infinite number of instruments" (Thomas Aquinas, *Summa theologica*, trans. Fathers of the Dominican Province [New York: Bezinger Brothers, 1946], pt. 1, Q. 91, art. 3).

102. Hugh of St. Victor, *Didascalicon*, trans. Jerome Taylor (New York: Columbia University Press, 1961), 1.9, 2.1. On Hugh's conception of human work and its influence, see Whitney, *Paradise Restored*, 77–127.

103. Paul Freedman, *Images of the Medieval Peasant* (Stanford: Stanford University Press, 1999), 34–35.

104. Chrétien de Troyes's description of Enide's saddle in *Erec et Enide* exposes this fact nicely: "The craftsmanship here was subtle and skilled, and the entire work was set off by fine gold. The Breton sculptor who had designed it labored for more than seven years, and during that time he worked on nothing else. I do not know whether he sold it, though he ought to have received a high price for it" (*The Complete Romances of Chrétien de Troyes*, trans. David Staines [Bloomington: Indiana University Press, 1993], 66).

105. "A craftsman absolutely master of his craft, and taking such pride in the exercise of it as all healthy souls take in putting forth their personal powers; proud also of the city and his people; enriching, year by year, their streets with loftier buildings, their treasuries with rarer possessions, and bequeathing his hereditary art to a line of successive masters, by whose tact of race, and honour of effort, the essential skills of metalwork in gold and steel, of pottery, glass-painting, wood-

work, and weaving, were carried out to a perfectness never to be surpassed" (John Ruskin, *The Stones of Venice*, in *The Works of John Ruskin*, 36 vols., ed. E. T. Cook and Alexander Wedderbum [London: Allen, 1908], 34:353–54). Similarly for Aron Gurevich, the medieval artisan's work "gave him satisfaction in itself," "was a means of asserting his human personality and heightening his social awareness," was a "union of productive, ethical, and aesthetic principles," and "carried the imprint of his personality" (*Categories of Medieval Culture*, trans. G. L. Campbell [London: Routledge and Kegan Paul, 1972], 208, 267).

106. Rodney Hilton, *Class Conflict and the Crisis of Feudalism*, 2nd ed. (London: Verso, 1990), 13–14.

107. Ibid., 14; Lee Patterson, *Chaucer and the Subject of History* (Madison: University of Wisconsin Press, 1991), 249. On the peasant land market, see P. D. A. Harvey, ed., *The Peasant Land Market in Medieval England* (Oxford: Clarendon Press, 1984) and P. R. Hyams, "The Origins of a Peasant Land Market in England," *Economic History Review* 23 (1970): 18–31.

108. "The social stratification in the sphere of urban craft production was analogous . . . to the familiar social stratification of the peasantry, for to the rich, middling and poor peasants corresponded rich and poor masters, the latter often merging with the journeymen, just as rural small-holders were often also hired labourers on demesnes or rich peasant holdings. . . . The resemblances between the rural and urban structures . . . are sufficiently coherent to suggest that the constant flow of rural immigrants who sustained the demographically vulnerable urban populations would not by any means be entering an unfamiliar world as they stepped through the gates in the city walls. In any case, many of them must have been there before" (Rodney Hilton, "Towns in English Medieval Society," in *The English Medieval Town*, ed. Richard Holt and Gervase Rosser [London: Longman, 1990], 24–25). See also Christopher Dyer, *Standards of Living in the Later Middle Ages* (Cambridge: Cambridge University Press, 1989), 23–26. On market relations between town and country, see Richard H. Britnell, *The Commercialization of English Society, 1000–1500*, 2nd ed. (Manchester: Manchester University Press, 1996), 112–15.

109. Rodney Hilton, *Bond Men Made Free* (New York: Viking Press, 1973), 35, 36.

110. As Hilton notes: "It is likely that [artisans] regarded the oligarchies' manipulation of the tax system much as the peasants regarded demands for ever more rents and services—as another form of non-economic and coercive appropriation of their earnings in return for nothing. . . . This exploitation was direct in the case of the unenfranchised towns, and was not entirely absent in the independent burroughs and communes which often had to pay a cash commutation for rents and tolls, as well as paying a high rate of taxation, whose weight fell more heavily on the artisans than on the ruling mercantile elites" (*Class Conflict*, 16, 215).

111. *Wimbledon's Sermon: Redde Rationem Villicationis Tue: A Middle English Sermon of the Fourteenth Century,* ed. Ione Kemp Knight (Pittsburgh: Duquesne University Press, 1967), lines 44–46. The Dominican John Bromyard makes the inclusion of craftsmen among the *laboratores* explicit: "God has ordained three classes of men, namely labourers such as husbandmen and craftsmen to support the whole body of the Church after the manner of feet" (G. R. Owst, *Literature and Pulpit in Medieval England,* 2nd ed. [New York: Barnes and Noble, 1961], 554). On the occupational and demographic heterogeneity of the Rising, see Hilton, *Bond Men Made Free,* 176–85.

112. Thorstein Veblen, "The Instinct of Workmanship and the Irksomeness of Labor," in *Essays in Our Changing Order,* ed. Leon Ardzrooni (New York: Viking, 1954), 81; Yves R. Simon, *Work, Society, and Culture* (New York: Fordham University Press, 1971), 21.

113. Weber, *Economy and Society,* 937.

114. Ibid., 935, 932.

115. Veblen, *Theory of the Leisure Class,* 27.

116. "Nam sunt revera omni peccanti animae duo ista poenalia, ignorantia et difficultas" (Augustine, *De libero arbitrio* 3.18, PL 32:1296).

117. "Nunc igitur maledictus eris super terram . . . Cum operatus fueris eam, non dabit tibi fructos suos" (Gen. 4.11).

118. As noted by Gregory I, "non offerens a muneribus, sed munera ab offerente placuerunt" (*Epistolae,* PL 77:1053). Cf. "Deus autem, qui est discretor cogitationum et intentionum cordis, nullo magis munere quam pia offerentis devotione placatur" (Bede, *Hexameron,* PL 91:64).

119. The *Glossa ordinaria* connects Cain's name, his possessiveness, and Augustine's interpretation of Cain as the founder of the earthly city: "Cain et Abel de una matre geniti, figura sunt omnium hominum qui de radice peccati in hanc vitam propagantur; et alii terrenam civitatem et mortiferas delicias sunt amaturi, et quantum in se est ambitione possessuri; quos significat Cain, qui interpretatur possessio" (PL 113:98).

120. Augustine, *City of God,* 3 vols., trans. Gerald Walsh and Grace Monahan (New York: Fathers of the Church, 1952), 2:425, 426.

121. Freedman, *Images,* 93.

122. Patterson, *Chaucer,* 262. On Cain and Ham in general, see Freedman, *Images,* 28, 34, 86–104; Oliver Farrar Emerson, "Legends of Cain in Old and Middle English," *PMLA* 21 (1906): 831–929; Gilbert Dahan, "L'exégèse de l'histoire de Cain et Abel du XIIe au XIVe siècle en Occident: Textes," *Recherches de Theologie Ancienne et Medievale* 50 (1983): 5–68; John Friedman, *The Monstrous Races in Medieval Art and Thought* (Cambridge, MA: Harvard University Press, 1981).

123. Freedman, *Images,* 93. The association of the Man in the Moon with Cain, which Dante refers to as common opinion (*Inferno* 20.124–28; *Paradiso*

2.49–51), is another instance of this. See Maddalena Mantovani, "La lirica 'Mon in þe mon stond & strit' e la leggenda dell'uomo sulla luna," *Quaderni di Filologia Germanica* 2 (1982): 25–45.

124. *Mactatio Abel*, in Happé, *English Mystery Plays*, 79–96.

125. Cf. "Shuld I leife my plogh and all thyng / And go with the to make offeryng? / . . . What gifys God the, to rose hym so? / Me gifys he noght bot soro and wo" (91–96); "Wenys thou now that I list gad / To gif away my warldys aght? / The dwill hym spede that me so taght! / What nede had I my travell to lose, / To were my shoyn and ryfe my hose?" (149–53).

126. The *contrapasso* of the curse God lays upon Cain's work—the loss of the goods that he withheld—was held as well to govern the punishment of bad tithing. As J. D. W. Crowther, citing the homily series *Jacob's Well*, points out, "The false tither will feel God's vengeance for breaking his law, and one of the forms that vengeance takes is 'þat god schal suffre flyes, foulys, & bestys, to wastyn & to dystryin here godys'" ("The Wakefield Cain and the 'Curs' of the Bad Tither," *Parergon* 24 [1979]: 20).

127. For a survey of this tradition, see Freedman, *Images*, 40–55.

128. Similarly, we see that the difficulty of work is the medium for the crediting of work with positive noneconomic value, as in monastic conceptions of work as a penitential and spiritual good: "To the extent that labor provided spiritual benefit, the latter derived from the voluntary self-deprivation involved, according to Cistercian opinion, not from any value inhering in the work itself" (Ibid., 26).

129. Cain's general character is hardly specific to him. As Owst points out, the Cain of the Towneley play, as a bad husbandman, is "little more than *a general pulpit type*" (Owst, *Literature and Pulpit*, 492, emphasis in original).

130. Cf. "'Ignoble because they worked, they had to work because they were poor, or risk being accused of pride and consigned to eternal damnation" (Georges Duby, *The Three Orders*, trans. Arthur Goldhammer [Chicago: University of Chicago Press, 1980], 325).

131. Weber, *Economy and Society*, 935. This is not to suggest, of course, that the status conception of work is simply the product of unmitigated greed and selfishness. These vices are mediated by social competition. For an account of aristocratic thrift and the more positive functions of aristocratic display, see Dyer, *Standards of Living*, 89–92. On the social function of generosity and wastefulness, see Aaron Gurevich, *Categories of Medieval Culture*, 246–58.

132. On medieval working conditions and work discipline in general, see Werner Rösner, *Peasants in the Middle Ages*, trans. Alexander Stützer (Urbana: University of Illinois Press, 1992), 85–143; Keith Thomas, "Work and Leisure in Pre-industrial Society," *Past and Present* 29 (1964): 49–66; E. P. Thompson, "Time, Work-Discipline, and Industrial Capitalism," *Past and Present* 38 (1967): 56–97; Jacques Le Goff, *Time, Work, and Culture in the Middle Ages*, trans.

Arthur Goldhammer (Chicago: University of Chicago Press, 1980), 43–52; G. G. Coulton, *The Medieval Village* (New York: Dover, 1989), 321–24.

133. "'Sir,' quod he, 'I am an hyne; / For I am wont to go to the plow, / And erne my mete yer that I dyne. / To swete and swinke I make avow, / My wyf and children therwith to fynd, / And servë god, and I wist how; / But we lewd men ben full[y] blynd. / For clerkes saye, we shullen be fayn / For hir lyvelod [to] swete and swinke, / And they right nought us give agayn, / Neyther to ete ne yet to drinke. / They mowe by lawë, as they sayn, / Us curse and dampne to hell[e] brinke; / Thus they putten us to payn, / With candles queynt and belles clinke'" (*Plowman's Tale*, lines 26–40, in *The Complete Works of Geoffrey Chaucer*, ed. Walter W. Skeat [Oxford: Clarendon Press, 1897]).

134. Weber, *Economy and Society*, 937.

135. "The sense of dignity that characterizes positively privileged status groups is naturally related to their 'being' which does not transcend itself, that is, it is related to their 'beauty and excellence.' Their kingdom is 'of this world.' They live for the present and by exploiting their great past" (Weber, *Economy and Society*, 934). The dignity of the negatively privileged is likewise related to their being, but it is a being that is transcendent and deferred in time. Their dignity "naturally refers to a future lying beyond the present, whether of this life or another. In other words, it must be nurtured by the belief in a providential mission and by a belief in a specific honor before God" (934). A good example of the concern of status with being, with personal essence, is the firmness of the noble-churl distinction—the impossibility of passing from one to the other and of permanently disguising either—in medieval romance. As E. K. Chambers notes regarding Malory's *Morte d' Arthur*, "[T]he distinction between noble and churl is fundamental. If there are sparks of nobility in a cowherd's son, like Tor, or a kitchen knave, like Gareth, you may be sure he will turn out to be a king's son in disguise" (quoted in G. G. Coulton, *Medieval Panorama* [New York: Norton, 1974], 240). The status-being connection is also evidenced by the conventional display of status through manners. In one sense, refined manners attest not to superior being but to the privileged act of private leisure: "Refined tastes, manners, and habits of life are a useful evidence of gentility, because good breeding requires time, application, and expense, and can therefore not be compassed by those whose time and energy are taken up with work. A knowledge of good form is *prima facie* evidence that that portion of the well-bred person's life which is not under observation of the spectator has been worthily spent in acquiring accomplishments that are of no lucrative effect" (Veblen, *Theory of the Leisure Class*, 31). At the same time, however, refined manners, to be accepted as representative of status, cannot bear association with study and discipline. They must not appear *labored*; rather, they must appear to be a direct, unmediated expression of superior nature. As Castiglione would explain:

"Ma avendo io già piú volte pensato meco onde nasca questa grazia . . . trovo una regula universalissima . . . e ciò è fuggir quanto piú si po . . . la affettazione . . . e . . . usar in ogni cosa una certa sprezzatura, che nasconda l'arte e dimostri ciò che si fa e dice venir fatto senza fatica e quasi senza pensarvi. Da questo credo io che derivi assai la grazia: perché delle cose rare e ben fatte ognun sa la difficultà, onde in esse la facilità genera grandissima maraviglia; e per lo contrario il sforzare e, come si dice, tirar per i capelli dà somma disgrazia" (*Il cortegiano*, ed. Silvano Del Missier [Novara: Istituto Geographico de Agostini, 1968], 1.26). While this passage confirms my earlier observation that the reduction of work to effort by status mentality is based on the principle that to act without effort is to display superior power, we may also see this reduction more generally as the result of the status-being relation insofar as to define work as effort is to reduce productive activity to a state of being.

136. Weber, *Economy and Society*, 938.

137. Britnell, *Commercialization of English Society*, 227.

138. In addition to the social and economic similarities between peasant and artisan enumerated above, the widely used general senses of *werk* and *craft* speak against this, as does the fact that agricultural work is referred to by them. There is nothing incongruous about the husbandman who sings, "Nou we mote worche" (*Song of the Husbandman*, line 5, in Elizabeth Danninger, *Sieben politische Gedichte der HS. B.L. Harley 2253: Textausgabe und Kommentar* [Würzburg: Könningshausen, 1980]), or a description of husbandry as a combination of natural resources and "crafte of men" (*Palladius on Husbondrie*, 1.19), or Walter of Henley's advice to "lette the bayly, mower, or reeve bee the whole day with the ploughe to see that they doe theire woorke truely and well" (Dorothea Oschinsky, ed., *Walter of Henley and Other Treatises on Estate Management and Accounting* [Oxford: Clarendon Press, 1971], 317).

139. Britnell estimates that only "one fifth of the population earned its living partly or wholly in the production and trading of goods and services" (*Commercialization of English Society*, 115).

140. Hilton, *Bond Men Made Free*, 35.

141. On the times and places of this change, see Georges Duby, *Rural Economy and Country Life in the Medieval West*, trans. Cynthia Postan (Philadelphia: University of Pennsylvania Press, 1998), 152–56. Cf. "long before the 13th century, industrial craftsmen had become separated both from their rural and feudal household contexts and appeared as apparently autonomous industrial households within urban communities, producing for sale to anybody who had money" (Hilton, *Class Conflict*, 214).

142. On the increase of occupational specialization in the late medieval England, see Britnell, *Commercialization of English Society*, 164–65.

143. Dyer, *Standards of Living*, 14–15.

144. C. H. Williams, ed., *English Historical Documents*, vol. 5, *1485–1558* (London: Eyre and Spottiswoode, 1971), 189.

145. Sylvia L. Thrupp, *The Merchant Class of Medieval London* (Ann Arbor: University of Michigan Press, 1962), 3.

146. Basil of Caesarea, *Hexameron* 1.7, in *A Select Library of Nicene and Post-Nicene Fathers of the Church: Second Series*, ed. Philip Schaff and Henry Wace (Grand Rapids, MI: Eerdmans, 1978), 8:55.

147. On the importance of this antithesis in Anglo-Saxon culture, see Fred C. Robinson, *"Beowulf" and the Appositive Style* (Knoxville: University of Tennessee Press, 1985).

148. Le Goff, *Time, Work, and Culture*, 75–76. Le Goff's principal examples are pagan artisan deities (cf. the devotion of Greek craftsmen to Hephaistos, on which see Alison Burford, *Craftsmen in Greek and Roman Society* [London: Thames and Hudson, 1972], 164–67), the higher *wergeld* of craftsmen (particularly ironsmiths and goldsmiths), and the later survival of these traditions in the personalization and sanctification of swords and the canonization of the royal goldsmith Eligius.

149. See Ovitt, *Restoration of Perfection*, 57–70.

150. See Whitney, *Paradise Restored*. The textual stronghold of this privileging of artisanal work is Hugh of St. Victor's *Didascalicon*, of which almost a hundred manuscripts survive from the twelfth to the fifteenth centuries (*Didascalicon*, p. 4). The very concept of the *artes mechanicae*, in which Hugh of St. Victor includes agriculture (*Didascalicon* 24.4), is a craft conception. Accordingly, while the techniques of other types of work are discussed in some detail, one sentence is given over to agriculture, dividing it not in terms of technique but in terms of the kind of land it works with. Hugh's tendency throughout is to laud human work in the form of craft: for example, "From this [want] the infinite varieties of painting, weaving, carving, and founding have arisen, so that we look with wonder not at nature alone but at the artificer as well." The purest expression of this tendency is his adoption of the concept of the three works from Chalcidius's commentary on the Timaeus: "'Now there are three works—the work of God, the work of nature, and the work of the artificer *[opus artificis]*, who imitates nature'" (*Didascalicon* 1.9). In this scheme God's work is to create out of nothing, nature's work is to make actual "that which lay hidden," and man's work is "to put together things disjoined or to do disjoin those put together." Obviously, agricultural work cannot be understood as any of these. Curiously, it was only when he came to comment upon "Tempus plantandi, et tempus evellendi, quod plantatum est" (Eccl. 3.2) that Hugh discovered the necessity of departing from the threefold model and distinguishing between "opus solius artificis sine natura" and "opus artificis cum natura," where

"opus artificis cum natura est: ea quae oriuntur de terra, studio et industria adju-vare" (*Homiliae in ecclesiasten*, PL 175:215).

151. The full passage: "Si enim in alicujus opificis officinam imperitus intra-verit, videt ibi multa instrumenta quorum causas ignorat, et si multum est insipi-ens, superflua putat. Jamvero si in fornacem incautus ceciderit, aut ferramento ali-quo acuto, cum id male tractat, seipsum vulneraverit, etiam perniciosa et noxia existimat ibi esse multa. Quorum tamen usum quoniam novit artifex, insipientiam ejus irridet, et verba inepta non curans, officinam suam instanter exercet. Et tamen tam stulti sunt homines, ut apud artificem hominem non audeant vituperare quae ignorant, sed cum ea viderint credant esse necessaria, et propter usus aliquos in-stituta: in hoc autem mundo cujus conditor et administrator praedicatur Deus, au-dent multa reprehendere quorum causas non vident, et in operibus atque instru-mentis omnipotentis artificis volunt se videri scire quod nesciunt" (*De Genesi contra Manichaeos* 1.16, PL 34:185). Cf. *Enarrationes in Psalmos* 148.12, PL 37:1945.

152. Roger Bacon, *De secretis operibus*, 4.533, cited from Lynn White Jr., *Medieval Technology and Social Change* (Oxford: Oxford University Press, 1962), 134; Chaucer, *SumT* III.1970, respectively.

153. "Craftsmen present in the monastery should practice their crafts with humility, as permitted by the abbot. But if anyone becomes proud of his skill and the profit he brings the community, he should be taken from his craft and work at ordinary labor. This will continue until he humbles himself and the abbot is satis-fied" (*The Rule of St. Benedict,* trans. Anthony C. Meisel and M. L. del Mastro [New York: Doubleday, 1975], ch. 57, p. 93). *The Smyth and His Dame* is in *Altenglische Legenden mit Einleitung und Anmerkungen,* ed. Carl Horstmann (Heilbronn, 1881), 322–28; lines 25–27 quoted above. For a thorough discussion of the tale and its cultural affiliations, see Lisa H. Cooper, "'These Crafty Men': Figuring the Arti-san in Late Medieval England" (PhD diss., Columbia University, 2003), 153–76.

154. Honoré Bonet, *The Tree of Battles,* trans. G. W. Coopland (Liverpool: Liv-erpool University Press, 1949), 4.8.

155. Freedman, *Images,* 31. On this aspect of the *Très riches heures,* see Jona-than Alexander, "*Labeur* and *Paresse:* Ideological Representations of Medieval Peasant Labor," *Art Bulletin* 72 (1990): 3–30.

156. A good example of this capacity is provided by the Cooke MS, which I will discuss more fully in the following chapter. The Cooke MS (British Museum, Add. MS. 23198) is one of two related compilations of the history and articles of masonry (*Two Earliest Masonic MSS.,* ed. Douglas Knoop, G. P. Jones, and Douglas Hamer [Manchester: Manchester University Press, 1938]). It might be expected that as a text "not simply about masons but for masons" and as an expression of "the conscience and pride of the craft, and its claim to antiquity and status" (p. 1) the Cooke MS would avoid terms that stressed the painfulness of work and bore

strong associations with servility and agriculture. Instead, the text employs a full range of words for work, using all except *swink,* and uses them not haphazardly but in ways that capitalize on their special meanings. The text's concern with the status and the nature of work is evident from its beginning, a giving thanks to God as a worker who established the conditions of man's work: "Thonkyd be god our glorious Fadir and founder and former of heuen and of erthe and of alle thyngis that in hym is that he wolde fochesaue of his glorious God-hed for to make so many thyngis of diuers vertu for mankynd" (lines 2–10). The introduction elides completely any sense of work as a postlapsarian institution. Instead, it echoes Gen. 1.26—"he made alle thyngis for to be abedient & soget to man" (11–12)—and defines the subjection of nature to man, not in terms of technological domination, but in terms of nature's own life-sustaining productivity: "For alle thyngis that ben comestible of holsome nature he ordeyned hit for manys sustynauns" (13–16). The text then introduces *craft* as the facilitator and modifier of this production: "And all-so he hath yif to man wittys and connynge of dyuers thyngys and craftys by the whiche we may trauayle in this worlde to get with our lyuyng to make diuers thyngis to goddis plesans and al-so for our ese and profyt" (16–24). Here the terms serve to express the important distinction between, one the one hand, the diversity of types of work and skills proper to them ("dyuers thyngys and craftys") and, on the other, working activity in general or the general application of effort to those forms of work ("trauayle"). Similarly, *labour* is elsewhere used to signify the common, binding element in all forms of work: "For alle men here in this worlde lyue by þe laboure of here hondys" (122–24). Throughout the text the vocabulary serves the distinction between the subjective and objective dimensions of work, between *travail-labour* and *werk-craft.* Both are an integral part of the duty of work and are consistently used in complementary constructions: "and truly do your *labour* and *craft* and takyth resonabulle your mede" (393–95); "thei may not fulfylle þer days *werke* and *traueyll*" (805–6); "þat þe mason *worche* apon þe werk day / Also trwly as he con or may / To deserue hys huyre for þe halyday / And trwly to *labrun* on hys dede / Wel deserue to haue hys mede" (Regius MS, British Museum Bibl. Reg. 17 A1, 270–74). To do one's labor and one's craft truly is to diligently and skillfully perform one's work as both an efficient and economically honest act, both to work well and to do good work. While the subjective and objective dimensions are thus recognized as blended in the work process, the terminological distinction also makes possible the isolation of effort or the expenditure of labor power as the remunerated element of work: "And he ordeyned conuenyent [wages] to pay for þer *trauayle*" (609–11); "for euery mann to be rewardyd after his *trauayle*" (738–39); "þey schuld tryuly fulfylle here dayes werke and *trauayle* for here pay" (917–20).

  157. Freedman, *Images,* 20.

158. Owst, *Literature and Pulpit*, 549.

159. *Wimbledon's Sermon*, lines 114–18.

160. Aristotle, *Politics* 1337b, in *The Basic Works of Aristotle*, ed. Richard McKeon (New York: Random House, 1941), 1306.

161. Whitney, *Paradise Restored*, 30.

162. "Cantica vero divina cantare, etiam manibus operantes facile possunt, et ipsum laborem tanquam divino celeumate consolari [Kleuma, cantus nautarum et remigum, quo se mutuo ad laborandum excitant]. An ignoramus, omnes opifices quibus vanitatibus et plerumque etiam turpitudinibus theatricarum fabularum donent corda et linguas suas, cum manus ab opere non recedant? Quid ergo impedit servum Dei manibus operantem in lege Domini meditari, et psallere nomini Domini Altissimi: ita sane ut ad ea discenda, quae memoriter recolat, habeat seposita tempora?" (Augustine, *De opere monachorum* ch. 17, PL 40:565). Cf. "aliud est enim corpore laborare animo libero, sicut opifex, si non sit fraudulentus et avarus, et privatae rei avidus; aliud autem ipsum animum occupare curis colligendae sine corporis labore pecuniae, sicut sunt vel negotiatores, vel procuratores, vel conductores: cura enim praesunt, non manibus operantur, ideoque ipsum animum suum occupant habendi sollicitudine" (*De opere monachorum* ch. 15, PL 40:561).

163. Hoccleve, *Regiment of Princes*, 1.997, 1.1009–15, in *Hoccleve's Works*, ed. Frederick J. Furnivall, EETS, e.s., 72 (Millwood, NY: Kraus Reprint Co., 1978).

164. As Knight explains, "[J]ust as modern representations of labourers have been refracted through the thought-systems of socialist politics or liberal sympathies, so the medieval materials were strongly affected and often redirected by the religious positioning of the bulk of the authors" ("The Voice of Labour in Fourteenth-Century English Literature," in Bothwell, Goldberg, and Ormrod, *Problem of Labour*, 102).

165. Whitney, *Paradise Restored*, 71.

166. Hugh of St. Victor, *Didascalicon* 2.20. William of Conches provides a fuller explanation of this likeness: "It is to be noted that as in the liberal arts there is the trivium concerned with eloquence and the quadrivium concerned with wisdom, so in the mechanical arts, the first three are called a trivium because they pertain to extrinsic goods—to fabric making, armament, and commerce; while four are a quadrivium because related to internal remedies or foods. It is asked how dramatics pertains to interior things. Two things are vitally necessary to man ... movement to keep the mind from languishing, joy to keep the body from exhaustion by too much work. So, plays and diversions were established" (*Un brano inedito della "Philosophia" di Guglielmo di Conches*, ed. Carmelo Ottaviano [Naples: Alberto Morano, 1935], 34, quoted in *Didascalicon*, p. 205 n. 68). Hugh's successors often eliminated theater from the list, making such contorted explanations unnecessary (Whitney, *Paradise Restored*, 103, 107, 118, 123).

167. "This art [commerce] is beyond all doubt a peculiar sort of rhetoric—strictly of its own kind—for eloquence is in the highest degree necessary to it. Thus the man who excels others in fluency of speech is called a *Mercurius,* or Mercury, as being a *mercatorum kirrius* (=*kyrios*)—a very lord among merchants" (Hugh of St. Victor, *Didascalicon* 2.4).

168. In brief, these phenomenal subclassifications are as follows. Armament is divided into "the constructional and the craftly," and "craftly armament is divided into the malleable branch . . . and the foundry branch" (Hugh of St. Victor, *Didascalicon* 2.22). Commerce comprises "purchase, sale, and exchange of domestic or foreign goods" (2.23). "Agriculture deals with four kinds of lands: arable, . . . plantational, . . . pastoral, . . . and floral" (2.24). To hunting belongs "gaming, fowling, and fishing" as well as "the preparation of all foods, seasonings, and drinks," with food subdivided into "bread and side dishes" (2.25). Medicine is divided into "'occasions' and operations," with medicinal operation subdivided into "interior or exterior" (2.26).

169. Whitney, *Paradise Restored,* 75–127; van den Hoven, *Work,* 159–200; Ovitt, *Restoration of Perfection,* 107–36.

170. Robert Kilwardby, *De ortu scientiarum,* ed. Albert G. Judy (Oxford: Clarendon Press, 1976), 40.378, p. 133, quoted in Whitney, *Paradise Restored,* 119.

171. Ibid., 42.393, p. 138, quoted in Whitney, *Paradise Restored,* 120.

172. In the following passage, for example, Kilwardby sets forth a web of relationships both between the mechanical and the liberal arts and between the mechanical arts themselves: "Under physics, indeed, are medicine and alchemy, which [itself] is not incongruously reduced to commerce, which itself is the science of wealth-getting. In the same way, wool-working, the making of arms, architecture, agriculture and food science, which examine with respect to their object, are much supported by physics. . . . Similarly, navigation, which pertains to commerce, and agriculture are much aided by astronomy because of their concern with seasons and movements of the heavens. . . . Similarly, the art of numbering, which because of its computations is well reduced to commerce, is under arithmetic and the instrumental art of harmony, which can be reduced to medicine, is under the mathematics of proportions. Similarly, architecture, construction, and arms-making with respect to their method of operating are under geometry. . . . Similarly, I think that wool-making is with respect to its method under arithmetic and geometry. It examines indeed the number and texture of threads and the measurement and form of the warp. . . . Again, medicine is aided not only by physics but by astrology, and consequently, by astronomy, without which astrology is not able to be known. Similarly, in other mechanical arts everywhere you find that they are under some speculative science or sciences" (*De ortu scientiarum,* 37.358, p. 127, quoted in Whitney, *Paradise Restored,* 122).

173. Edith Cooperrider Rodgers, *Discussion of Holidays in the Later Middle Ages* (New York: Columbia University Press, 1940), 35.

174. Steven A. Epstein, *Wage Labor and Guilds in Medieval Europe* (Chapel Hill: University of North Carolina Press, 1991), 159.

175. "Dominico item die lectioni vacent omnes: exceptis his qui variis officiis deputati sunt. Si quis vero ita negligens et desidiosus fuerit, ut non velit aut non possit meditari aut legere, injungatur ei opus quod faciat, ut non vacet" (*Regula Sancti Benedicti,* PL 66:704b).

176. Aquinas, for example, defines servile work as physical work "whereby one man serves another" and that "hinder[s] man from applying himself to Divine things" (*Summa theologica* pt. 1-2, q. 122, art. 5). For references to other similar definitions, see Rodgers, *Discussion of Holidays,* 35ff; Coulton, *Medieval Panorama,* 183; Epstein, *Wage Labor and Guilds,* 160. A comprehensive definition is provided in *Dives and Pauper:* "seruyl wark is clepyd euery bodely wark don principaly for temporel lucre & wordly wynnyng, as beyyng, sellyng, eryyng, sowyng, repynge, mowynge & alle craftis of wynnynge; also pletynge, motynge, marketis, feyris, seittynge of iusticis & of iugis, schadyng of blood and execucion, of punchinge be þe lawe, & alle warkys þat schuldyn lettyn man from Godis seruise & disposyn hym to couetyse or to þe fendis seruyce" (ed. Priscilla Heath Barnum, EETS, o.s., 275, 280 [London: Oxford University Press, 1976], 1:277–78).

177. Reginald Pecock, *Donet,* ed. Elsie Vaughan Hitchcock, EETS, o.s., 156 [London: Oxford University Press, 1921], 2.6, p. 128.

178. For examples, see Epstein, *Wage Labor and Guilds,* 160–63; Rodgers, *Discussion of Holidays,* 35–62, 76–79. For examples of actual infractions, see Coulton, *Medieval Panorama,* 183–85.

179. Rodgers, *Discussion of Holidays,* 77.

180. Ibid., 37. Rodgers provides a list of examples, such as putting the finishing touches on a painting and floating logs downstream.

181. As Rodgers points out, "[A]rranging terms for peace and repairing roads and bridges," for example, "were considered employments well suited to holidays, for to the medieval mind public utility constituted one of the manifold aspects of piety," and "hunting, fowling, and fishing were regarded as lawful holiday activities" provided they were undertaken for recreation alone (ibid., 39, 47). Cf. "it is not the part of an excellent man or of an eminent mind to busy oneself with agriculture . . . but it is praiseworthy only for the sake of leisure and alternation of cares" (Roderigo Sanchez de Arevalo, *Speculum vitae humanae,* ch. 21, quoted in Coulton, *Medieval Village,* 518); "Some [peasants] . . . go to fish, which is an act not unlawful in itself, but they offend in doing this on feast-days; to wit, they catch fish and sell them, thus breaking the commandment to do no servile work on holydays. It is different if they do this for recreation's sake, or to get a few small fish for

their own eating, provided that they do not on that account neglect to hear Mass"
(St. Antoninus of Florence, *Summa major* 3.2.4, quoted in Coulton, *Medieval Village*, 247).

182. "It is not contrary to the observance of the Sabbath to exercise any spiritual act, such as teaching by word or writing" (Aquinas, *Summa theologica* pt. 1-2, Q. 122, art. 4).

183. Rodgers, *Discussion of Holidays*, 55.

184. Ibid., 55.

185. On *sermones ad status*, see van den Hoven, *Work*, 201–43. On estates literature in general, see Jill Mann, *Chaucer and Medieval Estates Satire* (Cambridge: Cambridge University Press, 1973).

186. "Even as they plough and dig the earth all day long, so they become altogether earthy; they lick the earth, they eat the earth, they speak of earth; in the earth they have reposed all their hopes, nor do they care a jot for the heavenly substance that shall remain" (Alvarus Pelagius, *De planctu ecclesiae* 2.43, quoted in Coulton, *Medieval Village*, 244).

187. "Husbandmen, when they work their own lands, cannot commit fraud in their work, except in selling their produce at too high a price or too small a measure, or in selling bad for good" (Antoninus of Florence, *Summa major* 3.2.4, quoted in Coulton, *Medieval Village*, 246–47.)

188. "All craftsmen, says he [Bromyard], would at once refuse a job for which unsuitable materials were provided. If a carpenter were offered wages for the building of a house with planks that were too short or otherwise unsuitable, he would at once say—'I will not take the wage or have anything to do with it, because that timber is of no use.' Similarly, the physician who can see no hope of saving his patient. So, in every craft but that of the advocate and the lawyer" (Owst, *Literature and Pulpit*, 347).

189. Kilwardby, *De ortu scientiarum*, pp. 128–29, quoted in van den Hoven, *Work*, 194. Cf. "the other seven [arts] are called liberal either because they require minds which are liberal, that is, liberated and practiced . . . or because in antiquity only free and noble men were accustomed to study them, while the populace and the sons of men not free sought operative skill in things mechanical" (Hugh of St. Victor, *Didascalicon* 2.20).

190. Thomas Aquinas, *Summa theologica* pt. 2-2, Q. 187, art. 3. In another passage, an instance of the man unarmed topos, Aquinas more explicitly links hands and reason: "Horns and claws, which are the weapons of some animals, and toughness of hide and quantity of hair or feathers, which are the clothing of animals, are signs of an abundance of the earthly element; which does not agree with the equability and softness of the human temperament. Therefore such things do not suit the nature of man. Instead of these, he has reason and hands whereby he can make himself arms and clothes, and other necessaries of life, of infinite variety.

Wherefore the hand is called by Aristotle (*De anima* 3.8), 'the organ of organs.' Moreover this was more becoming to the rational nature, which is capable of conceiving an infinite number of things, so as to make for itself an infinite number of instruments" (*Summa theologica* pt. 1, Q. 91, art. 3). This is more in keeping, but still a departure, from Aristotle, who uses the hand simply to illustrate the nature of the soul: "[T]he soul is analogous to the hand; for as the hand is a tool of tools, so the mind is the form of forms and sense the form of sensible things" (*On the Soul* 3.8, in McKeon, *Basic Works of Aristotle*, 595).

191. "But the greatest thing by far is to be a master of metaphor. It is the one thing that cannot be learnt from others; and it is also a sign of genius, since a good metaphor implies an intuitive perception of the similarity in dissimilars" (*Poetics* 1459a, in McKeon, *Basic Works of Aristotle*, 1479).

192. See Arendt, *Human Condition*, 175–247.

193. Weber, *Protestant Ethic*, 85. Subsequent references are given in the text.

194. R. H. Tawney, *Religion and the Rise of Capitalism* (Gloucester, MA: Peter Smith, 1962), 241–42.

195. See Siegfried Wenzel, *The Sin of Sloth: Acedia in Medieval Thought and Literature* (Chapel Hill: University of North Carolina Press, 1967), esp. 88–91; Gregory M. Sadlek, *Idleness Working: The Discourse of Love's Labor from Ovid through Chaucer and Gower* (Washington, DC: Catholic University of America Press, 2004), 171–74.

196. The bourgeois context of Chaucer's source, Renaud de Louens's *Livre de Melibée et de Dame Prudence*, is underscored by its inclusion in the late-fourteenth-century *Le mesnagier de Paris*, a miscellany of moral instruction and domestic advice. Among other things, the *Mesnagier* contains Jean Bruyant's *Le chemin de povreté et richesse*, which features a quintessentially bourgeois allegorical construct, the *castle* of labor! See *Le mesnagier de Paris*, ed. Georgina E. Brereton and Janet M. Ferrier, trans. Karin Ueltschi (Paris: Livre de Poche, 1994), 813–37. Bruyant's poem is the source of Pierre Gringore's *Le chasteau du labour* (1499), itself the source of *The Castell of Labor* (1503), attributed to Alexander Barclay.

197. An interesting variation on the connection between work and good works (cf. n. 63 above, on Noah's work) occurs in a tale from the *Gesta Romanorum*, in which a hardworking smith, appropriately named Focus, refuses to keep the emperor's birthday as a holiday out of economic necessity and is moralized as a good worker in the moral sense: "By þis smyth focus is vnderstond euery goode cristyn man; þe which owith euery day to worch goode workys, and so ben worthi to be presentid to the Emperour of Hevene" (*Early English Versions of the Gesta Romanorum*, X.31). That the smith is chosen as the next emperor at the end of the tale points to another realm of action that work, especially artisanal work, was connected to in late medieval literature, that of politics and statecraft, on which see Cooper, "'These Crafty Men,'" 242–311.

CHAPTER 2.   "Cause & Fundacion of Alle Craftys"

1. G. R. Owst, *Literature and Pulpit in Medieval England,* 2nd ed. (New York: Barnes and Noble, 1961), 290–93; Albert B. Friedman, "'When Adam Delved . . .': Contexts of an Historic Proverb," in *The Learned and the Lewed: Studies in Chaucer and Medieval Literature,* ed. Larry D. Benson (Cambridge, MA: Harvard University Press, 1974), 213–30. Still, the radical and reformist possibilities of the proverb were recognized. Paul Freedman demonstrates how "this statement of original equality was both sufficiently well known and sufficiently subversive in its implication to be consistently put into the mouths of lower-class characters by learned observers" (*Images of the Medieval Peasant* [Stanford: Stanford University Press, 1999], 63).

2. In *Religious Lyrics of the XIVth Century,* ed. Carleton Brown, 2nd ed. (Oxford: Oxford University Press, 1965), p. 96. Brown dates the poem to the 1370s (xix), making it contemporary with John Ball's pre-Revolt activities.

3. In the N-town cycle, Adam and Eve announce their respective occupations after their banishment from Eden: "*Adam:* But lete vs walke forth in to þe londe / with ryth gret labour oure fode to fynde / with delvyng and dyggyng with myn hond / oure blysse to bale and care to-pynde. / And wyff to spynne now must þou ffonde / oure nakyd bodyes in cloth to wynde / tyll sum comforth of godys sonde / with grace releve oure careful mynde. / Now come go we hens wyff. *Eva:* Alas þat ever we wrought þis synne / oure bodely sustenauns for to wynne / ʒe must delve and I xal spynne / in care to ledyn oure lyff" (*Fall of Man,* in *Ludus Coventriae or The Plaie called Corpus Christi,* ed. K. S. Block, EETS, e.s., 120 [London: Oxford University Press, 1922], lines 237–49). In the Chester cycle, Adam and Eve speak of their delving and spinning in the context of Adam's assigning Cain and Abel their respective occupations: "*Adam:* Nowe for to gett you sustenance / I will you teach withoute distance. / For sythen I feele that myschaunce / of that fruite for to eate, / my leefe children fayre and free, / with this spade that yee may see / I have dolven. Learne yee this at mee, / howe yee shall wynne your meate. *Eva:* . . . This payne, theras had bine no neede, / I suffer on yearth for my misdeede; / and of this wooll I will spyn threede by threede, / to hill mee from the could" (*Cain and Abel,* lines 490–97 and 502–4, in *The Chester Mystery Cycle,* ed. R. M. Lumiansky and David Mills [New York: Oxford University Press, 1974]). Medieval visual representations of Adam and Eve at work frequently place the scene either outside Eden or after their expulsion from it (Michael Camille, "'When Adam Delved': Laboring on the Land in English Medieval Art," in *Agriculture in the Middle Ages,* ed. Del Sweeney [Philadelphia: University of Pennsylvania Press, 1995], 247–76, figs. 32 and 39). A poem by Hans Rosenplüt of Nuremburg (quoted in Freedman, *Images,* 63, and Sylvia Resnikow, "The Cultural History of a Democratic Proverb," *Journal of English and Germanic Philology* 36 [1937]: 395) makes the fallen nature

of Adam and Eve's work explicit: "When Adam tainted himself by eating [the apple] / Then God commanded him to win his bread / By tilling the soil and Eve by spinning / In sweat, their faces turned towards the earth."

4. *Cursor mundi,* ed. Richard Morris (London: Kegan Paul, 1874–93). The likening of laboring man to flying bird could carry a number of positive meanings: for example, that work is not only a curse but a power, that work is not only an objective but a subjective necessity through which man expresses and realizes himself, or that work is a kind of metaphoric "flight," an ascent to higher things otherwise inaccessible. These meanings are not entirely absent in the simile, but they remain tightly bound, both in this poem and during the Middle Ages in general, by the perspective that, befitting the ambiguity of Latin *labor,* identifies work with suffering and values it, like suffering in general, ascetically or as an activity whose good is deferred to the spiritual. The lines that follow those quoted above confirm this perspective: "In worlde we ware kast for to kare, to we be broght to wende / Til wele or wa, an of þa twa, to won with-outen ende." Likewise, the tradition of commentary on Job 5.7 consistently reads *laborem* as suffering or work-as-suffering, as an objective rather than subjective necessity, and as a worldly act whose highest value lies in driving the mind away from the world. For example: "*Homo ad laborem nascitur.* Quia impossibile est in hac peregrinatione sine labore esse: sed in eo quod caro affligitur, mens ad petenda alta levatur" (*Glossa ordinaria,* PL 113:768). See also Alan of Lille, *Distinctiones dictionum theologicalium,* PL 210:716; Innocent III, *De contemptu mundi,* PL 217:706–7; Richard of St. Victor, *Explicatio in Cantica canticorum,* PL 196:405.

5. Thomas Walsingham, *Historia Anglicana,* 2.32–33, quoted in R. B. Dobson, *The Peasants' Revolt of 1381* (New York: Macmillan, 1970), 375.

6. Stephen Justice, *Writing and Rebellion: England in 1381* (Berkeley: University of California Press, 1994), 109.

7. See James Dean, "The World Grown Old and Genesis in Middle English Historical Writings," *Speculum* 57 (1982): 548–68. Dean divides this movement into "five stages of antediluvian and one stage of postdiluvian decline: Original Sin, fratricide, development of the city, technocracy, illicit sexuality and giants, and empire. The last phase, the establishment of empire in Nimrod's generation, occurs after the Flood but continues the pattern instituted in the earlier age" (549).

8. Augustine, *De civitate Dei* 14.26, PL 41:434.

9. A rare instance of Gen. 3.7 ("consuerunt folia ficus, et fecerunt sibi perizomata") considered as work is provided by Hugh of St. Victor, who associates it with craft work: "the work of the artificer is to put together things disjoined or to disjoin those put together, whence we read, 'They sewed themselves aprons'" (*Didascalicon,* trans. Jerome Taylor [New York: Columbia University Press, 1961], 1.9, p. 55).

10. "Canticum de Creatione," lines 451–62, ed. Carl Horstmann, *Anglia: Zeitschrift für Englische Philologie* 1 (1878): 287–331. Cf. "And oure Lord God sente Miȝhel þe archaungel to sowe dyuerse seedis, and ȝaf hem to Adam, and tauȝte Adam to wirke and to tilye þe lond and to haue fruyt to lyue by, and all þe generaciouns aftir hem" (*Life of Adam and Eve*, lines 24–28, in *The Wheatley Manuscript*, ed. Mabel Day, EETS, o.s., 155 [London: Oxford University Press, 1921], p. 86). The source in the Latin *Vita* is "dominus autem per Michaelem archangelum semen transmisit Ade docens eum laborare tellurisque legere fructum quatinus vivere quivissent ipse ac generationes post eum cuncte" (*Vita Adae et Evae*, ed. Wilhelm Meyer [Munich: Verlag der k. Akademie, 1879], p. 63). On this genre in general, see Michael E. Stone, *A History of the Literature of Adam and Eve* (Atlanta: Scholars Press, 1992), and Marinus de Jonge and Johannes Tromp, *The Life of Adam and Eve and Related Literature* (Sheffield: Sheffield Academic Press, 1997). On other Middle English versions, see James Dean, *The World Grown Old in Later Medieval Literature* (Cambridge, MA: Medieval Academy of America, 1997), 117–20.

11. "Thanne þei wenten and souȝten nyne dayes, but þei founden not siche as þei hadden in Paradys; naþeless siche þei founden as beestis eeten. Thanne seyde Adam to Eue: Oure Lord God delyueride mete to beestis, but to us he deliueride mete of aungels. But make we sorowe and doo penaunce bifore þe siȝt of oure Lord þat made us fourty dayes, if happily oure Lord God þat made us forȝeue us and ordeyne us where-wiþ to lyue" (*Life of Adam and Eve*, p. 81, lines 17–25). Cf. *Canticum de Creatione*, lines 91–102, and *Vita Adae et Evae*, p. 61.

12. Elspeth Whitney, *Paradise Restored: The Mechanical Arts from Antiquity through the Thirteenth Century* (Philadelphia: American Philosophical Society, 1990), 93.

13. For example: "But it is not without reason that while each living thing is born equipped with its own natural armor, man alone is brought forth naked and unarmed. For it is fitting that nature should provide a plan for those beings which do not know how to care for themselves, but that from nature's example, a better chance for trying things should be provided to man when he comes to devise for himself by his own reasoning those things naturally given to all other animals. Indeed, man's reason shines forth much more brilliantly in inventing these very things than ever it would have had man naturally possessed them" (Hugh of St. Victor, *Didascalicon* 1.9). Cf. Origen's "the Providence who in comparison with the irrational animals made the rational in a state of need which was advantageous" (*Contra Celsum* 4.76, quoted in George Boas, *Essays on Primitivism and Related Ideas in the Middle Ages* [Baltimore: Johns Hopkins Press, 1948], 194), and Reginald Pecock's description of how men, "bi liȝt of her natural resoun," made discoveries "boþe in sciencis and in craftis soon aftir þe bigynnyng of þe world and alwey contynuely siþen" (*The Reule of Crysten Religioun*, ed. William Cabell Greet, EETS, o.s., 171 [London: Oxford University Press, 1927], 4.12, p. 431).

14. Quoted in Dobson, *Peasants' Revolt,* 375.

15. As Paul Freedman explains, "In order to deny that servitude among Christians was licit, two assertions were necessary: first, that there was no basis for a differentiated penalty for general human sinfulness that imposed servitude on some but not on others, and second, that servitude violated not only original equality but a continuing intention of God to uphold it" (*Images,* 248).

16. Ibid., 61.

17. Cited from Owst, *Literature and Pulpit,* 555. Similar examples are referenced in Freedman, *Images,* 36–37. Cf. "idlenesse . . . is a fulle grete synne, for it is ayeins the commaundement that Godde made to Adam. For he commaunded hym and seide to hym that he sholde labour and lyve with his swote" (*The Mirroure of the Worlde: A Middle English Translation of "Le Miroir du Monde,"* ed. Robert R. Raymo and Elaine E. Whitaker [Toronto: University of Toronto Press, 2003], lines 3803–7, p. 142).

18. Walsingham, *Historia Anglicana,* 2.32–33, quoted in Dobson, *Peasants' Revolt,* 375. Investigating how "both [Ball and Langland] use the concrete vocabulary of labor as a vocabulary of reform," Stephen Justice argues for Langland's influence on Ball in *Writing and Rebellion,* 102–39.

19. The notable exceptions, mostly concerned with the rarer forms of medieval production, are *De diversis artibus,* a compendium of ornamental techniques by a twelfth-century Benedictine, Theophilus; the thirteenth-century *Sketchbook* of Villard de Honnecourt; various works on farming and estate management; treatises on book production and illumination techniques; and four small technical treatises written by German master masons between 1450 and 1516. On Theophilus, see Theophilus, *De diversis artibus,* ed. and trans. C. R. Dodwell (London: Thomas Nelson, 1961); Theophilus, *On Diverse Arts,* ed. and trans. John G. Hawthorne and Cyril Stanley (Chicago: University of Chicago Press, 1963); D. V. Thompson, "Theophilus Presbyter: Words and Meaning in Technical Translation," *Speculum* 42 (1967): 313–39; Lynn White, "Theophilus Redivivus," *Technology and Culture* 5 (1964): 224–33; Erhard Brepohl, *Theophilus Presbyter und das Mittelalterliche Kunsthandwerk* (Köln: Böhlau, 1999). On Villard de Honnecourt, see *The Sketchbook of Villard de Honnecourt,* ed. Theodore Bowie (Bloomington: Indiana University Press, 1959); Carl F. Barnes, *Villard de Honnecourt: The Artist and His Drawings* (Boston: G. K. Hall, 1982); Roland Bechmann, *Villard de Honnecourt: La pensée technique au XIIIe siècle et sa communication* (Paris: Picard, 1991). On medieval model books in general, see R. W. Scheller, *A Survey of Medieval Model Books* (Haarlem: De Erven F. Bohn N. V., 1963). On Middle English agricultural, estate management, and technical books, see George R. Reiser, *Works of Science and Information,* in ed., *A Manual of the Writings in Middle English 1050-1500,* ed. Albert E. Hartung (New Haven: Connecticut Academy of Arts and Sciences, 1998), 10:412–37. Medieval works treating of artists' techniques, mostly painting and

book decoration, are covered in S. M. Alexander, "Towards a Survey of Art Materials: A Survey of Published Technical Literature in the Arts. Part I. From Antiquity to 1599," *Art and Archaeology, Technical Abstracts* 7 (1969): 123–61. The German masonry books are referenced and summarized in Paul Frankl, *The Gothic: Literary Sources and Interpretations through Eight Centuries* (Princeton: Princeton University Press, 1960), 144–53, and Paul Booz, *Der Baumeister der Gotik* (Munich: Deutscher Kunst-verlag, 1956), 80–104. Vitruvius's *De architectura* (on which see Pamela O. Long, "The Contribution of Architectural Writers to a 'Scientific' Outlook in the Fifteenth and Sixteenth Centuries," *Journal of Medieval and Renaissance Studies* 15 [1985]; 265–98) was not well known in the Middle Ages. See also Bernhard Bischoff, "Die handschriftliche Überlieferung der technischen Literatur," in *Artigianato e tecnica nella società dell'alto medioevo occidentale*, Settimane di studio del Centro Italiano di Studi sull'Alto Medioevo 18 [Spoleto: Presso la sede del Centro, 1971], 267–96.

20. See James C. Webster, *The Labors of the Months in Antique and Mediaeval Art to the End of the Twelfth Century* (Princeton: Princeton University Press, 1938); Wilheim Hansen, *Kalenderminiaturen der Stundenbücher: Mittelalterliches Leben im Jahreslauf* (Munich: Georg D. W. Callaway, 1984); Bridget Ann Henisch, "In Due Season: Farm Work in the Medieval Calendar Tradition," in Sweeney, *Agriculture in the Middle Ages*, 309–33; and Bridget Ann Henisch, *The Medieval Calendar Year* (University Park: Pennsylvania State University Press, 1999).

21. Andrew Galloway, "Writing History in England," in *The Cambridge History of Medieval English Literature*, ed. David Wallace (Cambridge: Cambridge University Press, 1999), 255.

22. Virgil, *Georg.*, in *P. Vergili Maronis opera*, ed. R. A. B. Mynors (Oxford: Clarendon Press, 1969). On the mingling of these traditions, see Jean Delumeau, *History of Paradise: The Garden of Eden in Myth and Tradition*, trans. Matthew O'Connell (New York: Continuum, 1995), 3–21.

23. Camille, "'When Adam Delved,'" figs. 31 and 34.

24. Guillaume De Lorris and Jean De Meun, *The Romance of the Rose*, trans. Charles Dahlberg (Hanover, NH: University Press of New England, 1983), 155.

25. John Lydgate, *Fall of Princes*, ed. Henry Bergen (Washington, DC: Carnegie Institution, 1923–27), lines 1195–1201. For similar later representations of the Golden Age, see Harry Levin, *The Myth of the Golden Age in the Renaissance* (New York: Oxford University Press, 1969), 29–31.

26. George Ovitt Jr., *Restoration of Perfection: Labor and Technology in Medieval Culture* [New Brunswick: Rutgers University Press, 1987], 164–65.

27. Mircea Eliade, *Cosmos and History: The Myth of the Eternal Return*, trans. Willard R. Trask (New York: Harper and Row, 1959), 34.

28. Lee Patterson, *Chaucer and the Subject of History* (Madison: University of Wisconsin Press, 1991), 85.

29. Gerhart B. Ladner, *The Idea of Reform: Its Impact on Christian Thought and Action in the Age of the Fathers* (Cambridge, MA: Harvard University Press, 1959), 9.

30. "Definitions and assertions of temporal communities, dominion, and other social ideals and institutions were . . . emphatically based on historical circumstances or claims, in everything from monastic land tenures to England's dominion over Scotland; from aristocratic and royal inheritance and status to peasants' justifications of rebellion" (Galloway, "Writing History in England," 255). See also Gabrielle M. Spiegel, *The Past as Text: The Theory and Practice of Medieval Historiography* (Baltimore: Johns Hopkins University Press, 1997), esp. 83–110.

31. Boas, *Essays on Primitivism,* 192.

32. Augustine, *City of God,* 3 vols., trans. Gerald Walsh and Grace Monahan (New York: Fathers of the Church, 1952), 22.24.

33. Guy H. Allard, "Les arts méchaniques aux yeux de l'idéologie médiévale," in *Les arts méchaniques au moyen âge,* ed. G. H. Allard and A. Lusignan (Montréal: Bellarmin, 1982), 21, 19. Similarly, Augustine emphasizes the difference between a superficial knowledge of and a proficiency in the practical arts when he defines the former as a hermeneutic necessity: "A knowledge of these arts is to be acquired casually and superficially in the ordinary course of life unless a particular office demands a more profound knowledge. . . . We do not need to know how to perform these arts but only how to judge them in such a way that we are not ignorant of what the Scripture implies when it employs figurative locutions based on them" (*On Christian Doctrine,* trans. D. W. Robertson Jr. [New York: Macmillan, 1958], 2.30, pp. 66–67). More pointed in its disdain for practical technology is the concluding remark of a twelfth-century lexicographical treatise on tools that, says Allard, "révèle à merveille la mentalité littéraire de l'époque" ("Les arts méchaniques," 20): "Il est plus honorable *(praestantior)* de dénommer les outils correctement que d'en posséder une grande quantité" (B. Haureau, *Notices et extraits de quelques manuscrits latins . . .* [Paris, 1891], 3.216, quoted in Allard, "Les arts méchaniques," 20).

34. Freedman, *Images,* 33.

35. William Langland, *Piers Plowman: The C-Text,* ed. Derek Pearsall (Exeter: University of Exeter Press, 1978). On the history of this metaphor, see Stephen A. Barney, "The Plowshare of the Tongue: The Progress of a Symbol from the Bible to *Piers Plowman,*" *Mediaeval Studies* 35 (1973): 261–93.

36. Lisa H. Cooper, "The 'Boke of Oure Charges': Constructing Community in the Masons' Constitutions," *Journal of the Early Book Society* 6 (2003): 6.

37. Ladner, *Idea of Reform,* 222.

38. "Video enim per totum textum divinarum Scripturarum sex quasdam aetates operosas, certis quasi limitibus suis esse distinctas, ut in septima speretur requies; et easdem sex aetates habere similitudinem istorum sex dierum, in quibus

ea facta sunt quae Deum fecisse Scriptura commemorat" (*De Genesi contra Manichaeos* 1.23, PL 34:190).

39. " . . . incipiat quinto die in actionibus turbulentissimi saeculi, tanquam in aquis maris operari, propter utilitatem fraternae societatis" (*De Genesi contra Manichaeos* 1.25, PL 34:194).

40. Similarly, in the *City of God* Augustine establishes a correspondence between the human life span and the workweek in describing an individual's good works by analogy to weekly occupational work: "For, although our good works are, in reality, His, they will be put to our account as payment for this Sabbath peace, so long as we do not claim them as our own; but, if we do, they will be reckoned as servile and out of place on the Sabbath, as the text reminds us: 'The seventh day . . . is the rest of the Lord . . . Thou shalt not do any work therein'" (*City of God* 22.30).

41. *Sermones de Scripturis,* Sermo 43, PL 38:255, quoted in Ladner, *Idea of Reform,* 194.

42. " . . . recte dicitur paterfamilias aedificare domum, cum hoc non opere suo faciat, sed eorum quibus servientibus imperat" (*De Genesi contra Manichaeos* 1.25, PL 34:194).

43. Cited from John Lydgate, *Lydgate's Troy Book,* ed. Henry Bergen, EETS, e.s., 97, 103, 106, 126 (London: K. Paul, Trench, Trübner, 1906–35).

44. See Guido delle Colonne, *Historia destructionis Troiae,* trans. Mary Elizabeth Meek (Bloomington: Indiana University Press, 1974), 5.148–69, p. 46.

45. The construction of the lists in Chaucer's *Knight's Tale* provides another example of the identification of aristocratic with industrial power. Like Priam, Theseus is described as the "maker" of the lists (I.1861, 1907). But Chaucer, who as clerk of the king's works oversaw the construction of the lists at Smithfield in 1390, more realistically foregrounds the cost of this production, specifically Theseus's expense (I.1881–84, 2090), the payment of "mete and wages" to the workers (I.1900), and the high cost of materials (I.2087–88). This emphasis both describes and dispels the illusion that expenditure equals production, or, in the words of the Knight, the idea that "the dispence / Of Theseus . . . *gooth so bisily* / *To maken up the lystes*" (I.1882–84).

46. *The Two Earliest Masonic MSS.,* ed. Douglas Knoop, G. P. Jones, and Douglas Hamer (Manchester: Manchester University Press, 1938), 1. On merchant-class imitation of the nobility, see Sylvia L. Thrupp, *Merchant Class of Medieval London* (Ann Arbor: University of Michigan Press, 1962), 12–13, 249–56.

47. Knoop, Jones, and Hamer, *Two Earliest Masonic MSS.,* 6–8.

48. Cooke MS, 421–24, 564–65. Cf. Cooke MS, 534–35, 640–41 and Regius MS, 2. "The editors argue that this earlier version was probably composed sometime in the second half of the fourteenth century, principally on the reasoning that

the manuscripts' fixing of fellows' wages according to the cost of victuals (Cooke MS, 733–39; Regius MS, 90–93) suggests a date after the Black Death (1348) when prices rose sharply and scarcity of labour caused wage questions to become acute" (21). Master masons, unlike other master craftsmen who sold their products, were themselves paid by wage or salary. The issue of fellows' wages is part of the larger issue of how the master should make use of the goods of his employer, concerning which the Cooke MS lays down a kind of golden rule that clearly worked to the benefit of masters: "Maister of þis art schulde be wysse and trewe to þe lorde þat he seruyth dispendyng his godis trule as he wolde his awne were dispendyd" (729–33). On masons' wages in general, see Douglas Knoop and G. P. Jones, *The Mediaeval Mason: An Economic History of English Stone Building in the Later Middle Ages and Early Modern Times*, 3rd ed. (Manchester: Manchester University Press, 1967), 98–115.

49. The martyrs were put to death by the emperor Diocletian for refusing to make an idol and to offer sacrifice. See Jacobus de Voragine, *The Golden Legend*, trans. William Granger Ryan, 2 vols. (Princeton: Princeton University Press, 1993), 2.290–91. There is no evidence for the commemoration of the Quatuor Coronati in England before the middle of the fifteenth century. See Knoop, Jones, and Hamer, *Two Earliest Masonic MSS.*, 44–51, and Knoop and Jones, *Mediaeval Mason*, 107, 139.

50. Idolatry, as explained in the Book of Wisdom, is both a failure to recognize the *omnipotens artifex* and a deification of the work of human hands: "But all men are vain, in whom there is not the knowledge of God: and who by these good things that are seen, could not understand him that is, neither by attending to the works have acknowledged who was the workman" (Wisd. of Sol. 13.1); "But unhappy are they, and their hope is among the dead, who have called gods the works of the hands of men" (Wisd. of Sol. 13.10).

51. Since Gen. 11.3 specifies that the builders of the tower had "lateres pro saxis, et bitumen pro caemento" (bricks for stones and bitumen for mortar), it is possible that the Regius author deliberately altered this detail to apply more accurately to masons.

52. On the reasons for this mistaken attribution of the tower to Nebuchadnezzar, see Knoop, Jones, and Hamer, *Two Earliest Masonic MSS.*, 183 n.583. Cf. "Also þey dradde þat anoþer flod schulde come, and bulde a wel hiȝe place of brent tyle and glewe instede of morter" (Ranulph Higden, *Polychronicon*, 9 vols., ed. Churchill Babington and Joseph R. Lumby [London: Longmans, 1865–86], 2.249, citing Trevisa's translation). On Babel as an attempt for heaven, see also Augustine, *City of God* 16.4.

53. The general meaning of this interesting phrase is clearly that the craftsman who leads a good Christian life within his estate, who "uses" it well in the

Augustinian sense, will go to heaven. At the same time, "vseþ hem wel" seems to posit an identity between the moral and technical aspects of artisanal work. In other words, it implicitly defines good work, in the sense of well-executed work, as a good work. In this sense, the phrase is comparable to the distinction between "true" and "false" work frequently made in trade regulations. Lisa H. Cooper has noted that both texts "draw connections between bad work and bad behavior, as if to suggest that faulty craftsmanship is the natural result of improper living" ("'Boke of Oure Charges,'" 19).

54. On the origin of the *artes,* see Ernst Robert Curtius, *European Literature and the Latin Middle Ages,* trans. Willard R. Trask (New York: Harper and Row, 1953), 39–41.

55. Pamela O. Long, *Openness, Secresy, Authorship: Technical Arts and the Culture of Knowledge from Antiquity to the Renaissance* (Baltimore: Johns Hopkins University Press, 2001), 102.

56. What the Cooke author, in glossing the "vii liberalle scyens" as "vii sciens or craftys that ben fre in hem selfe the whiche vii lyuen onle by Gemetry" (82–86), means by "fre in hem selfe" is not exactly clear. He may mean that the arts are free insofar as they serve their own particular ends or that the arts are free in that they are not practiced as part of servile or feudal obligation, but he clearly does not mean that the liberal arts are free in the sense of being opposed to the manual arts as merely material and degrading.

57. The editors of the Cooke MS assert, without explanation or consideration of the consequences thereof, that in "alle men here in this worlde lyue by þe labour of here hondys" *man* is used not in its general sense but to mean "a hired man as distinct from a master-workman" (155 n. 123). This reading is contrary to a) the intensifying inclusiveness of "in this worlde," b) the patently general meaning of *man* in the preceding phrase and in the following phrases "men lyuen alle by Gemetrye" (121–22) and "the sciens þat alle resonable menn lyue by" (127–28), and c) the direction of the Cooke author's whole argument, which is to demonstrate the utilization of geometry by grammar, dialectic, rhetoric, arithmetic, music, astronomy, and their practitioners (certainly not all hired laborers). Their reading disrupts the parallelism developed in the text between "alle sciens lyuen alle only by the sciens of Gemetry" (100–103), "men lyuen alle by Gemetrye" (121–22), "alle men here in this worlde lyue by þe laboure of here hondys" (122–24), and "Gemetry is the sciens þat alle resonable menn lyue by" (127–28). Nevertheless, it is possible to construct a reading, albeit an implausible one, on the basis of the editors' restrictive reading of *men,* whereby "men lyuen alle by Gemetrye" would mean that all people are sustained by geometric principles insofar as they are sustained, directly or indirectly, by labor that makes use of them. Similarly, the author's initial statement that geometry is the "causer of alle" other arts would mean that geometry enables all forms of production, which in turn enable the pur-

suit of nonproductive arts. However, this reading relies on distinctions between meanings of *men* not distinguished in the text.

58. Boas, *Essays on Primitivism*, 186.

59. Dean, "World Grown Old," 550. The primitivist outlook is well evidenced in the Middle English translations of Pseudo-Methodius's *The Beginning and the End of the World*: "in þe secunde þousand of þe world, þere were men wikked doeris & fynderis of worst crafte of þe sones of Caym, & of al vnclennesse & filþe, þat is Obal & Tubal . . . Þese fonden firste þe werkes of bras & of iren, of gold & of silver, & of grindinge; and þei firste fonde alle þe artes of musik" (in Trevisa's "Dialogus inter Militem et Clericum," *Sermon by Fitzralph, and "Þe Bygynnyng of þe World,"* ed. Aaron Jenkins Perry, EETS, o.s., 167 [London: Oxford University Press, 1925], 96).

60. "Genuitque Ada Iabel, qui fuit pater habitantium in tentoriis, atque pastorum." The Cooke author turns the first herdsman into the first mason with the unconvincing gloss, "That is to sey fader of men dwellyng in tentis þat is dwellyng howsis" (175–78). That Jabal, Lamech's son, was Cain's mason is a generational impossibility evidently invented by the author.

61. On the legend of the two pillars, see Knoop, Jones, and Hamer, *Two Earliest Masonic MSS.,* 39–44, and Dean, "World Grown Old," 559.

62. Mistaking Nimrod for his grandfather Ham, the MS actually reads, "And this same Cam . . . ," with "Nembroth" crossed through beneath "Cam," though the editors do not indicate whether this incorrect correction is in a different hand. On Nimrod in Middle English historiography, see Dean, "World Grown Old," 564–68, and *World Grown Old,* 134–39.

63. "Uniformity of customs would tend to be brought about partly by the influence of the King's Master Masons and the Office of the Works, established in 1253, but principally by mobility amongst masons, which had doubtless existed to some extent from the earliest times. The use of the system of impressment in connection with the erection of Welsh castles at the end of the thirteenth century could hardly fail to lead to some interchange of ideas and practices. The influence exerted, however, was probably slight compared with that exercised by the greatly increased use of impressment from 1344 onwards and in particular by its wholesale adoption in 1360–63, when masons from almost every county in England were assembled in such large numbers at Windsor Castle, that the continuator of the *Polychronicon* could write that William Wykeham had gathered at Windsor almost all the masons and carpenters in England. Though the chronicler's statement was doubtless an exaggeration, the vast gathering of masons at Windsor in 1360–63 must have marked an epoch in masonic history and probably contributed more than any other event to the unification and consolidation of the masons' customs, and very possibly led to their first being set down in writing" (Knoop, Jones, and Hamer, *Two Earliest Masonic MSS.,* 23). On masons' self-government,

intinerancy, and impressment, see Knoop and Jones, *Mediaeval Mason*, 135–64, 127–34, and 80–85, respectively. On masons in towns, see Heather Swanson, *Medieval Artisans: An Urban Class in Late Medieval England* (Oxford: Blackwell, 1989), 89–92.

64. See John H. Harvey, *Henry Yevele: The Life of an English Architect* (London: B. T. Batsford, 1944).

65. Lon R. Shelby, "The Education of Medieval English Master Masons," *Mediaeval Studies* 32 (1970): 3–4. The building contracts are edited in L. F. Salzman, *Building in England down to 1540: A Documentary History* (Oxford: Clarendon, 1967).

66. Thrupp, *Merchant Class*, 161.

67. Shelby, "Education," 11.

68. The Cooke author cites the *Polychronicon* seven times, Peter Comestor thrice, Bede twice, *De imagine mundi* of Honorius Augustodunensis twice, Isidore's *Etymologies* four times, and Methodius twice. He seems to thinks that "Beda" is the title of a work, referring to "the stories þat is named Beda" (142). None of these texts contain the statements attributed to them, though the references are generally appropriate or plausible insofar as these texts do treat of the biblical episodes that the Cooke author recasts.

69. Knoop and Jones, *Mediaeval Mason*, 3.

70. Ibid., 4.

71. The "difficulties experienced in obtaining a supply of labour were similar in nature"; "experts in the difficult business of directing contemporaneous labours of large numbers of men were necessary"; "piece-work was by no means unfamiliar"; and "the craftsmen employed approximated more nearly than did other mediaeval artificers to modern workmen, being mere wage-earners, paid for working on raw material owned by their employer, and with very little prospect of rising above this condition" (Knoop and Jones, *Mediaeval Mason*, 3)

72. Ibid., 128.

73. Lisa H. Cooper similarly argues that the Constitutions "provide a kind of substitute home . . . an imagined community among artisans whose actual community was frequently dispersed and then reformulated at new construction sites" and connects this interesting relationship between text and space to the dimensions of the manuscripts themselves: "The portability of these two volumes, neither or which was ever bound with another document and each of which would easily fit into a satchel or pocket, suggests that like the diminutive books of hours cherished by hundreds of late medieval laity, they were texts that the master masons who probably owned them did not choose to leave home without" ("'Boke of Oure Charges,'" 4).

74. David Nicholas, *The Later Medieval City, 1300–1500* (London: Longmans, 1997), 227.

75. "Manual labor is useful, so that man may live through daily deeds and the course of life. But he who endures mental labors for the sake of learning prevails and prepares perpetual merits."

76. For example: "Justice of lawe tho was holde, / The privilege of regalie / Was sauf, and al the baronie / Worschiped was in his astat; / The citees knewen no debat, / The people stod in obeissance / Under the reule of governance, / And pes, which ryhtwisnesse keste, / With charite tho stod in reste" (Gower, *CA* Pro. 103–10).

77. R. F. Yeager finds that Gower's "oddly diverse congeries of human achievements . . . show evidence of order" (*John Gower's Poetic: The Search for a New Arion* [Cambridge: D. S. Brewer, 1990], 164. The order that Yeager describes, however, consists of "verbal and logical connectives" (165) and is essentially associative rather than causal or historical.

78. As Paul Strohm notes, "The principal characteristic of viciousness in the *Confessio* is a tendency to thrust oneself into or overturn the rightful order of things—to alter one's station, to supplant others, to disrupt sanctioned relationships. The righteous, on the other hand, are content with their station and responsibilities, and observe estate, degree, and the natural balance of nature" ("Form and Social Statement in *Confessio amantis* and *The Canterbury Tales*," *Studies in the Age of Chaucer* 1 [1979]: 29).

79. In G. C. Macaulay, ed., *The Complete Works of John Gower*, 4 vols. (Oxford: Clarendon Press, 1899–1902).

80. The thematic situation of Gower's history of work has drawn some direct critical attention. R. F. Yeager, arguing against the "view of Gower as an artlessly digressive—even formless—writer," has considered its connections to Genius's discourse on *gentilesse* and to Gower's "logocentric" worldview (*John Gower's Poetic*, 158–70). For Yeager, the thematic transition from *gentilesse* to labor derives from Gower's practice-oriented conception of virtue: "[V]irtue, like promised love, was meaningless to Gower until manifested in deeds. Only then could it be considered 'real,' through action and—ideally—reciprocal exchange. True gentility thus requires effort; achieving it becomes a kind of work. Hence, the discussion of 'gentilesse' leads to one of 'Labor,' with its particularly non-courtly forms of human action" (161). Gower's privileging of intellectual over physical labor, especially his greater interest in alchemy and language, exemplifies the fact that "all events in Gower's universe are, or have been, wrought by divine words—or man's, in approximation of the Word of God" (166). As Yeager notes, the most direct expression of this logocentric worldview, and its moral implications for the use of language, occurs in *CA* 6.1545–49: "In Ston and gras vertu ther is, / Bot yit the bokes tellen this, / That word above alle erthli thinges / Is vertuous in his doinges, / Wher so it be to evele or goode." Accordingly, Gower "offers us a narrative of history beginning—not, as historians teach us, with an evolving agriculture—but with the

acquisition of letters" (165). (It is significant that Gower begins his list of inventors with "Cham . . . [who] ferst the lettres fond" [4.2396–97], but it is not clear whether Gower meant by this that letters actually preceded the other arts. Moreover, this possibility would seem to contradict Genius's portrayal of the double origins of manual and mental work [4.2381–87].) Last, Yeager argues that the logocentric orientation of Gower's history of work, bound up as it is with Gower's own vocational identity as "poet of moral and political reform" (169) and his granting to "poetry the highest potential for accomplishing good or ill" (166), is in turn teleologically related to "the call to poetic labor which concludes his poem" (169).

Where Yeager's reading of Gower's history of work subsumes the poet's interest in work into the larger moral themes and purpose of the *Confessio*, Gregory M. Sadlek has addressed Gower's history of work from a historicist perspective "as a site of action at which both literary and social forces (the literary tradition of love's labor as well as traditional and evolving ideologies of labor) are brought into a sustained literary engagement" ("John Gower's *Confessio amantis,* Ideology, and the 'Labor' of 'Love's Labor,'" in *Re-visioning Gower,* ed. R. F. Yeager [Asheville, NC: Pegasus, 1998], 149). For Sadlek, Gower's work history is part of "a dialogue among various ideologically colored voices" (157): "There is the voice of the traditional medieval ideology of work based on the schema of the Seven Deadly Sins. There are aristocratic voices which speak, on the one hand, of 'tariinges' (the fruit of aristocratic *otium*) being the true work of love and, on the other, of knightly combat as love's proper work. There is also, I would argue, the voice of a new work ethic, which insists that legitimate work must also produce concrete results" (157). Sadlek does not trace this multifaceted representation of work to any specific authorial purpose or work mentality. Rather, Gower's discourse represents a "site of action" that "does not speak with a single ideological voice" (158), and Gower's own "ideology of labor" is described as "an ideology in process, mirroring to some extent ideological shifts in his language and society" (157).

81. John H. Fisher, *John Gower: Moral Philosopher and Friend of Chaucer* (New York: New York University Press, 1964), 41.

82. Ibid., 97.

83. Sadlek, "John Gower's *Confessio amantis,*" 157. Sadlek's argument calls for some qualification. He argues that Gower's allegiance to the idea that "just keeping busy, just countering the vice of sloth, is not enough," that "one's work must produce results" (156)—an idea most directly expressed by Amans with respect to love's labor: "Bot thogh my besinesse laste / Al is bot ydel ate laste, / For whan theffect is ydelnesse, / I not what thing is besinesse" (4.1757–60)—constitutes a departure from "traditional medieval work ideology" because it runs counter to the fact that "in the traditional schema of the Seven Deadly Sins, the antidote to idleness was simply to be busy" (156). While the idea of busyness is a feature of this schema, this overlooks the importance traditionally placed on ob-

jectively valuable good works as the means of avoiding idleness as well as the emphasis that social theory placed upon the *performance* of occupational functions. Rather, it seems that Gower is not so much departing from this notion of simple busyness as using it, just as *besinesse,* as Sadlek observes (153), is Gower's favorite word for work. The value of *besinesse* for Gower lies precisely in the fact that it is both content-free and the simple opposite of idleness, first, because the word does not carry, as Sadlek points out, "the negative connection to *physical* labor" (154)— an aristocratic prejudice—and second, because it offers a way of giving ethical value to work without reference to its objective character—a requirement of the moral suspicion attached to merchant-class work, or business. This alone can explain, it seems to me, why Gower both gives emphasis to productivity and results and at the same time privileges a word whose meaning is so detachable from them, as Chaucer's Man of Law makes clear (fittingly, given his links with Gower): "Nowher so bisy a man as he ther nas, / And yet he semed bisier than he was" (*GP* I.321–22).

84. Patterson, *Chaucer,* 324.

85. *Romance of the Rose,* lines 18607ff., pp. 308–9.

86. See Thrupp, *Merchant Class,* 191–287, and Michael J. Bennet, "Education and Advancement," in *Fifteenth-Century Attitudes,* ed. Rosemary Horrox (Cambridge: Cambridge University Press, 1994), 79–96.

87. K. B. McFarlane, *The Nobility of Later Medieval England* (Oxford: Clarendon Press, 1973), 275.

88. Patterson, *Chaucer,* 333.

89. This is not to deny that Gower's valorization of intellectual work is related, as Yeager has shown, to his own vocational identity as a poet. Rather, his poetic identity, as one that seeks to subsist outside the socioeconomic order, is itself dialectically related to his interest in work as a means of achieving freedom from work. Just as Gower's poetic voice is a "commun vois" (*CA* Pro. 124) that "seeks to efface the specificity of its social origins in the generality of its prescriptions and the universality of its tone" (Patterson, *Chaucer,* 332), so does his separation of the origins of intellectual and physical work articulate a desire to pursue intellectual work free from economic and social constraint, a desire that is more directly expressed in the colophon attached to many manuscripts of the *Vox* and the *Confessio:* "John Gower, desirous of lightening somewhat the account for the intellectual gifts God gave to his keeping, while there is time, between work and leisure, for the knowledge of others, composed three books of instructive material" (cited from Fisher, *John Gower,* 59).

90. Cf. "But every craft (by giving sustenance to him who lives from his trade) is substantially good, if it is under good direction, if no one puts it to bad use. Therefore the craft itself is not bad" (*Mirour de l'Omme,* trans. William Burton Wilson [East Lansing, MI: Colleagues Press, 1992], p. 341, lines 25969ff).

91. Ovid, *Metamorphoses,* 2 vols., LCL (Cambridge, MA: Harvard University Press, 1916), 1.90–112 and 15.96–110. The vegetarianism of the Golden Age is implicit in *Metamorphoses* 1.103 and in *Roman de la Rose* lines 8355ff, but not in Boethius. In writing "No flesh ne wiste offence of egge or spere" (19), a line that clearly applies to both animals and humans, Chaucer may have had in mind Pythagorus's vivid descriptions of the killing of animals as a precursor and counterpart to human bloodshed. Man's original vegetarianism was also argued in a biblical context, on the basis of Gen. 1.29–30 ("And God said: Behold I have given you every herb bearing seed upon the earth, and all trees that have in themselves seed of their own kind, to be your meat"), by Alexander Neckam in the thirteenth century. See Boas, *Essays on Primitivism,* 82–85.

92. The *Roman de la Rose* also uses the myth in other ways. For a full description, see F. W. A. George, "Jean de Meung and the Myth of the Golden Age," in *The Classical Tradition in French Literature,* ed. H. T. Barnwell et al. (Edinburgh: Authors, 1977), 31–39. See also Dean, *World Grown Old,* 143–71.

93. John Norton-Smith, "Chaucer's *Etas Prima,*" *Medium Aevum* 32 (1963): 122.

94. A. V. C. Schmidt, "Chaucer and the Golden Age," *Essays in Criticism* 26 (1976): 114.

95. Andrew Galloway, "Chaucer's *Former Age* and the Fourteenth-Century Anthropology of Craft: The Social Logic of a Premodernist Lyric," *ELH* 63 (1996): 536.

96. "As the revolt at St. Albans dramatically witnessed, milling rights were a perpetual irritant between tenants and landlords. Lords had the right to license mills and tallage their (mandatory) use. Tenants would sometimes evade this costly arrangement by using handmills small enough to be concealed from the bailiff: at St. Albans, these mills had been confiscated 'in the time of Abbot Richard' and been put to a symbolic use [as paving stones in the abbey] that proclaimed the abbey's right to multure" (Justice, *Writing and Rebellion,* 136). For more on the regulation of milling rights, see Richard Holt, "Whose Were the Profits of Corn Milling?" *Past and Present* 116 (1987): 3–23.

97. L. O. Purdon, "Chaucer's Use of *Woad* in the *Former Age,*" *Papers on Language and Literature* 25 (1989): 216–19.

98. Norton-Smith, "Chaucer's *Etas Prima,*" 122–24.

99. "In part, the 'blisful lyf', peaceful and sweet (1) enjoyed by the people of the 'golden age' is evoked in its pastoral simplicity using the terms of Chaucer's sources, but largely it is suggested by describing what it lacks (for the poem is full of negatives); and what it lacks are the benefits of late fourteenth-century civilization, questionable benefits as far as the argument of the poem is concerned" (A. J. Minnis, *Oxford Guides to Chaucer: The Shorter Poems* [Oxford: Clarendon Press, 1995], 487).

100. The figure stems from *Metamorphoses* 1.137–40, where it pertains to the Iron Age. Boethius thus contracts Ovid's scheme of the four ages to foreground the human agency behind the world's corruption.

101. Norton-Smith, "Chaucer's *Etas Prima*," 122.

102. Schmidt, "Chaucer and the Golden Age," 100 and 113.

103. Minnis, *Oxford Guides to Chaucer: The Shorter Poems*, 489.

104. Cf. "Chaucer was possessed by a certain experience—perhaps through contemplating the life of his time—the wars, the trade, the growing commercialism, the avarice, luxury and lack of 'trouthe' that seem also to have preoccupied Gower and Langland. He also had a realization about the 'quality' of life in his time—a realization, surely, of a certain depth and import, which he sought to communicate" (Schmidt, "Chaucer and the Golden Age," 110).

105. Galloway, "Chaucer's *Former Age*," 539, 538.

106. "If we must needs scrupulously observe and keep up all that was customary in the rude years of the nascent world, let us roll all time back on its tracks right up to the beginning, and decide to condemn step by step all that successive experience has found out in later ages." Prudentius continues in this vein for many lines (Prudentius, *Contra orat. Symm.* 276ff, 2.27ff, in *The Poems of Prudentius*, ed. and trans. H. J. Thompson, 2 vols., LCL 387 and 398 [Cambridge, MA: Harvard University Press, 1949–53]).

107. John Wyclif, *Select English Works*, ed. Thomas Arnold, 3 vols. (Oxford: Clarendon Press, 1869), 1:384.

108. John Wyclif, *Tractatus de mandatis divinis, Tractatus de statu innocencie*, ed. Johann Loserth and F. D. Matthew (London: Wyclif Society, 1922), 4.4, pp. 495–99.

109. Roger Dymmok, *Liber contra XII errores et hereses lollardorum*, ed. H. S. Cronin (London: Wyclif Society, 1922), 12.1, p. 292. Galloway compares the *Former Age* to Wyclif's *De statu innocencie* and Dymmok's *Liber* as part of "a newly broadened and intensified contemporary perception and discussion of practical and vocational uses of knowledge" ("Chaucer's *Former Age*," 544). He finds that the *Former Age*, intentionally or not, both "resists reformist or revolutionary optimism" and "offers a rebuttal to those who would deny reformers like the Lollards the trenchancy of the disenchanted vision of history" (545).

110. See Anne Hudson, *The Premature Reformation: Wycliffite Texts and Lollard History* (Oxford: Clarendon Press, 1988), 144ff.

111. Gower, *Mirour de l'Omme*, 26449ff, p. 347.

112. Dean, *World Grown Old*, 313. On the whole, however, Dean finds "Chaucer's attitude about the world grown old . . . ironic and somewhat elusive" (313).

113. Obviously, the "besinesse" Chaucer attributes to the father of *gentilesse* is different from the "swety bysinesse" of the *Former Age*. The latter overtly signifies physical labor where the former does not. Yet *Gentilesse*'s "besinesse"

certainly encompasses labor within its signification of diligent activity in general, first, because *besinesse* was used to denote not only the state of being busy but occupational tasks themselves (*MED,* s.v. "bisinesse," 2ab)—"And the same Salomon seith that 'he that travailleth and besieth hym to tilien his land shal eten breed, but he that is ydel and casteth hym to no bisynesse ne occupacioun shal falle into poverte and dye for hunger'" (*Mel* VII.1589–90)—and second, because "besinesse" (*Gent* 10), in its opposition to "the vyce of slouthe" (*Gent* 11), partakes of the labor-sloth opposition defined in contemporary discussion of the nature of the vices and virtues: "Agayns this roten-herted synne of Accidie and Slouthe sholde men exercise hemself to doon goode werkes . . . Usage of labour is a greet thyng, for it maketh, as seith Seint Bernard, the laborer to have stronge armes and harde synwes; and slouthe maketh hem feble and tendre" (*ParsT* X.688–89). For similar examples, see *Book for a Simple and Devout Woman: A Late Middle English Adaptation of Peraldus's "Summa de Vitiis et Virtutibus" and Friar Laurent's "Somme le Roi,"* ed. F. N. M. Diekstra (Groningen: Egbert Forsten, 1998), p. 138, and Siegfried Wenzel, *The Sin of Sloth: Acedia in Medieval Thought and Literature* (Chapel Hill: University of North Carolina Press, 1960), 91–92. Cf. "Oure fader Adam bygan with sore travaile, / When he was flemed out of Paradice. / Lord! what myght than gentillesse availe, The *firste stokke of labour* toke his price" (John Lydgate, *A Thoroughfare of Woe,* lines 33–36, printed in *The Minor Poems of John Lydgate,* ed. Henry Noble MacCracken, EETS, e.s., 107 and o.s., 192 [London: Oxford University Press, 1910–34])—a reference to *Gentilesse's* "firste stok" as Adam?

114. Scogan includes the whole text of *Gentilesse* in his *Moral Balade,* which is printed in Walter W. Skeat, *The Chaucer Canon* (Oxford: Clarendon Press, 1900).

115. See Boas, *Essays on Primitivism,* 15–86, and Levin, *Myth of the Golden Age,* 32–34. The Cockaynge tradition is surveyed in Elfriede Marie Ackerman, "*Das Schlaraffenland* in German Literature and Folkson: Social Aspects of an Earthly Paradise, with an Inquiry into Its History in European Literature" (PhD diss., University of Chicago, 1944). See also Louise O. Vasvari, "The Geography of Escape and Topsy-Turvy Literary Genres," in *Discovering New Worlds,* ed. Scott D. Westrem (New York: Garland, 1991), 178–92; Guy Demerson, "Cocagne, utopie populaire?" *Revue Belge de Philologie et d'Histoire* 59 (1981): 529–53.

116. As James Dean explains, "We can discern a new moral phase in the development of *senectus mundi* . . . in the writings of eleventh- and twelfth-century writers on the contempt of the world, including Peter Damian, Bernard of Cluny, Benzo of Alba, Serlo of Wilton, and Hugh of St. Victor. These writers, who exposed human sins on an epic scale and sometimes in lurid language, wrote of the world's senescence to explain by the world should be held in contempt. . . . As Cardinal Lotario dei Segni, later Pope Innocent III, explained the case, the greater world de-

generates because of the moral failings of men and women, and mankind falls further because of the world's general viciousness" (*World Grown Old*, 54).

117. "The lost ages striving after good morals were superior, but now those who seek to live without sin are without a name. The Golden Age and kisses of peace have perished. Now the age is faithless, the age is truly foul. The age is foul; I do not call the age filthy, but I call it filth itself" (*Scorn for the World: Bernard of Cluny's "De Contemptu Mundi,"* ed. and trans. Ronald E. Pepin [East Lansing, MI: Colleagues Press, 1991], 3.1–5).

118. Bernard begins his discussion of the Golden Age in just this fashion: "Aurea tempora primaque robora praeterierunt, / Aura gens fuit et simul haec ruit, illa ruerunt" (Ibid., 2.1–2).

119. Dean, *World Grown Old*, 309. E.g., "But Deeth, that wol nat suffre us dwellen heer, / But as it were a twynklyng of an ye, / Hem bothe [Petrarch and Giovanni da Lignano] hath slayn, and alle shul we dye" (*ClT* IV.36–38).

120. There are, in addition to the Clerk's statement about the decline of the world (lines 1139–40), other suggestions of Griselda's embodiment of specifically Golden Age values. As James Dean has explained, "Griselde . . . seems to step out the *Former Age* in that she personifies moderation, gentility, and Boethian *trouthe* and stedfastness" (*World Grown Old*, 310). To his description I would add that Griselda's way of life, though poor and laborious, is associated with earthly abundance and beauty. The Clerk describes Griselda's village as "of site delitable" (199) and emphasizes that though the villagers sustained themselves through labor "the erthe yaf hem habundance" (203). Also, the Clerk associates Griselda with gold itself. First, the public acknowledgment of Griselda's virtue is marked by her changing out of "her rude array" into "a clooth of gold that brighte shoon" (1116–17), the moral symbolism of which is underscored by "And ther whe was honoured as hire oghte" (1120). Second, the Clerk's closing comparison of Griselda with modern women, whose "gold . . . hath now so badde alayes / With bras" (1166–67), evokes the conventional metal symbolism of successive ages of moral decline.

121. The Monk asks to be excused of his "ignorance" (VII.1990) of his tragedies' historical order (VII.1985–87), and he is interested in no more than the *quia* of worldly downfall. As Helen Cooper remarks on the tale, "There is no theological or philosophical differentiation of the two principles [Fortune vs. God], nor much attempt to make the assignment of the downfalls to one or the other look anything but haphazard. This lack of theological distinction is made worse by the lack of moral distinction. The good, the innocent, the high-born, and the evil are all jumbled together, not to show the goodness of virtue or the viciousness of vice, but simply as *ensamples* of downfalls" (*The Canterbury Tales*, 2nd ed. [Oxford: Oxford University Press, 1996], 333). The Monk is also suspicious of his audience's interest in his histories—"if yow list to herkne hyderward" (VII.1969); "if yow liketh for to

heere" (VII.1983)—a suspicion that both proves true—"Youre tale anoyeth al this compaignye.... Whereas a man may have noon audience, / Noght helpeth it to tellen his sentence" (VII.2789–802)—and seems to express his own disinterestedness and sense of the arbitrariness of his tale: "I wol ... telle yow a tale, or two, or three" (VII.1966–68); "I wol yow seyn the lyf of Seint Edward; / Or ellis, first, of tragedies wol I telle" (VII.1970–71).

122. Norton-Smith, "Chaucer's Etas Prima," 119. Frederick J. Furnivall "probably created the title *The Former Age*" (*The Minor Poems, Part I*, vol. 5 of *A Variorum Edition of the Works of Geoffrey Chaucer*, ed. George B. Pace and Alfred David [Norman: University of Oklahoma Press, 1982], 97). The *MED* maintains that ME *former* could be used to mean "(a) First (in time), earliest; (b) original, primitive; ~ age, first age of the world, the Golden Age" (s.v. "former a.," 1b) and the *OED* explains that "In ME, it [*former*] sometimes took the place of the earlier *forme*, first, primeval, as in *former father, days*" (s.v. "former a.," 1c). But it is highly unlikely that *The Former Age* uses *former* in this way. First, Chaucer does not use *former* anywhere else to mean "first," and in *Boece* he translates *prior aetas* as "first age" (*Boece*, 2.m5.1). Second, ME *former* meaning "first" is very rare. Third, the evidence given in the *MED* is suspect. For "first (in time), earliest" the *MED* provides Middle English translations of "Statuto tempore revertetur, et veniet ad astrum; et non erit priori simile novissimum" (Dan. 11.29) and "hoc significante Spiritu sancto, nondum propalatam esse sanctorum viam, adhuc priore tabernaculo habente statum" (Heb. 9.8), neither of which necessarily uses *prior* to mean "first." And for "original, primitive; ~ age, first age of the world, the Golden Age" the *MED* cites only the two instances of *former* in *The Former Age*, "A blisful lyf ... / Ledden the peples of the former age" (2) and "... the flees was of his former hewe" (18).

123. David Aers, *Chaucer* (Brighton: Harvester, 1986), 9. Cf. " [Chaucer's] characteristic relation to the world was analytic rather than rhetorical.... [and] his analysis focused, finally, neither on moral standards nor on social conditions but on attitudes; that is to say, on socially determined and therefore historically contingent value and beliefs" (Patterson, *Chaucer*, 167–68).

124. Arthur Lovejoy and George Boas, *Primitivism and Related Ideas in Antiquity* (Baltimore: John Hopkins University Press, 1935), 7.

125. Fred Davis, *Yearning for Yesterday: A Sociology of Nostalgia* (New York: Free Press, 1979), 16.

126. Dean, *World Grown Old*, 276.

127. "Chaucer's attitude toward civilization and technology in the poem is wholly negative; but he would not have found support, let alone inspiration, for this view in the Bible, whether or not he was familiar with Augustine's Commentary on it. For Genesis shows technology not as *caused* by the Fall, but as occasioned by it, whereas the Golden Age myth seems to describe a 'Fall' caused by *technology*"

(Schmidt, "Chaucer and the Golden Age," 113). This is not true, of course, of all versions of the Golden Age myth.

128. The Diogenes tradition is surveyed in Niklaus Largier's *Diogenes der Kyniker: Exempel, Erzählung, Geschichte in Mittelalter und Früher Neuzeit* (Tübingen: Max Niemeyer Verlag, 1997). On the one hand, Diogenes exemplified temperance and ascetic poverty. On the other, his extreme minimalism made him an impracticable model of virtue, and his moral authority was tarnished by his reputed sexual shamelessness (see, e.g., Augustine, *City of God* 14.20). In short, Diogenes embodies a contempt for the world and civilization that borders on animality—a threat underscored by the name of the Cynic school. Diogenes is not generally associated with the Golden Age, and Chaucer does not refer to him in any other context. In making him a spokesman for Golden Age values, Chaucer may be following Boccaccio: "Modicis equidem et nulla mortalium solertia preparatis simplex contentatur natura, quod non absque rubore presentium etas aurea sub Saturno testata est, cui ad sedandam famem sitimque suffecisse glandes et rivulos tradidere veteres. Hoc idem lactucis agrestibus et radicibus approbavit recentior Dyogenes" (*De casibus virorum illustrium,* 7.7, in vol. 9 of *Tutte le opere di Giovanni Boccaccio,* ed. Vittore Branca [Milan: Arnoldo Monadori, 1983], p. 630).

129. Origen, *Contra Celsum* 4.76, quoted in Boas, *Essays on Primitivism,* 194.

130. Persius, *Satires* Pro., lines 10–11, in *Juvenal and Persius,* trans. G. G. Ramsay, LCL 91 (Cambridge, MA: Harvard University Press, 1979).

131. *Romance of the Rose,* lines 20175ff.

132. Galloway, "Chaucer's *Former Age,*" 538–39.

133. Schmidt, "Chaucer and the Golden Age," 106.

134. The unfitness of acorns for human consumption is memorably recorded in Dante's description of the inhabitants of the Arno valley as "bruti porci, piú degni di galle / che d'altro cibo fatto in uman uso" (*Purgatorio* 14.43–44).

135. The *Former Age* urges the problem of necessity more than any of its sources. In the *Metamorphoses,* the perennial temperateness and bountifulness of the earth in the Golden Age, which includes streams of milk and honey (1.111), obviate any need for labor.

136. *Bibliotheca historica* 1.8, quoted in Lovejoy and Boas, *Primitivism,* 221. Cf. Horace: "When, as beasts, they sprang from the earth in its beginning, a dumb and squalid herd, they fought for acorns and for dens with claw and fist" (*Satires* 1.3.99–101, quoted in Lovejoy and Boas, *Primitivism,* 372). And Vitruvius: "In the olden days men were born like wild beasts in woods and caves and groves and kept alive by eating rough food" (*De architectura* 2.1, quoted in Lovejoy and Boas, *Primitivism,* 375). Manilius emphasized the ignorance of primitive man: "life was uniformly rough and, entirely occupied with the appearance of things, lacked reason. . . . Nor yet had they the skill to produce the learned arts, and the great earth

lay sterile beneath its rude inhabitants . . . each thought he knew enough" (*Astro-nomicon* 1.66–78, quoted in Lovejoy and Boas, *Primitivism,* 377). In the eighth cen-tury Paul the Deacon retold the legend of King Saturn to similar effect: "Now he [Saturn] showed the people who had been savages up to that time how to build houses, cultivate the soil, plant vines, and to live in human ways, for before that time they had sustained life like half-wild beasts, living merely on acorns. And they dwelt either in caves or in shelters woven from leaves and twigs. He was also the first to strike bronze coins. Because of these benefactions, he was called a god by the untaught and rustic crowd" (Preface to *Brev. ab urbe condit.,* quoted in Boas, *Essays on Primitivism,* 197).

137. Ranulf Higden, *Polychronicon,* 2.5, citing Trevisa's translation. The pas-sage is based on Isidore, *Etymologiae* 15.2, PL 82:537.

138. See E. P. Anderson, "Some Notes on Chaucer's Treatment of the *Som-nium Scipionis,*" *Proceedings of the American Philological Association* 33 (1902): xcviii–xcix, and Macrobius, *Commentary on the Dream of Scipio,* trans. William Harris Stahl (New York: Columbia University Press, 1952), 52–55.

139. Quoted in Lovejoy and Boas, *Primitivism,* 381. The original: "Nam nam quis facile mundum semper fuisse consentiat, cum et ipsa historiarum fides multa-rum rerum cultum emendationemque vel ipsam inuentionem recentem esse fatea-tur; cumque rudes primum homines et incuria silvestri non multum a ferarum asperitate dissimiles meminerit vel fabuletur antiquitas; tradatque nec hunc eis quo nunc utimur victum fuisse sed, glande prius et bacis altos sero sperasse de sul-cis alimoniam; cumque ita exordium rerum et ipsius humanae nationis opinemur ut aurea primum saecula fuisse credamus, et inde natura per metallia viliora de-generans ferro saecula postrema foedaverit?" (Macrobius, *Commento al Somnium Scipionis,* ed. and trans. Mario Regali, 2 vols. [Pisa: Giardini, 1983], 2.10.6, 2.307).

140. The strategy is very Chaucerian. Cf. "And every turment eke in helle / Saugh he [Aeneas], which is longe to telle; / Which whoso willeth for to knowe, / He moste rede many a rowe / On Virgile or on Claudian, / Or Daunte, that it telle kan" (*HF* 445–50).

141. " . . . atque ita contingit ut non rudi mundo rudes homines et cultus in-scii . . . terris oberrent et asperitatem paulatim vagae feritatis exuti conciliabula et coetus natura instituente patiantur, fitque primum inter eos mali nescia et adhuc astutiae inexperta simplicitas, quae nomen auri primis saeculis praestat. Inde quo magis ad cultum rerum atque artium usus promovet, tanto facilius in animos serpit aemulatio quae primum bene incipiens in invidiam latenter evadit, et ex hac iam nascitur quicquid genus hominum post sequentibus saeculis experitur" (Macro-bius, *Commento al Somnium Scipionis,* 2.10.15–16, p. 310), my translation.

142. In addition to the implication in both of the passages cited above that the arts arose of necessity, Macrobius characterizes labor and the arts as positive values in other ways, referring to "cultus quo nunc utimur" (2.10.8) [the culture

that we now enjoy], "litterarum usus, quo solo memoriae fulcitur aeternitas" (2.10.8) [the use of letters, by which the immortality of memory is sustained], and "multa . . . quae nobis inventa placuerunt" (2.10.8) [many invented things that have satisfied us].

143. Fredric Jameson, *The Ideologies of Theory*, 2 vols. (Minneapolis: University of Minnesota Press, 1988), 2:159.

CHAPTER 3.   "My Werk"

1. As Johan Huizinga noted, it was in England that "earlier than in other countries, eyes were opened to an appreciation of the economic factors in life" (*The Autumn of the Middle Ages*, trans. Rodney J. Payton and Ulrich Mammitzsch [Chicago: University of Chicago Press, 1996], 205. See also Arthur B. Ferguson, *The Articulate Citizen and the English Renaissance* (Durham, NC: Duke University Press, 1965), 91–106.

2. Jill Mann, *Chaucer and Medieval Estates Satire* (Cambridge: Cambridge University Press, 1973), 202.

3. Cited from R. B. Dobson, *The Peasants' Revolt of 1381* (New York: Macmillan, 1970), 64.

4. In *The Complete Works of John Gower*, ed. G. C. Macaulay, 4 vols. (Oxford: Clarendon Press, 1899–1902).

5. John Gower, *Mirour de l'omme*, trans. William Burton Wilson (East Lansing, MI: Colleagues Press, 1992).

6. James Bothwell, P. J. P. Goldberg, and W. M. Ormrod, introduction to *The Problem of Labour in Fourteenth-Century England*, ed. James Bothwell, P. J. P. Goldberg, and W. M. Ormrod [York: York Medieval Press, 2000], vii.

7. Siegfried Wenzel, *The Sin of Sloth: Acedia in Medieval Thought and Literature* (Chapel Hill: University of North Carolina Press, 1967).

8. Cited from G. R. Owst, *Literature and Pulpit in Medieval England*, 2nd ed. (New York: Barnes and Noble, 1961), 554.

9. "If one country had all goods together, then it would be too proud. And therefore God established, quite rightly, that any one country would properly have need of the others. Thereupon God ordained merchants, who should go seek in another country whatever any one country did not have. Therefore, he who conducts himself well and trades honestly is blessed by God and man. The law allows, and it is only right, that he who can lose in a venture should also be allowed to gain from it when his fortune brings it about. Therefore I say to you that he who wants to become a merchant and risk his money is not to be blamed if he earns a profit, provided he earn it in moderation and without fraud" (Gower, *Mirour de l'omme*, 25189ff). It is striking how Gower both defends mercantile practices as materially

necessary and saves them from the taint of mere utility by assigning them the providential function of saving nations from excessive pride.

10. Langland's idea of the intrinsic morality of manual labor is most clearly expressed by Piers's description of his work as commanded by Truth: "Som tyme I sowe and som tyme I thresshe, / In taillours craft and tynkeris craft, what Truthe kan devyse, / I weve and I wynde and do what Truthe hoteth" (*PPl* B.5.546–48). The most obvious and basic meaning of these lines is that manual and especially agricultural labor, being the most necessary form of work, is also the most legitimate (materially, socially, morally, and spiritually). The ideal commensurability of the various functions of the three estates is a central theme of the plowing of the half-acre (B.6), and merchants are included in Piers's pardon on the condition of their recirculation of profits into public works and charity (B.7.25–32).

11. Louise M. Bishop, "Hearing God's Voice: Kind Wit's Call to Labor in *Piers Plowman*," in *The Work of Work: Servitude, Slavery, and Labor in Medieval England*, ed. Allen J. Frantzen and Douglas Moffat (Glasgow: Cruithne Press, 1994), 198.

12. James Simpson, *Piers Plowman: An Introduction to the B-Text* (New York: Longman, 1990), 224. On Langland's fusion of work and good works, see also Justine Rydzeski, *Radical Nostalgia in the Age of Piers Plowman: Economics, Apocalypticism, and Discontent* (New York: Peter Lang, 1999), esp. ch. 2.

13. William Langland, *Piers Plowman: The C-Text*, ed. Derek Pearsall (Exeter: University of Exeter Press, 1978).

14. On the nature of Langland's clerical profession, see E. Talbot Donaldson, *Piers Plowman: The C-Text and Its Poet* (New Haven: Yale University Press, 1949). On the *apologia* and the issue of Will's work, see the important collection *Written Work: Langland, Labor, and Authorship*, ed. Steven Justice and Kathryn Kerby-Fulton (Philadelphia: University of Pennsylvania Press, 1997).

15. Donaldson, *Piers Plowman: The C-Text*, 226.

16. Mann, *Chaucer*, 12.

17. Traugott Lawler, *The One and the Many in the Canterbury Tales* (Hamden, CT: Archon Books, 1980), 52.

18. Lee Patterson, *Chaucer and the Subject of History* (Madison: University of Wisconsin Press, 1991), 27.

19. For a useful survey, see Lee Patterson, "Perpetual Motion: Alchemy and the Technology of the Self," *Studies in the Age of Chaucer* 15 (1993): 26–27; Peter Brown, "Is the 'Canon's Yeoman's Tale' Apocryphal," *English Studies* 64 (1983): 481–90.

20. Joseph Grennen, "Saint Cecilia's 'Chemical Wedding': The Unity of the *Canterbury Tales*: Fragment VIII," *Journal of English and Germanic Philology* 65 (1965), 466–67. Alchemical texts conventionally named the alchemical process the "work" (*opus*) or the "great work," as in "erat enim iste multum intentus in

opere maiore" [he was assiduous in his quest for the Great Work] (Morienus, *A Testament of Alchemy*, ed. and trans. Lee Stavenhagen [Hanover, NH: University Press of New England, 1974), p. 2. As in the many other hagiographical narratives in which a saint defends the unseen spiritual reality by arguing that the world gives evidence to the Creator, Cecilia banishes Tiburce's fear of death by describing the world and man's soul as the work of God: "That Fadres Sone hath alle thyng ywroght, / And all that wroght is with a skillful thoght / The Goost, that fro the Fader gan procede, Hath sowled hem" (*SNT* 326–29). On the various contrasting senses of *werk* in the two tales, see Bruce Rosenberg, "The Contrary Tales of the Second Nun and the Canon's Yeoman," *Chaucer Review* 2 (1968): 282.

21. *The Rule of St. Benedict,* ed. and trans. Anthony C. Meisel and M. L. del Mastro (New York: Doubleday, 1975), ch. 48.

22. *Ancrene Wisse: A Guide for Anchoresses,* ed. and trans. Hugh White (New York: Penguin, 1993), p. 195.

23. "Few nuns were occupied in agricultural work, and that only in the poorest nunneries and the Cistercian nunneries. In the poorer houses the nuns themselves carried out the household tasks: cooking, laundry, spinning and weaving. Most nunneries were almost self-sufficient where food was concerned. . . . In the richer nunneries all household chores were done by lay sisters or servant women and the nuns occupied themselves with embroidery, delicate spinning, illumination of books and reading" (Shulamith Shahar, *The Fourth Estate: A History of Women in the Middle Ages* [London: Methuen, 1983], 44).

24. For specific examples, see Eileen Power, *Medieval English Nunneries* (Cambridge: Cambridge University Press, 1922), 330–40.

25. For example: "No one shall choose for herself what work or task she shall do; but it shall be up to the superior to order what seems useful. . . . No one is to work on anything of her own, unless the abbess has given her an order or permission; but let all your work be done in common, with such holy zeal and such fervent alacrity as you would give to it if it were your own" (Caesarius of Arles, *Rule for Nuns,* rules 8 and 29, quoted in Emilie Amt, ed., *Women's Lives in Medieval Europe: A Sourcebook* [New York: Routledge, 1993], 223 and 226); "The sisters . . . are to work faithfully and devotedly . . . at work which pertains to a virtuous life and to the common good. They must do this in such a way that, while they banish idleness, the enemy of the soul, they do not extinguish the Spirit of holy prayer and devotion to which all other things of our earthly existence must contribute" (*The Rule of St. Clare,* 7.1–2, in St. Francis of Assisi and St. Clare, *Francis and Clare: The Complete Works,* trans. Regis J. Armstrong and Ignatius C. Brady [New York: Paulist Press, 1982], 219); "Per totum diem cum operamini manibus, meditatio sancta de corde non cesset: propter illud Apostoli: *Psalmis, hymnis, canticis spiritualibus cantantes et psallentes in cordibus vestris Domino* [Col. 3]" (Aurelianus Arelatensis, *Regula ad virgines,* PL 68:402). Similar conditions on nuns' labor are also

discussed in Ulla Sander Olsen, "Work and Work Ethics in the Nunnery of Syon Abbey in the Fifteenth Century," in *The Medieval Mystical Tradition in England, Exeter Symposium V,* ed. Marion Glasscoe (Cambridge: D. S. Brewer, 1992), 129–43.

26. Power, *Medieval English Nunneries,* 288; Shahar, *Fourth Estate,* 49.

27. See Paul Lee, *Nunneries, Learning and Spirituality in Late Medieval English Society* (York: York Medieval Press, 2001), 136–38. In other words, the Second Nun is a self-conscious translator, and it is also possible to understand this self-consciousness as reflecting an anxiety about being both a counterexample to the decline in Latin learning among nuns and, as a translator into the vernacular, a co-agent of that decline. In these terms, her reference to "ydelnesse, / *That cause is of so greet confusion*" (22–23) may be read as an institutional critique.

28. See, for example, Derek Pearsall, *The Canterbury Tales* (London: Routledge, 1985), 252, and Helen Cooper, *Oxford Guides to Chaucer: The Canterbury Tales,* 2nd ed. (Oxford: Oxford University Press, 1996), 358–59. There is plenty of evidence that "sone of Eve" (62), as a liturgical formula, is appropriate to a nun. See William B. Gardner, "Chaucer's 'Unworthy Sone of Eve,'" *Studies in English* 26 (1947): 77–83.

29. See Elizabeth Makowski, *Canon Law and Cloistered Women: "Periculoso" and Its Commentators, 1298–1545* (Washington, DC: Catholic University of America Press, 1997), and Power, *Medieval English Nunneries,* 371ff.

30. "Prius ergo demonstrare debemus beatum apostolum Paulum opera corporalia servos Dei operari voluisse, quae finem haberent magnam spiritualem mercedem, ad hoc ut ipso victu et tegumento a nullo indigerent, sed manibus suis haec sibi procurarent" (Augustine, *De opere monachorum,* 3.4, PL 40:551).

31. George Ovitt Jr., *The Restoration of Perfection: Labor and Technology in Medieval Culture* (New Brunswick: Rutgers University Press, 1987), 106.

32. Ibid.

33. As John Scattergood says of the *Canon's Yeoman's Tale,* "it is hard to escape the conclusion that in [Chaucer's] view the potential for growth and change and the energy to turn the world upside-down lay beyond the comfortably reassuring town walls in the suburban tenements of those who were by choice and necessity outsiders" ("Chaucer in the Suburbs," in *Medieval Literature and Antiquities: Studies in Honour of Basil Cottle,* ed. Myra Stokes and T. L. Burton [Cambridge: D. S. Brewer, 1987], 161). See also John Reidy, "Alchemy as Counter-Culture," *Indiana Social Studies Quarterly* 24 (1971): 41–51. On medieval alchemy's anticipation of modern attitudes to technology, see William Newman, "Technology and Alchemical Debate in the Late Middle Ages," *Isis* 80 (1989): 423–45. Newman shows that "alchemists of the Middle Ages developed a clearly articulated philosophy of technology, in which human art is raised to a level of appreciation difficult to find in other writings until the Renaissance" (424–25). Appropriately, Lee Patterson argues that alchemy "functioned in late-medieval culture as one of the sites where

the modernizing impulse took root" and that the *Canon's Yeoman's Tale* "expresses Chaucer's awareness of *himself* as a modern poet oriented toward a dynamic future" ("Perpetual Motion," 31).

34. As Joseph Grennen points out, "The *preef* (L. *probatio*), or testing of the quality of the golf by cupellation or some other method, was the final stage of the alchemical process. . . . [T]he technical cast of the phrasing suggests a substance which has been led through the stages of the alchemical *Opus* but which, because treatment has not been arrested in time, can not withstand the final test" ("Chaucer's Characterization of the Canon and His Yeoman," *Journal of the History of Ideas* 25 [1964]: 284). In these terms, the Yeoman characterizes the Canon's success as sabotaged by excessive thought, as in the case of the proverbial painter who must be hit over the head before he ruins his work by trying to perfect it.

35. Patterson, "Perpetual Motion," 54.

36. Peggy A. Knapp, "The Work of Alchemy," *Journal of Medieval and Early Modern Studies* 30 (2000): 582.

37. 381 Cf. "Estranged labor . . . estranges man's own body from him, as it does external nature and his spiritual essence, his *human* being. . . . An immediate consequence of [this] fact . . . is the *estrangement of man* from *man*" (Karl Marx, *Economic and Philosophical Manuscripts of 1844,* trans. Martin Milligan [Amherst, NY: Prometheus Books, 1988], 78). The Yeoman similarly recognizes the continuity between individual and social alienation: "And whan he thurgh his madnesse and folye / Hath lost his owene good thrugh jupartye, / Thanne he exciteth oother folk therto / To lesen hir good as he hymself hath do" (742–45).

38. Edgar H. Duncan has demonstrated that "the lists of alchemical substances, apparatus, processes, etc., thrown out by the yeoman [are] more nearly paralleled in Geber's *Sum* than in any other treatise" ("The Literature of Alchemy and Chaucer's Canon's Yeoman's Tale: Framework, Theme, and Characters," *Speculum* 43 [1968]: 642).

39. Pseudo-Geber, *The Summa perfectionis of Pseudo-Geber,* ed. and trans. William R. Newman (Leiden: E. J. Brill, 1991), pp. 635–40. Cf. "this science was nevir taght to man / But he were prouyd perfitly with space / whether he were able to receyve this grace / For his trouth, vertu, & for his stable witt, / which if he fawte, he shal nevir haue itt" (Norton, *Ordinal of Alchemy,* lines 210–14).

40. Richard Kieckhefer, *Magic in the Middle Ages* (Cambridge: Cambridge University Press, 1989), 138. See, for example, Gower's definition of the powers of the three philosophers' stones *(lapis vegetabilis, lapis animalis, lapis mineralis)* in *CA* 4.2531–72.

41. Newman, "Technology and Alchemical Debate," 437.

42. Morienus, *Testament of Alchemy,* 11.

43. Norton, *Ordinal of Alchemy,* line 3071.

44. Quoted in David McLellan, *Karl Marx* (New York: Penguin, 1975), 71.

45. Pseudo-Geber, *Summa perfectionis,* pp. 632, 768.

46. Ibid., p. 768.

47. Marx, *Economic and Philosophical Manuscripts,* 76–77. For example: "[W]e see certain astute and ingenious men knowing very well the works of nature and pursuing her in those principles in which it is possible. . . . But when these men have been pushed down beyond poverty, they are forced to set this very excellent magistery aside, out of indigence. There are also many other eager men beyond those already described, detained by the vain cares and temptations of this world, occupying themselves wholly in every sort of secular business, from whom this precious science of ours flees" (Pseudo-Geber, *Summa perfectionis,* pp. 637–38); "the tyncture of holye Alchymye . . . was nevir for money sold ne boght / Bi any man which for it hath sowghl, / Bot govyn to an able man bi grace / wroght with grete cost with long leiser & space" (Norton, *Ordinal of Alchemy,* lines 182–90). Cf. "an animal . . . produces only under the dominion of immediate physical need, while man produces even when he is free from physical need and only truly produces in freedom therefrom" (Marx, *Economic and Philosophical Manuscripts,* 77).

48. Of the Yeoman's education and literacy there are also a few preliminary hints, both concerned with moral commonplaces, as when he mentions that he was "ones lerned of a clerk" (748) and notes, "as witnessen thise olde wyse" (1067).

49. The first passage is from the *Book of Crates,* here cited from Patterson, "Perpetual Motion," 39. The second is from Petrus Bonus's *Precious New Pearl,* here cited from Joseph Grennen, "Chaucer and the Commonplaces of Alchemy," *Classica et Mediaevalia* 26 (1965): 319.

Index

NICOLA MASCIANDARO

is assistant professor of English at Brooklyn College.